To thank you for sending in the postage-paid feedback card in the back of this book, you'll receive a free two-year subscription to the **NOLO** *News*—our quarterly magazine of legal, small business and consumer information. With each issue you get updates on important legal changes that affect you, helpful articles on everyday law, answers to your legal questions in Auntie Nolo's advice column, a complete Nolo catalog and, of course, our famous lawyer jokes.

Legal information online–24 hours a day

Get instant access to the legal information you need 24 hours a day.

Visit a Nolo online self-help law center and you'll find:

- hundreds of helpful articles on a wide variety of topics
- selected chapters from Nolo books
- online seminars with our lawyer authors and other experts
- downloadable demos of Nolo software
- frequently asked questons about key legal issues
- our complete catalog and online ordering info
- our ever popular lawyer jokes and more.

Here's how to find us:

America Online Just use the key word Nolo.

On the **Internet** our World Wide Web address (URL) is: http://www.nolo.com.

Prodigy/CompuServe Use the Web Browsers on CompuServe or Prodigy to access Nolo's Web site on the Internet.

NOLO PRESS

25 YEARS

LAW FOR ALL

Nolo's Pocket Guide

to

Family
LAW

by Attorneys

Robin Leonard & Stephen Elias

NOLO PRESS · BERKELEY

YOUR RESPONSIBILITY WHEN USING A SELF-HELP LAW BOOK

We've done our best to give you useful and accurate information in this book. But laws and procedures change frequently and are subject to differing interpretations. If you want legal advice backed by a guarantee, see a lawyer. If you use this book, it's your responsibility to make sure that the facts and general advice contained in it are applicable to your situation.

KEEPING UP-TO-DATE

To keep its books up-to-date, Nolo Press issues new printings and new editions periodically. New printings reflect minor legal changes and technical corrections. New editions contain major legal changes, major text additions or major reorganizations. To find out if a later printing or edition of any Nolo book is available, call Nolo Press at (510) 549-1976 or check the catalog in the *Nolo News,* our quarterly newspaper.

To stay current, follow the "Update" service in the *Nolo News.* You can get a two-year subscription to the paper free by sending us the registration card in the back of the book. In another effort to help you use Nolo's latest materials, we offer a 25% discount off the purchase of your Nolo book when you turn in the cover of an earlier edition. (See the "Recycle Offer" in the back of the book.)

This book was last revised in February 1996.

PRINTING HISTORY

Fourth Edition	FEBRUARY 1996
Editors	Mary Randolph and Albin Renauer
Design	Jackie Mancuso
Proofreading	Susan Cornell
Production	Nancy Erb and Linda Wanczyk
Index	Jean Mann
Printing	Delta Lithograph

Leonard, Robin.
    Nolo's pocket guide to family law / by Robin Leonard & Stephen Elias. -- 4th ed.
        p.   cm.
    Includes index.
    ISBN 0-87337-322-7
    1. Domestic relations--United States--Dictionaries. I. Elias, Stephen. II. Title.
KF503.6.L46   1996
346.7301'5'03--dc20
[347.3061503]
                                                                95-26806
                                                                CIP

Quantity Sales: For information on bulk purchases or corporate premium sales, please contact the Special Sales department. For academic sales or textbook adoptions, ask for Academic Sales. (800) 955-4775, Nolo Press, Inc., 950 Parker St., Berkeley, CA 94710.

DEDICATIONS

To Lee, who has helped me broaden the definition of "family," and to the memory of Cheryl, one of the first people to tell me it was okay to stop practicing law.

—RL

To Rubin, who patiently suffered the loss of his father from time to time during the writing of this book.

—SE

ACKNOWLEDGMENTS

Nolo's Pocket Guide to Family Law was originally published in 1988 (the second edition came out in 1990) as the *Family Law Dictionary*.

Our specific thanks for work on the first edition go to:

Mary Randolph (and her father, retired Judge William Randolph of Macomb, Illinois) and Albin Renauer, whose editorial skills, humor and patience made the book a reality. Thanks especially for suggesting "a rare type of pasta" as an alternative definition of Vinculo Matrimonii.

Carol Bohmer, Robin's Family Law professor at Cornell University, who spent cold, wintry Ithaca days reading the manuscript so that those terms not commonly used in California would be accurate and understandable.

Jake Warner who plopped down at least 50 family law books on our desks for sources of terms and who was the favorite player of "stump the authors."

For the second edition, specific thanks go to:

Kate McGrath, who did much of the research and actually understands the difference between an embryo and a zygote.

James Dean Bolding, Sr., Helyne Briggs, Elaine Dean and Wendy Miller, whose "stump the authors" contributions were added to the second edition.

Doing the third edition was a bigger challenge than updating the book for the second edition, primarily because we turned an alphabetical dictionary into a topic-arranged pocket guide. Our thanks go to:

Katherine Jaramillo, who did much of the new research, suggested the chapters for this guide and took the first stab at putting the original dictionary entries into their appropriate pocket guide chapters.

Patti Gima, who refined the chapters and created subtopics within the chapters.

Jackie Smith Arnold, Carlton Biggs, Freddy Estrada, Patti Greene, Al Harven, Raymond G. Hernandez, John Ilerenas, Ron Kleber, Scott-Robert Loos, Angella O'Byrne and J. Ray Renteria, whose "stump the authors" contributions appeared in the third edition.

For the fourth edition, we'd like to thank Stan Jacobson for his research assistance.

CONTENTS

ABOUT THIS BOOK

Nolo's Pocket Guide to Family Law is a compilation of laws, concepts, words and phrases used in the legal arena known as "family law." The pocket guide includes discussions of marriage, divorce, adoption, support, custody, living together, property, abortion and more.

Trying to read up about the law on our own is often a frustrating experience. Most books about law are written for lawyers and stay tucked away on law library shelves. Even if we do manage to get our hands on them, we find they are filled with nearly impenetrable jargon.

This book is Nolo's attempt to gather key family law rules and concepts into a readable, affordable little book that fits in your pocket, briefcase or your car's glove compartment. If you're contemplating divorce, trying to adopt your stepchild or wanting to leave property to your non-marital partner, you'll have the basic information you need at your fingertips. And if you're working with a lawyer through a legal procedure, you can quickly find the meaning of the "legalese" that went right over your head during your last conversation.

WHY THE *POCKET GUIDE* IS UNIQUE

Family law is an area in which non-legal terms have developed vast importance. For example, we include discussions of "extended family," "marriage of convenience" and "same-sex marriage" as well as *Alimony, Child Support* and *Custody.*

We also provide extensive charts showing the law for all 50 states in many important areas, such as the grounds for divorce and marital prohibitions. Did you know, for example, that in Iowa you can't marry your grandchild's spouse and that in Kentucky you can't marry your first cousin once removed? (In case you're wondering who exactly your first cousin once removed is, that's in the chart called "Who Is Your Kin," Table 8.1, in the appendix.)

HOW THE BOOK IS ORGANIZED

To make it easy to find the information you need, we have grouped topics into broad categories: *Adoption, Child Support, Custody and Visitation, Court Procedures, Family Relationships, Minors and Parents, Reproductive Rights and Reproductive Technology,* and *Rights of Unmarried People,* for example. The table of contents lists them all.

At the beginning of each section, you will find a list of the topics covered there. You may need to look at several entries to find the information you need, especially if your question doesn't fit neatly into any one category. Check the index for keywords you're interested in.

LEGAL CITATIONS

The *Pocket Guide* summarizes most laws of general interest; there may be times, however, when you will want to go further and read the full text of a statute. For this reason, citations to state and federal statutes (and occasionally, crucial court cases) appear throughout the book. The section on "Looking Up the Law" at the front of the book explains how to use these citations.

A NOTE ABOUT STATE VARIATIONS

Family law, probably more than any other area of law, differs among states tremendously. What is called "visitation" in one state is called "parental contact" in another. Some states have done away with the term "divorce" and now use "dissolution." "Alimony" is gone in a number of states and has been replaced by either "spousal support" (such as in California) or "maintenance" (the term used in New York). And some states call parental sharing of custody "joint custody" while other states call it "shared custody."

Terminology isn't the only thing that differs. The laws themselves do as well. For example, when it is necessary to determine how a married couple's property is divided at divorce, eight states follow community property principles, one follows a modified community property principle, 40 use a system known as "equitable distribution of property" and one uses traditional common law property principles. Also, some states have made laws preferring joint custody whenever possible; other states have laws rejecting joint custody.

What all this means is that where terminology differs, the most frequently used term is the major heading, but all other used terms are given as alternatives. Where the law differs, we have tried to be comprehensive in explaining the differences.

A NOTE FROM THE AUTHORS

Please be aware that any omission is unintentional. We encourage feedback. If you think we've left something out, complete the registration card at the back of the book and send it to Nolo Press. If we include your suggestion in the next edition, we'll list your name in the acknowledgments.

LOOKING UP THE LAW

Nolo's Pocket Guide to Family Law not only summarizes many laws, but serves as a way to find the text of laws you may want to read word-for-word. And once you find the law, you will probably also find with it references to articles and court cases that discuss the law.

This brief discussion tells you how to use a reference from this book to look up a state or federal statute or court decision.

FINDING A LAW LIBRARY

To look up state or federal statutes or court decisions, go to your county law library (usually in the county courthouse) or the library of a law school funded by the state. Some, but not all, large public libraries also have collections of state or federal statutes; call before you go.

If it's a local (city or county) ordinance you're curious about, you can probably find it at the main branch of your local public library. Or call the city or county attorney's office and ask for a copy.

FINDING STATUTES

When you go to look up a statute, try to use what is called an "annotated" version of the statutes. Annotated statutes include not only the text of the statutes themselves, but also brief summaries of court cases that have discussed each statute. After you look up a statute, you may well want to read the cases listed, too, to see how courts have construed the language of the statute.

Federal statutes. Federal statutes are organized by subject in a set of books called the United States Code (U.S.C.), which is available in virtually every law library. If you know the statute's common name or its citation, you should be able to find it easily.

Example: You want to read some of the provisions of the Family Support Act of 1988, 42 U.S.C. § 666 and following. You would look in Title 42 of the United States Code (the numbers are on the spine of the books) and find section 666. The statute begins with section 666 and covers many sections.

State statutes. State statutes, which fill many volumes, are often organized into "codes." Each code covers a separate area of law, such as Marriage and Divorce or Husbands and Wives. If you have a citation from this book, you'll be able to look up the statute easily.

MAKING SURE YOU HAVE THE MOST RECENT VERSION OF THE STATUTE

Every year, state legislatures and Congress pass hundreds of new laws and change (amend) lots of existing ones. When you look up a statute, it's crucial that you get the most recent version.

To do that, always look for a pamphlet that is inserted in the back of the hardcover volume of statutes. It's called a pocket part, and it contains any changes made to the statute in the hardcover book since the hardcover was printed. Pocket parts are updated and replaced every year—it's much cheaper than producing a whole new hardcover volume every year.

Look up the statute again in the pocket part. If there's no entry, that means the statute hasn't been changed as of the date the pocket part was printed. If there is an entry, it will show you what language in the statute has been changed.

To check for changes that are even more recent—made since the pocket part was printed—you can check something called the Advance Legislative Service. It's a series of paperback pamphlets that contain the very latest statutory changes.

FINDING CASES

If you want to look up a case (court decision) and have the citation (either from this book or from an annotated code), all you need to do is decipher those strange numbers and abbreviations.

The proper citation for the case allowing women to have an abortion is *Roe v. Wade*, 410 U.S. 133 (1973).

The name of the case includes the name of the plaintiff (Roe) followed by a v. (meaning versus) followed by the defendant's name (Wade). 410 is the volume number where the case is found in the series called United States Reports (abbreviated by U.S.) at page 133. The case was decided in 1973.

MAKING SURE THE CASE IS STILL GOOD LAW

Judges don't go back and change the words of their earlier decisions, like legislatures amend old statutes, but cases can still be profoundly affected by later court decisions. For example, any state's highest court, usually called the Supreme Court, has the power to overrule a decision of a trial court or an appellate court. If it does, the trial court or an appellate court's written decision no longer has any legal effect.

There are several ways to check to make sure a case you're relying on still represents valid law. The most common is to use a collection of books called *Shepard's*, which lets you compile a list of all later cases that mention the case you're interested in. Unfortunately, the *Shepard's* system is too complicated to explain here. If it's important to you, consult one of the legal research tools mentioned below.

MORE LEGAL RESEARCH

Legal research is a subject that can (and does) easily fill a whole book of its own. Here are some good resources if you want to delve further into the subject:
- For a thorough, how-to approach to finding answers to your legal questions, see *Legal Research: How to Find and Understand the Law*, by Stephen Elias and Susan Levinkind (Nolo Press).
- For an entertaining and informative video presentation of the basics of legal research, take a look at *Legal Research Made Easy: A Roadmap Through the Law Library*, by Professor Robert Berring of the University of California-Berkeley (Nolo Press/LegalStar).

FAMILY LAW ONLINE

For people with computers who have joined the online community, vast number of legal resources are available in cyberspace. In addition to basic legal resources such as statutes, regulations and cases, you can find online books, discussion groups (called newsgroups), electronic newsletters (called listservers), collections of articles and public forums. Nolo Press publishes a book—*Law on the Net*, by James Evans—that explains how and where to find these resources. (Order information is at the back of the book.)

Nolo Press also maintains a Nolo Press Self Help Law Center on the Internet's World Wide Web, America Online and the Microsoft Network (MSN). The family law resources include:
- informative and topical articles about various family law issues
- an online bookstore detailing Nolo's family law books (they are also listed in the catalog at the back of this book).

- an online update service for Nolo products
- periodic seminars by Nolo authors, and
- links to other useful online law sites.

Here are Nolo's online addresses:

World Wide Web
http://www.nolo.com

America Online
keyword Nolo

Nolo Press can be reached by e-mail at nolopress.com.

Probably the best online site that is purely dedicated to family law is Divorce Helpline Webworks, a World Wide Web service accessed at: http://www.divorcehelp.com.

This site offers:

- a marvelous tutorial called *A Short Divorce Course* that helps people think intelligently about divorce and the many issues that typically arise
- a series of articles about all facets of a divorce
- a registry of 350 professionals, including attorneys, paralegals, mediators and mental health professionals available to help people who are doing their own legal work
- forms to help divorcing couples sort out their situation
- a bookstore that offers a wide selection of family law books, and
- links to other family law resources on the World Wide Web.

Some additional sources of family law information online include:

Legal Information Network on America Online (keyword Legal). This site offers questions and answers in its legal discussion—Section I.

Divorce Online (http://www.divorce-online.com/). This World Wide Web site provides general topical information, including articles written about mediation, win-win divorces and joint custody. The site also contains answers to frequently asked family law questions.

Divorce Home Page (http://www.primenet.com/[tilde]dean/). This World Wide Web site offers support to people going through divorce or ending a relationship. It offers something for everyone, including a good catalog of divorce-related resources, but tends to focus on issues of interest to men.

Divorce, mediation and California family law (http://www.catalog.com/rmg/famlylaw.htm). This site provides links to a number of family-related newsgroups (discussions) including:

- alt.support.divorce
- alt.support.step-parents
- alt.support.loneliness
- alt.support.depression
- alt.support.anxiety.panic
- alt.psychology.help

Cornell family law database (http://www.law.cornell.edu/topics/topic2.html#family law). This site provides links to the laws available on the Internet. As of January 1996, you could find family law statutes for California, Colorado, Florida, Indiana, Minnesota, New York, Texas, Utah, Washington and Wyoming.

GETTING PROFESSIONAL HELP

A divorce, legal separation, paternity action, or custody or child support dispute often involves a complex interplay between law, economics and highly-charged emotions. Not surprisingly, many professionals are out there to help you.

ATTORNEYS

Traditionally, each spouse or parent hires an attorney to represent his or her separate interests in a divorce, legal separation, paternity, custody or child support proceeding. The attorneys then fight it out in court under what is known as the "adversarial system" of justice. This system tends to generate large fees for the attorneys and seriously deplete the resources of the spouses or parents. As the old saying goes, one lawyer in a town starves while two lawyers in the town prosper.

In addition to large attorneys' fees, the adversarial system tends to foster extreme bitterness, which in turn makes divorce and other procedures very difficult on children—who all too often become pawns in the struggle.

Recognizing these problems, many attorneys are starting to change the way they practice family law. Some become mediators and work with couples to arrive at the best possible agreement. Others offer their services on a piecemeal basis—the client is in charge of the case and purchases services from the lawyer as needed. This "lawyer coach" model tends to dramatically lower the costs of a legal entanglement and the type of fighting that naturally flows from attorney representation. The lawyer coach model works best when the client has independent access to competent self-help law resources. Lawyers who offer these types of services can be located on the Divorce HelpLine home page on the World Wide Web (http://www.divorcehelp.com).

As a general rule, you are best served by an attorney who:

- makes you feel comfortable
- shares his or her expertise with you so you can participate in the case as fully as you want
- will resolve disputes out of court whenever possible, and
- has experience with the types of issues in your case—such as taxes, custody or valuing a family business.

MEDIATORS

Family law mediation has become a growth industry in recent years. Mediation is a process in which a skilled intermediary helps couples arrive at a mutually satisfactory agreement, rather than submitting their dispute to a court for decision. Studies show that divorce-related mediation produces a satisfactory resolution of all outstanding issues in over 80% of cases mediated.

Many states offer court-sponsored mediation for disputes over child custody. Mediation of other types of issues—such as property division or alimony—is voluntary and must be agreed to and paid for by the couple. Even so, the cost of mediation tends to be hundreds of dollars per person rather than the thousands of dollars per person usually paid if a case proceeds to court.

Many mediators prefer to have each party find a separate attorney to consult with before signing an agreement hammered out in the mediation. This assures that neither side gives up valuable rights without at least knowing about them.

Private mediators can be found in the telephone directory under "Mediation" or "Divorce Assistance," or through a community mediation program, the family court, a public mental health agency or a local bar association. Referrals may be obtained from the following organizations:

Conflict Resolution Center, Inc.
2205 E. Carson St.
Pittsburgh, PA 15203
Voice: (412) 481-5559
Fax: (412) 481-5601
e-mail: crcii@igc.apc.org

Academy of Family Mediators
4 Militia Drive
Lexington, MA 02173
Voice: (617) 674-2663
Fax: (617) 674-2690
email: afmoffice@igc.apc.org

Society of Professionals in Dispute Resolution
815 15th St. NW, Suite 530
Washington, DC 20005
Voice: (202) 783-7277
Fax: (202) 783-7281

Independent Paralegals

Many people conclude that attorneys may be bad for their family's mental health and devastating to their pocketbooks, and so they have chosen to handle their own legal matters. This usually requires the use of self-help law books and sometimes assistance from a non-lawyer typing service generally referred to as an "independent paralegal."

Because they are not lawyers, independent paralegals cannot give legal advice or represent you in court. They can, however:

- steer you to appropriate written resources
- provide appropriate court forms
- type the papers in an acceptable format, and
- have the papers filed and served on the other party.

The degree to which independent paralegals flourish in a particular state is directly connected to how vigorously that state's lawyers oppose them. As a general matter, independent paralegals—especially those who help with divorce and custody or child support modifications—are much more prevalent in the western states than in other parts of the country. No state regulates independent paralegals—that is, they don't have a professional license—and potential customers are well advised to pay close attention to an independent paralegal's experience and reputation in the community. The best approach to finding an independent paralegal is to look in the classified ads under Referral Services or in the Yellow Pages under "divorce assistance" or "legal help."

Counselors, Therapists and Other Mental Health Professionals

Counseling, therapy or other mental health assistance can be an important part of dealing with a separation, divorce or other legal concern. Counselors and therapists can:

- help adults and children deal with the emotional issues, and
- help resolve a child custody dispute in a way that benefits the children.

In addition, a child custody evaluator can offer an independent view of what custody arrangement would be best for the children if the parents cannot decide. And a mental health professional with training in domestic violence or child abuse may help fashion a treatment plan that leads to a more healthy relationship between an abusive parent and the children.

Mental health professionals are fairly easy to find. Referrals from the family law court, friends or relatives, the local mental health department, a battered women's shelter, a school counselor, a religious advisor or a family physician are common ways. Also, the Yellow Pages normally carry listings under counseling, mental health, psychiatrists, psychologists, psychotherapists and social workers.

Appraisers and Financial Planners

When a couple splits up, one common type of dispute involves how to value certain property—such as real estate or a family business. For instance, if you want to sell the family home, you may claim it's worth $200,000 while your mate (who wants to buy you out) may claim its value to be half that amount. To resolve this, you can jointly hire an appraiser, a person with special expertise on valuing property, or you can each hire an appraiser and then split the difference.

Appraisers may be found in the Yellow Pages or through the following resources:

American Society of Appraisers (referral to a business appraiser)
Washington, DC
(800) 272-8258

Appraisal Institute (referral to a real estate appraiser)
875 N. Michigan Avenue, Suite 2400
Chicago, IL 60611
(312) 335-4100

Institute of Business Appraisers
P.O. Box 1447
Boynton Beach, FL 33425
(407) 732-3202

Certified financial planners can be very helpful if you want to know the value of a pension or the tax consequences of keeping or selling a particular asset. These professionals can be located through the Yellow Pages or:

International Association of Financial Planning
2 Concourse Parkway, Suite 800
Atlanta, GA 30328
(404) 395-1605

ADOPTION

TOPICS

FOUR TYPES OF ADOPTION
OTHER TERMS USED TO DESCRIBE ADOPTIONS
THE ADOPTION PROCESS
UNIFORM ADOPTION ACT (UAA)

Adoption is a court procedure by which an adult becomes the legal parent of someone who is not his or her biological child. Adoption creates a parent-child relationship recognized for all purposes—including child support obligations, inheritance rights and custody. While in most cases adults adopt minors, it is possible in most states for one adult to adopt another.

FOUR TYPES OF ADOPTION

Stepparent Adoption
In a stepparent adoption, the child is living with a legal parent who has remarried, and the new spouse wants to adopt. Most states have special provisions making it relatively easy for a stepparent to adopt, if the child's noncustodial parent agrees, is dead or missing, or has abandoned the child.

Agency Adoption
Adoptions arranged by licensed charities or publicly-funded social service agencies are called agency adoptions. Agency adoptions involve more court or welfare department involvement than do private adoptions. When a child lives at an orphanage and is adopted, the adoption is usually an agency adoption.

County Adoption
A county adoption happens when a county has custody of a child because the parents have abused, neglected or abandoned the child, or the child has been declared beyond the parents' control. These children are usually placed in foster homes while efforts are made to reunite the family. If reunification doesn't occur, the parents' rights are terminated and the child is made available for adoption.

1

ADOPTION

HOW A CHILD BECOMES AVAILABLE FOR AGENCY OR COUNTY ADOPTION

When a parent fails to provide any financial assistance to, and/or communicate with, his child over a period of time, a court may deem the child abandoned by that parent. Abandonment also describes situations where a child is physically abandoned—left on a doorstep, delivered to a hospital or placed in a trash can, for example. These children are usually placed in orphanages or foster homes and made available for adoption.

When a parent or guardian fails to provide a child with adequate necessaries, education, supervision or general guidance, the adult may be guilty of child neglect. If child neglect is suspected, the local welfare department will conduct an investigation. In severe cases, the child will be removed from the home after a court hearing and placed in a foster home. If the parents do not improve their situation within a reasonable time (usually between six months and two years, depending on the state), the child may be taken away permanently and placed for adoption.

Independent Adoption

An adoption arranged privately between the birth mother and the adoptive parent(s) rather than through a public agency is termed an independent (or private) adoption. A court must approve an independent adoption for it to be valid.

OTHER TERMS USED TO DESCRIBE ADOPTIONS

Open Adoption

An open adoption is an adoption where the birth mother remains in contact with the adoptive parents and the child throughout the child's life. In most adoptions, birth and adoption records are sealed by court order, and the child and adoptive parents may never know the mother's identity. A growing number of families (especially where the adoptive parents are related to the birth mother) are choosing an open adoption route for a number of reasons, including:
- minimizing the birth mother's feelings of guilt and isolation
- reducing the likelihood that the birth mother will rescind the adoption
- having future easy availability to medical histories of the biological parents
- minimizing the trauma to the child in finding out that she was adopted, and
- maximizing the loving adult contacts the child has.

Equitable Adoption

In some states, when a close relationship like that of parent and child exists between a child and an unrelated adult, the courts recognize that an equitable adoption (sometimes called a putative or constructive adoption) has occurred. Often, the adult had agreed or intended to adopt the child but had not validly done so. The effect of calling the relationship an equitable adoption is that the adult must support the child and may be ordered to pay child support if the adult and child no longer live together (as would be the case if the adult and the child's legal parent split up).

Single-Parent Adoption

A single-parent adoption is an adoption by one unmarried person.

Second-Parent Adoption

A second-parent adoption (also called a co-parent adoption) is an adoption of a child by the unmarried partner of the child's legal parent. Second parent adoptions have been granted to lesbians and gay men who are the partners of biological parents or parents who adopted previously as a single parent.

Two-Parent Adoption

A two-parent adoption is an adoption of a child by an unmarried couple. Like second-parent adoptions, a number of two-parent adoptions have been granted to lesbian and gay couples.

States that have granted second-parent or two-parent adoptions to lesbian or gay couples include Alaska, California, Illinois, Indiana, Massachusetts, Michigan, Minnesota, New Jersey, New York, Oregon, Pennsylvania, Texas, Vermont and Washington. They've also been granted in Washington, DC.

Adult Adoption

The reason why one adult might want to adopt another is to create a legally binding relationship when marriage is not available—for example, if the two people are of the same sex, one is already married to another person or they are related too closely to permit marriage (such as first cousins, in a few states). The relationship created by an adult adoption is that of parent and child.

The obstacles the adoptive parent and adopted adult child face include:

- state laws prohibiting adult adoptions—Alabama, Arizona, Hawaii, Michigan, Nebraska and Ohio prohibit one adult from adopting another
- incest laws, if the adoptive parent and adopted adult child are involved in a sexual relationship
- sodomy laws, if the adoptive parent and child are involved in a same-sex sexual relationship, and
- adoption laws specifying an age difference between the adoptive parent and child.

The struggle states engage in over adult adoptions can be demonstrated by the laws in New York and Delaware. New York's adoption law (Domestic Relations Law Art. VII § 110) is silent on the issue of adult adoptions. After a few lower courts granted them to gay couples (one partner adopting the other) in the early 1980s, the state's highest court ruled otherwise. It held that the state's adoption law could not be used as a "quasi-matrimonial vehicle" to legally formalize an adult relationship between sexual partners. (*Matter of Robert Paul P.*, 63 N.Y.2d 233 (1984).)

Delaware's adoption law, on the other hand, specifically allows adult adoptions. (Delaware Code § 13-951.) In a case in which one gay partner sought to adopt his lover, the lower court denied the adoption saying that an adoption must be between two people with a "parent-child" relationship, even if they are both adults. The Supreme Court of Delaware reversed, noting that there was nothing wrong with an adult adoption done primarily to create inheritance rights. (*In re Adoption of Swanson*, 623 A.2d 1095 (1993).)

THE ADOPTION PROCESS

Best Interests of the Child

Regardless of type, adoptions can be granted (or in the case of an equitable adoption, recognized) only by a court and are allowed only when the court declares the adoption to be in the best interests of the child. (The best interest of the child does not apply in adult adoptions; see discussion, above.) To assist the court in making this determination, the state (or local) welfare department conducts an investigation into the home maintained by the prospective adopting parents. The court looks at:

- the occupations, earnings and stability of the prospective parents
- the medical, emotional and physical needs of the child
- religious and racial compatibility (religion and race need not be the same, but the court looks at the potential societal difficulties if they are not)
- whether the prospective parent has any criminal record or history of child abuse, and
- the age of the child.

Federal law requires preference be given to the following people in the adoption or foster placement of an Indian child:

- a member of the child's family
- other members of the child's tribe, or
- other Indian families.

The law requires that the tribe be notified of most foster-adoption placements. If these laws are not followed, some state adoptions can be set aside by tribal courts.

Child's Consent

In addition, most states require the consent of the person being adopted if she is over a certain age, usually about 12.

Preferred Parents

In county and agency adoptions, most state welfare departments give preference to married people in granting adoptions. This is done by placing children to be adopted in the homes of married couples and by giving married couples more favorable recommendations than single people in adoption recommendation reports. In a growing number of states, however, anyone capable of being a good parent may adopt, including single people. In fact, increased numbers of single people and lesbians and gay men as single people and as couples are being allowed to adopt to encourage adoption of hard-to-place children.

New Hampshire (Revised Statutes Annotated § 170-B:4) and Florida (Statutes Annotated § 63.042), however, expressly prohibit lesbians and gay men from adopting. The Florida law is being challenged in court.

HARD-TO-PLACE CHILDREN

Counties and agencies often have a hard time finding adoptive parents for older children (above age five), minority children, children with special needs (such as abused or neglected children), children with physical and mental disabilities and underprivileged children. Children in these categories are sometimes referred to as "unadoptable." As single, lesbian and gay people seek to adopt, however, more children with special needs may be adopted. This is because single, lesbian and gay people have traditionally been prohibited from adopting and are often more flexible than married couples about adopting older, disabled or underprivileged children.

Grandparents' Rights

When a child is adopted, the biological parents' rights are usually terminated. Similarly, in a few states, the grandparents' visitation rights cease as well. More than 20 states, however, allow visitation by the grandparents when the grandchild is adopted by a stepparent, particularly when the biological parent is deceased.

Probation Department Investigation

When an adoption is pending, the court handling the matter will want the family environment investigated. The investigation usually consists of a series of visits to the home by a social worker who physically views the surroundings and talks to whomever is present. Most visits are scheduled; often, however, the social worker makes at least one unannounced visit. Depending on the state, the investigation will be conducted by the juvenile probation department, the adult probation department or the welfare department.

Agency and county adoptions usually require substantially more investigation by the probation department. This is because a child placed for adoption by an agency or the county is considered a "ward of the state" and the state is responsible for representing the interests of the child. In stepparent and independent adoptions, however, the social workers may make only one or two visits to the adoptive parents' home. This is because in stepparent and independent adoptions, the biological parent or parents have selected adoptive parents and are representing the interests of the child.

Adoption Records

Because of the potential psychological trauma to both the adopted child and the birth mother, nearly all states have laws denying adopted persons access to court information containing the identities of the birth mother, or other information which would lead to the discovery of her identity—such as the location of the adoption or the person who arranged the adoption.

Some states, however, including Alabama (Code § 26-10A-31), Alaska (Statutes § 25.23.150) and Kansas (Statutes Annotated § 65-2423), allow adoptees who have reached adulthood access to this information. A few other states allow an adult adoptee access to the records only if the birth mother consents. Arizona adoptees and birth parents may sign up to be "found" by the other, or, conversely, to request that no contact be made. (Revised Statutes § 8-121.) And most states permit limited access to the birth parents' medical histories when necessary.

Birth Certificates

A birth certificate is a document completed by a county official or a person delivering a baby, and then filed with the county shortly after a baby is born. Its purpose is to record the birth. A birth certificate can be modified to reflect an adoption—the adoptive parents' names replace the biological parents' names and the child's name is changed to whatever name is given to her by the adoptive parents.

Birth certificates specifically request the names of the child, the mother and the father, if he is known. In California, same-sex parents who are adopting a child (or the same-sex partner of a biological parent who is adopting her partner's child) may have both names listed as parents on the birth certificate.

UNIFORM ADOPTION ACT (UAA)

This law was proposed by the National Conference of Commissioners on Uniform State Laws, and endorsed by the American Bar Association, in early 1995. As of yet, no state has adopted the law.

The UAA distinguishes among the various types of adoptions—agency/county, independent and stepparent—and sets up standardized procedures for consents and relinquishments by biological parents. It gives biological fathers 30 days to make a claim after the proposed adoption of a child. A birth mother has eight days to change her mind. It requires an evaluation of all prospective adoptive parents, no matter what kind of adoption. If an adoption is contested, the county must expedite the hearing. Finally, the UAA explicitly recognizes open adoptions by authorizing continuing contact between the adoptive and birth families.

ALIMONY

TOPICS

**HOW ALIMONY IS DETERMINED
ALTERNATIVES TO MONTHLY ALIMONY PAYMENTS
MODIFYING ALIMONY PAYMENTS
ENFORCING ALIMONY
TERMINATING ALIMONY**

Alimony (also called maintenance or spousal support) is money paid under the terms of a court order or settlement agreement following a divorce by one ex-spouse to the other for support. Until the 1970s, alimony was a natural extension of the financial arrangement in "traditional" marriages, where the husband was the breadwinner and the wife stayed home, caring for the house and children but not earning any income. Alimony was paid only by the husband to the wife. The amount of alimony was determined by a number of factors—the needs of the parties, their status in life, their wealth and their relative fault in causing the divorce—if a husband was committing adultery or treating his wife cruelly, he would pay a relatively large amount. If, however, the wife was having an affair or treating her husband cruelly, she would receive little or no alimony.

Except in marriages of long duration (ten years or more) or in the case of an ill or ailing spouse, alimony today usually lasts for a set period of time with the expectation that the recipient spouse will become self-supporting.

Temporary Alimony

When a couple separates or files for divorce, the spouses often need the immediate intervention of a court to establish alimony, especially to help determine who pays the bills and lives in the house pending the divorce proceedings. Either spouse may request a hearing before the judge to have the issue temporarily resolved pending a final hearing in the divorce action. The orders made in these preliminary hearings are often, but not necessarily, included in the final judgment.

In some states or counties, legislatures or courts publish tables that calculate a range of alimony to be paid. Judges use these tables as guidelines to determine the amount of temporary alimony to be paid until the divorce becomes final. If the parties cannot agree on an amount, these temporary amounts are imposed at a preliminary hearing and may be altered when the court has a better understanding of what will be best in the long run.

ALIMONY

Permanent Alimony

Permanent alimony is permanent because it is from a final court order. It is intended to continue at the same payment rate indefinitely into the future or until a time specified in the court order. In reality, however, permanent alimony may be modified if the parties agree or if the party wanting the modification petitions the court and the court changes the amount or duration. The only time alimony cannot be modified is when it is specifically made non-modifiable by agreement between the spouses or when it is part of an integrated property settlement agreement, where alimony is paid as part of the property division. (See "Alternatives to Monthly Alimony Payments," below, for more on integrated property settlement agreements.)

Permanent alimony is unavailable in Texas. Temporary support may be granted, but only until the final divorce decree is issued.

Separate Maintenance

In some states, a spouse may obtain separate maintenance (alimony) from her husband while she lives apart from him, even though no divorce has been filed.

Family Support

When alimony and child support are combined into one payment without regard to which portion is alimony and which is child support, some states call it family support. Because of the increased concern over enforcement of child support, however, most courts require that child support and alimony be specified separately.

Non-Support

Non-support refers to the failure of a husband (in all states) or a wife (in some states) to support his or her spouse.

HOW ALIMONY IS DETERMINED

Ability to Pay

Courts always consider a person's ability to pay when setting his alimony obligation. A court looks at the payer's gross income from all sources (wages, public benefits, interest and dividends on investments, rents from real property, profits from patents and the like, and any other sources of income), less any mandatory deductions (income taxes, Social Security, health care and mandatory union dues). The result is the payer's net income.

In most states, deductions for credit union payments and wage attachments are not subtracted when calculating net income. Thus, if John makes $2,000 per month, and income tax, Social Security, unemployment insurance benefits and other government deductions reduce his income to $1,500, this is his net income. The fact that $300 more is withheld to pay a credit union loan does not further reduce his net income for the court's purposes. The reason for this rule is that the law accords support payments a higher priority than other types of debts, and would rather see other debts not paid than have a spouse go without adequate support.

Ability to Earn

When a court computes the amount of alimony to be paid by a spouse, both parties' ability to earn is usually taken into account. Actual earnings are an important factor in determining a person's ability to earn, but are not conclusive where there is evidence that a person could earn more if she chose to do so. Some states, however, set alimony payments based only on actual earnings—that is, the ability to pay.

Example: Jane Doctor, who has earned $100,000 a year for the past three years while married, quit her job when she and her husband separated in order to become a TV repairperson with an annual income of approximately $20,000. During the divorce trial, Jane's husband, Lionel, requested alimony for himself. Because Jane abruptly changed her income, the court imposed a larger alimony obligation on Jane than she can afford earning $20,000 a year. The court has reasoned that Jane can return to the world of medicine if she needs to and that her ex-husband should not be penalized because of her employment decision. In some states, however, the court would reason that ability to earn is too speculative and would set alimony on the basis of Jane's $20,000 income.

Ability to Be Self-Supporting

The ability of an ex-spouse to support herself is normally considered by a court when setting the amount and duration of alimony to be paid to that spouse. A court looks to whether the ex-spouse possesses marketable skills and whether she is able to work outside the home (having custody of pre-school children and not having access to day care could make this impossible). The ability to be self-supporting differs from actually being self-supporting. If a spouse has marketable skills and is able to work outside the home, but has chosen not to look for work, the court is very likely to limit the amount and length of alimony.

In many states, no alimony is awarded if both spouses are able to support themselves. If, however, one spouse was dependent on the other for support during the marriage, the dependent spouse is often awarded alimony for a transition period or until she becomes self-supporting. If a spouse receiving alimony becomes self-supporting before the time set by the court for the alimony to end, the paying spouse can go to court and file a request for modification or for a termination of alimony. Conversely, if at the end of the support period the ex-spouse does not have the ability to support herself, she may request an extension of alimony, which may be difficult to obtain. For example, New York courts may extend alimony only to keep the supported spouse from going on to welfare. (General Obligations Law § 5-311.)

> ### FINANCIAL STATEMENT
>
> A financial statement is a court paper which requires a party to specify her monthly income and expenses. The court often requires each divorcing spouse to fill out a financial statement so that the court has a complete picture of the parties' financial situations before making a decision on alimony and other financial matters.

Standard of Living During Marriage

When a court sets alimony, it often considers the family's pre-divorce standard of living and attempts to continue this standard for both spouses, if feasible. Mrs. Rockefeller, therefore, would be entitled to more alimony than most divorced spouses. If only one spouse worked outside the home, and in many marriages where both spouses worked outside the home, it is usually impossible to continue the same standard of living for both people after the spouses have gone their separate ways. Maintenance of the same standard of living is therefore more of a goal than a guarantee.

Length of Marriage

When a marriage is relatively short—approximately three years or fewer—and no children were born or adopted, courts often refuse to award alimony. If there are children under school age, however, alimony may be awarded to the parent given physical custody because the court wants to enable the custodial parent to care full-time for the child.

Tax Consequences of Alimony

For federal income tax purposes, alimony paid under a written agreement or court order is deductible by the payer and is taxable to the recipient. Child support, on the other hand, is tax-free to the recipient but not deductible by the payer.

In the past, when ex-spouses had more flexibility in negotiating the amount of child support and alimony, many ex-spouses agreed to greater alimony and less child support because of the resulting tax advantage to the payer. Because all states determine the basic child support obligation by formula, however, shifting the amounts of child support and alimony to take advantage of tax deductions is increasingly difficult.

Debts

Upon divorce, the court allocates debts incurred during marriage between the spouses based on who can pay and who benefits most from the asset attached to the debt. If the court orders a spouse to pay a large portion of marital debts, it often reduces the amount of alimony that spouse is ordered to pay.

Professional Degree or License

Some spouses support their mates financially as well as emotionally through professional, graduate or trade school. When they divorce, alimony is rarely awarded to the spouse who supported the couple. Yet, she often made sacrifices (such as delaying her own education) in order to support the other. Some states try to compensate the spouse who put the other through school in the alimony award. For more information on this topic, see "When One Spouse Puts the Other Through School" in the *Property and Debts* chapter.

Agreement Before Marriage

Before a couple marries, the parties may make an agreement concerning certain aspects of their relationship, including whether alimony will be paid in the event the couple later divorces. These agreements are also called ante-nuptial, pre-nuptial or pre-marital agreements. They are usually upheld by courts unless one person shows that the agreement is likely to promote divorce (for example, by including a large alimony amount in the event of divorce), was written and signed with the intention of divorcing or was unfairly entered into (for example, a spouse giving up all of his rights in his spouse's future earnings without the advice of an attorney).

The Uniform Pre-Marital Agreement Act provides legal guidelines for people who wish to make agreements prior to marriage regarding ownership, management and control of property; property disposition on separation, divorce and death; alimony; wills and life insurance beneficiaries. The statute expressly prohibits couples from including provisions concerning child support. Pre-marital agreements are permitted in states that haven't adopted this uniform statute, but are subject to different guidelines in those states. The Act has been adopted in 20 states—Arizona, Arkansas, California, Hawaii, Illinois, Iowa, Kansas, Maine, Montana, Nebraska, Nevada, New Jersey, North Carolina, North Dakota, Oregon, Rhode Island, South Dakota, Texas, Utah and Virginia.

For additional information on how alimony is determined, see Table 2.1 in the Appendix.

ALTERNATIVES TO MONTHLY ALIMONY PAYMENTS

Lump Sum Support

In several states, a spouse may pay his total alimony obligation at the time of the divorce by giving the other spouse a lump sum payment equal to the total amount of future monthly payments.

States which expressly allow lump sum support include:

- Alaska (Statutes § 25-25.24.160(3))
- Florida (Statutes Annotated § 61-08)
- Kansas (Statutes Annotated § 60-1610(b)(2))
- Louisiana (Civil Code, article 160)
- Maine (Revised Statutes Annotated § 19-721)
- Michigan (Compiled Laws Annotated § 552.23)
- Nevada (Revised Statutes Annotated § 125.150)
- New Mexico (Statutes Annotated § 40-4-7)
- North Carolina (General Statutes § 50-16.1)
- Ohio (Revised Code § 3105.18)
- Oregon (Revised Statutes § 107-105)
- South Carolina (Code of Laws § 20-3-130)
- Virginia (Code § 20-107.1)
- West Virginia (Code § 48-2-15), and
- Wyoming (Statutes Annotated § 20-2-114).

Alimony in Gross

This is another term for lump sum support.

Periodic Support

Occasionally, alimony obligations are paid less frequently than monthly. This is called periodic support. Traditionally, periodic support was paid until the recipient died or remarried. Today, however, because alimony is usually paid for a fixed period, periodic support is more like lump sum support divided over a few periodic payments.

Integrated Property Settlement Agreement

Upon divorce, couples commonly enter into a divorce agreement which divides marital property and may set alimony. The agreement is called integrated if the property settlement and alimony payments are combined into either one lump sum payment or periodic payments. Integrated agreements are often used when the marital property consists of substantial intangible assets (for example, future royalties, stock options or future pension plans) or when one party is buying the other's interest in a valuable tangible asset (for example, a home or business). In addition, if a spouse is entitled to little or no alimony, but is not financially independent, periodic payments may help that spouse gain financial independence.

MODIFYING ALIMONY PAYMENTS

There are several ways in which alimony may be modified.

NON-MODIFIABLE ALIMONY

In many states, divorce agreements or decrees (court judgments) may state that alimony amounts and periods are non-modifiable, which means that they cannot be changed once they are established.

Agreement to Modify Alimony

After a final decree of divorce is filed with a court, former spouses may agree to modify the alimony terms. This modified agreement (also called a stipulated modification) may be made without court approval. If one person later reneges on the agreement, however, the other person may not be able to enforce it unless the court has approved the modification. Thus, it is advisable to obtain court approval before relying on such agreements. Courts routinely approve agreed-upon modifications to alimony.

Cost of Living Adjustment (COLA) Clause

A COLA clause in an alimony order means that payments are to increase annually at a rate equal to the annual cost of living increase, as determined by an economic indicator (such as the Consumer Price Index). Some judges include COLAs in their orders when setting alimony. This eliminates the need for any requests for modifications from the recipient based on the change in the cost of living.

Escalator Clause

An escalator clause sometimes is included in a divorce agreement or decree to provide an alimony recipient with an automatic specified share of any increase in the payer's earnings.

Temporary Modification of Alimony

When the needs of an ex-spouse receiving alimony change temporarily, or if the payer's ability to pay is temporarily impaired by illness, loss of job or other condition, a court may modify an existing alimony order for a specific period of time to account for the temporary condition. At the end of the set period, the temporary modification terminates and the alimony reverts to the prior terms unless an order for permanent alimony is obtained. Although desirable, a temporary modification of alimony may not be easy to obtain without a lawyer's assistance.

Changed Circumstances

When parties are unable to agree on a modification of alimony, the party wanting the change will have to file a request for a modification of alimony with the court. She must usually show that circumstances have changed substantially since the time of the previously issued order. This rule encourages stability of arrangements and helps prevent the court from becoming overburdened with frequent and repetitive modification requests. Below are several examples of a change of circumstances.

Change in law. When a law affecting alimony is amended or a new law enacted, this by itself can sometimes constitute the changed circumstance necessary to file a request for modification of a prior alimony order.

Cohabitation. In some states, an alimony recipient who begins cohabiting (usually living intimately with a person of the opposite sex, but a few courts have applied this rule to women who begin living with female lovers) is presumed to need less alimony than originally awarded. If the recipient objects, it is her burden to show that her needs have not decreased.

Cost of living increase. When inflation reduces the value of alimony payments, the recipient may cite her increased cost of living as a changed circumstance and request an increase.

Decrease in income/decreased ability to pay/loss of job. When an ex-spouse paying alimony suffers a decrease in earnings, she may be able to obtain from the court a downward modification of alimony. The modification may be temporary or permanent, depending on her prospects for new work or increased hours.

Decreased need for alimony. When a former spouse's need for alimony decreases or ceases, the court may reduce or terminate the alimony if the paying spouse files a request for modification. Such a request can be made if the alimony recipient gets a job, an increase in pay or sometimes if she begins intimately living with someone of the opposite sex (cohabiting).

Disability. Disability in family law generally means the inability to earn enough income to support oneself through work because of a physical or mental condition. A temporary disability suffered by a person paying alimony may warrant a temporary decrease of alimony. A permanent disability may warrant a request for modification of alimony based on changed circumstances. Similarly, if a recipient of alimony becomes disabled, a court may order an increase if her earnings decreased or her expenses increased (for example, health care or child care) as a result.

Financial emergency. A financial emergency occurs when a person is unexpectedly required to lay out money (for example, to pay sudden medical bills). When a person who pays alimony suffers a financial emergency, he may file a request with the court for a temporary decrease of alimony. When a person who receives alimony suffers a financial emergency, she may ask the court for a temporary increase.

Hardship. Hardship means suffering or adversity. If compliance with a legal obligation would cause a hardship on a person or his family, he may be excused from the obligation. For example, a payer's inability to meet an alimony obligation without great economic suffering himself is a hardship. If a court finds this hardship substantial, the payer may be relieved of all or a part of his support obligation for a temporary or indefinite period.

Increase in income. When an alimony recipient's income increases, her ex-spouse may file with the court a request for modification of the alimony, claiming that the changed circumstance means his ex-spouse needs less alimony. Whether the court will agree depends on the particular facts of the situation. When the paying spouse's income increases, alimony may stay the same if the recipient's needs are being met. If her ex did not have the ability to pay enough alimony to meet her true needs before the increase in income, however, a court might grant a request for a modification based on the increase.

Medical emergencies. Medical emergencies that require large expenditures of money are the kind of temporary and catastrophic circumstances that may support a temporary modification of alimony. If the recipient suffers the emergency, the payer may be required to temporarily increase payments (if he is able).

Likewise, if the payer is the one with the emergency, his duty to support may temporarily be eased by the court.

New support obligation. When an ex-spouse paying alimony assumes a new legal support obligation (for example, adopts, remarries or has a child), the court may reduce the earlier alimony order if it would be a hardship to pay the prior alimony and meet the new obligation. On the other hand, if the new support obligation is voluntarily assumed (for example, helping to support stepchildren when there is no duty to do so), rather than required by law, a court is unlikely to order a reduction.

Retroactive Modification of Alimony

In theory, courts are supposed to refuse to retroactively modify an alimony obligation. This means if a person is unable to pay support, he may petition the court for a reduction, but even if the court reduces future payments, it should hold him liable for the full amount of support due and owing. Many courts, however, do not follow this rule. Although the courts will state that they refuse to make retroactive modifications, they frequently excuse the payers from some of the arrearages. The courts' reasoning is that if the recipients survived the months (or years) without the support, they truly can get by without it.

ENFORCING ALIMONY

Arrearages or Arrears

Each installment of court-ordered alimony is owed and to be paid according to the date set out in the order. When an ex-spouse ordered by a court to pay alimony does not comply, the overdue payments are called arrearages or arrears. Because the majority of people ordered to pay alimony don't, and a growing number of women who are awarded (but not paid) alimony are poor, many (but unfortunately, not enough) courts are becoming more strict than they were a few years ago about enforcing alimony orders and collecting alimony arrearages.

No federal laws have been passed specifically to aid in the collection of alimony. The Child Support Enforcement Act of 1984 and some state laws, however, allow district attorneys to pursue alimony arrearages when seeking back owed child support. In addition, a number of states are using enforcement laws such as wage attachments and contempt of court proceedings to collect alimony arrearages.

Revised Uniform Reciprocal Enforcement of Support Act (RURESA)

This law (or its predecessor, the Uniform Reciprocal Enforcement of Support Act), was enacted by every state. It permits an ex-spouse who is owed alimony to collect it by using the court in her state to enforce her alimony order against her ex living in another state. The court in the state where the recipient lives contacts a court in the other parent's state, which in turn requires her ex to pay.

As a practical matter, this procedure often falls short of its stated goals. District attorneys commonly give RURESA and URESA alimony cases low priority. If any time and effort goes into collecting support by the D.A.s, it is usually to collect child support. (See *Child Support* chapter for more information on RURESA.)

Uniform Interstate Family Support Act (UIFSA)

This law has been enacted by nearly half of the states. Its purpose is to provide uniform laws for enforcing alimony obligations when one ex-spouse lives in one state and the other ex-spouse lives in another state. Some terms have been copied verbatim from URESA and RURESA, however, many terms give courts expanded the powers to enforce alimony orders. (See *Child Support* chapter for more information on UIFSA.)

Wage Attachment

A wage attachment is a court order requiring an employer to deduct a certain amount of money from an employee's paycheck each pay period in order to satisfy a debt. Wage attachments are often used to collect alimony or child support arrearages and to secure payment in the future.

TERMINATING ALIMONY

Automatic Termination

Alimony usually ends automatically when the recipient remarries, when either ex-spouse dies, or when a condition set out by the court order occurs (for example, a recipient becomes self-supporting or begins cohabiting). Alimony may also end at a specific date set by the court's alimony order. If periodic payments are part of a divorce agreement or an integrated property settlement agreement, however, the alimony may continue even after the recipient remarries.

Cohabitation

In a few states, cohabitation brings about a termination of alimony, if the paying spouse can show that the recipient spouse and new lover live together, share expenses and are generally recognized as a couple. All state laws of this kind specifically apply to heterosexual cohabitation. Two California courts applied the spirit of the law to a case in which a woman receiving alimony moved in with her lesbian lover. And although Minnesota does not have a statute authorizing the reduction of alimony because of cohabitation, an ex-wife's alimony was terminated in a case where her husband proved she had "entered into an apparently stable relationship with a woman." (5 Family Law Rptr. 2127 (1979).)

Remarriage

When an alimony recipient remarries, there is usually a termination of alimony on the theory that the recipient is now obtaining additional income from the remarriage. When the alimony payer remarries, the recipient is unlikely to be able to obtain an increase in alimony unless she can show an increased need which happened to coincide with or predate the payer's remarriage.

EXTENSION OF ALIMONY

Although alimony is usually set for a limited amount of time, the period is usually extended by the court if the recipient presents evidence of changed circumstances. The recipient must file a request for a modification of alimony before the existing alimony expires. This is because once there is a termination of alimony, the court cannot reinstate it.

Example: As part of Jody and Tim's divorce agreement, Tim is to pay Jody $400 per month in alimony for three years or until she obtains a job, whichever comes first. Jody and Tim agree that the purpose of the alimony is to give Jody adequate time to learn a skill and find work. Six months ago, Jody completed a computer course in which she learned how to program. En route to a job interview, however, she was in a car accident and has been laid up ever since. The three-year period ends in two months. Jody has filed a motion requesting an extension of the alimony until she is well enough to interview and work. Because she did her best to obtain a skill and find a job, the court is likely to grant her an extension until she gets a job.

If a divorce agreement or decree states that alimony amounts and periods are non-modifiable, however, a judge cannot extend alimony beyond the termination date.

CHILD SUPPORT

TOPICS

WHO MUST PAY CHILD SUPPORT?
FOR WHOM MUST CHILD SUPPORT BE PAID?
LAWS AND PROCEDURES TO ESTABLISH CHILD SUPPORT
STANDARDS USED TO DETERMINE CHILD SUPPORT
ENFORCEMENT OF CHILD SUPPORT PAYMENTS
MODIFICATION OF CHILD SUPPORT
TAX CONSEQUENCES OF CHILD SUPPORT

All states require natural parents and adoptive parents to support their children until:
- the children reach the age of majority (and sometimes longer)
- the children go on active military duty
- the children are declared emancipated by a court, or
- the parents' rights and responsibilities are terminated (such as when a child is adopted).

In a divorce, this means that the noncustodial parent is often required to pay child support while the custodial parent is deemed to be meeting his support duty through the custody itself. For parents awarded joint physical custody, the support obligation of each is often based on the ratio of each parent's income to their combined incomes, and the percentage of time the child spends with each parent.

All states require their courts to set child support by plugging certain numbers into a formula. Most formulas take into consideration the parents' incomes and necessary expenses. In addition, most states permit judges to modify the amount generated by the formula to take into consideration some of the following factors:
- needs of the child
- standard of living of the child before the divorce or separation
- the noncustodial parent's ability to earn and ability to pay
- relative income and assets of the parents, and
- tax consequences of alimony and child support.

Unfortunately, a large percentage of parents ordered to pay child support do not. Society has become less tolerant of these parents, and the federal government requires all state governments to enact laws to facilitate enforcement of child support orders; these laws work to some extent, but are still far from adequate.

CHILD SUPPORT

Temporary Child Support

When a couple separates or files for divorce, the spouses often need the immediate intervention of a court to establish child support. Either spouse may request a hearing before the judge to have the issue resolved pending a final hearing in the divorce. In some states, legislatures publish tables that calculate a range of temporary child support to be paid. No matter how the judge arrives at the amount, the orders made in these preliminary hearings are not necessarily included in the final judgment.

Permanent Child Support

Permanent child support is permanent because it is from a final court order. Payments are to continue until the child reaches the age of majority, the child is emancipated or the court order modifies the amount upon the request of either parent.

Family Support

When alimony and child support are combined into one payment without regard to which portion is alimony and which is child support, some states call it family support. Because of the increased concern over enforcement of child support, however, many states require that child support and alimony be specified separately.

WHO MUST PAY CHILD SUPPORT?

When a mother is not married, it's not always clear who the father is—and whether or not he must pay child support.

Acknowledged Father

An acknowledged father is any biological father of a child born to unmarried parents for whom paternity has been established by either the admission of the father or the agreement of the parents. An acknowledged father must pay child support.

Presumed Father

If any of the following are true, a man is presumed to be the father of a child, unless he or the mother proves otherwise to a court:

- he was married to the mother when the child was conceived or born, although some states do not consider a man to be a presumed father if the couple has separated
- he attempted to marry the mother (even if the marriage was not valid) and the child was conceived or born during the "marriage"
- he married the mother after the birth and agreed either to have his name on the birth certificate or to support the child, or
- he welcomed the child into his home and openly held the child out as his own. In some states, the presumption of paternity is considered conclusive, which means it cannot be disproven, even with contradictory blood tests. In Michael H. v. Gerald D., 491 U.S. 110 (1989), the U.S. Supreme Court upheld California's presumed father statute as a rational method of protecting the integrity of the family against challenges based on the due process rights of the father and the child. A presumed father must pay child support.

Unwed Father

An unmarried man who impregnates a woman is referred to as an unwed father. Unwed fathers have few rights concerning their children, unless they are also presumed fathers. For example, an unwed father does not have the right to require the mother of the child to obtain his consent, or even notify him, before she undergoes an abortion or places the child for adoption. If the mother decides to bear and keep the child, however, the unwed father will be required to pay child support if a court determines or he acknowledges that he's the father; in addition, he has the right to visitation with his child and may seek custody.

Stepfather

A stepfather is not obligated to support the children of the woman to whom he is married unless he legally adopts the children.

ADULTERINE BASTARD

Adulterine bastard, though not used in many places, is a term used to describe a child born to a married woman when the woman's husband is not the father of the child. This may occur if a woman becomes pregnant by someone other than her husband during the marriage; if a woman enters the marriage already pregnant (by someone other than her husband); or if a woman, without her husband's consent, becomes pregnant through artificial insemination by donor.

In the past, many divorcing husbands attempted to evade paying child support in these situations, claiming that the children were adulterine bastards and therefore not "theirs." Many states, however, have laws which irrebuttably presume (that is, the presumption cannot be disproved) that a child born during a marriage is the child of the husband, regardless of who the biological father is.

Equitable Parent

In Michigan (*Atkinson v. Atkinson*, 408 N.W.2d 516 (1987)) and Wisconsin (*In re Paternity of D.L.H.*, 419 N.W.2d 283 (1987)), a spouse who is not a legal parent (biological or adoptive) may be granted custody or visitation under the notion of equitable parent. Courts apply this concept when a spouse and child have a close relationship and consider themselves parent and child or where the biological parent encouraged this relationship. If the court grants an equitable parent custody or visitation, then the parent will also be required to pay child support.

FOR WHOM MUST CHILD SUPPORT BE PAID?

All states require natural parents and adoptive parents to support their children until:
- the children reach the age of majority (and sometimes longer, particularly if a child is disabled)
- the children go on active military duty
- the children are declared emancipated by a court, or
- the parents' rights and responsibilities are terminated (such as when a child is adopted).

Illegitimate Child

A father is obligated to support all of his children, regardless of whether he was married to the mother. Children born to parents not legally married to each other are sometimes termed illegitimate unless and until the parents later marry. This term is used infrequently today, and has little legal effect except where the law expressly gives rights only to legitimate children. For instance, illegitimate children are denied the right to inherit from their fathers in some states.

Emancipated Minor

A minor demonstrating freedom from parental control or support is considered emancipated, or may be declared emancipated by a court. Child support obligations to the parents of emancipated minors may be canceled by the court. For obvious reasons, most states do not allow parents to unilaterally declare their children emancipated; rather, a special proceeding must be brought to have the child declared emancipated by a court and the support obligation terminated.

LAWS AND PROCEDURES TO ESTABLISH CHILD SUPPORT

Guidelines for Temporary Child Support

In some states, legislatures publish tables or formulas that calculate a range of child support to be paid. Courts use these tables as guidelines to determine the amount of temporary child support to be paid while the divorce is pending. If the parties cannot agree on an amount, the temporary amount is imposed at a preliminary hearing and may be altered when the court has a better understanding of what will be best in the long run.

Family Support Act of 1988 (42 U.S.C. § 666)

The Family Support Act of 1988 reformed the U.S. welfare system by emphasizing enforcement of child support orders against delinquent parents and expanded job training and educational opportunities to reduce parents' reliance on welfare.

Under the act, all states must include automatic wage attachments in new or modified child support orders, with few exceptions. The act also encourages states to use paternity tests to establish responsibility for child support, and requires the use of guidelines in making support awards. States must also develop automatic tracking and monitoring systems for parents not paying support. And because refusal to pay child support is often linked to frustrated visitation, the act funds projects to improve noncustodial parents' access to their children.

Aid to Families with Dependent Children (AFDC)

The Aid to Families with Dependent Children program is a joint federal-state program that provides assistance to almost five million families nationwide every month. It is the main source of income for families with children and no parent who is employed full-time.

A family must meet all these requirements to be eligible for the AFDC program:

- Family income and resources must be within limits set by the state. The family must own less than $1,000 worth of resources. Many types of property are exempt from this limit, including most furniture and clothing, a burial plot, the full value of a home and the value of a car up to $1,500. The family's gross income must be no higher than 185% of the state subsistence level.
- The children in the family must be deprived of parental support or care. This means at least one of the child's parents must be absent from the home or incapacitated, or the family's main breadwinner must be employed less than 100 hours per month. Most often, the deprivation requirement is met because only one parent lives in the home.
- The children must be living either with a parent or with another relative who qualifies as a caretaker relative (most relatives qualify).

- The family must either be U.S. citizens or have legal alien status.
- The caretaker must not be involved in a strike on the last day of the month for which benefits are sought.

Families don't necessarily get what they need under this program, only what the state is willing to pay. And the amount the state pays is subject to change by the state legislature, and when budget constraints exist, families may be paid even less.

With some exceptions, if the family has income, it is deducted from the need standard (which is always a little higher than the payment standard), and AFDC pays the difference. Generally, all cash receipts count as income, except:

- the first $50 per month in child support received by the family
- a small portion of earned income
- certain expenses (such as child care) associated with the job
- all of the earned income of a student under 16, and
- educational loans and grants.

Once a family qualifies for AFDC, it must meet certain requirements to stay eligible. It must:

- report its income and resources accurately to the welfare department
- provide a Social Security number for each member of the family
- cooperate with work or education requirements, which means looking for a job or undergoing training, and
- cooperate with the District Attorney's office in collecting child support from an absent parent.

A family that is denied AFDC or has its benefits cut or terminated is entitled to a hearing before a judge. The judge is employed by the welfare department but is required to be impartial. The judge will examine the facts in light of the welfare rules and decide whether or not the welfare department's actions were appropriate. For families already on AFDC, the hearing is held before the actions take effect.

OTHER TERMS OF THE FAMILY SUPPORT ACT

The act also creates a new Job Opportunities and Basic Skills Training (JOBS) Program to help welfare recipients enter or reenter the job market. Participation is required, except for parents who are pregnant or caring for children under age three. Parents with children under six need only participate part-time. If a parent fails to participate, she loses her Aid to Families with Dependent Children (AFDC) benefits.

While each state's program is different, all offer basic education and skills training, and may offer on-the-job training, community work experience and job searching. They focus on unemployed custodial and noncustodial parents who are, or are likely to become, long-term welfare recipients. The states must provide child care and Medicaid for up to one year to assist the transition from welfare to work.

Before the act, in some states, AFDC was available for only single parents. Now it offers benefits, including cash assistance, job training, Medicaid and child care, for intact families whose principal earner is unemployed.

Paternity Action

A court suit filed to have a man declared the father of a child is called a paternity action (or establishment, filiation or parentage action). It can be brought by either the mother or the father. If paternity is established, the court will order the father to pay child support and grant him custody or visitation rights. Today, blood and DNA tests can affirmatively determine paternity with a 99.99% accuracy, and can rule out paternity with 100% accuracy.

Once paternity has been established, a judge determines the frequency of child support payments and visitation in something called an establishment hearing.

A man sued for paternity can reduce the likelihood of a court ruling against he if he can show:

- he has low sperm count
- he has poor quality sperm
- they used contraception
- that the mother had intercourse with more than one man at the time of conception
- comments from the mother stating that the man was not the father, and
- that his name is not on the birth certificate.

Conversely, the likelihood that he will be ruled the father will increase if:

- he lived with the mother
- they had unprotected intercourse
- he acknowledged that he was the father or admitted to paternity
- he has ever claimed the child as a dependent on his tax return
- he was present when the child was born, or
- he supported or bought gifts for the child.

Most paternity actions are initiated by welfare officials who provide AFDC to the mother and are required by law to seek reimbursement from the father. The mother must cooperate in these proceedings; failure to do so can result in a reduction or loss of her AFDC grant.

Financial Statement

A financial statement is a court paper which requires a party to specify her monthly income and expenses. The court often requires each divorcing spouse to fill out a financial statement so that the court has a complete picture of the parties' financial situations before making a decision on child support.

STANDARDS USED TO DETERMINE CHILD SUPPORT

Under the Child Support Enforcement Act of 1984 (42 U.S.C. 651 and following), federal law requires each state to develop guidelines to calculate a range of child support to be paid, based on the parents' incomes and expenses.

Courts are supposed to strive for fairness to the parents in establishing the dollar amount of child support obligations. They are thus given discretion to apportion child support responsibility between parents according to their relative financial circumstances. Some states' laws specify factors which must be considered in determining who pays child support, and how much. These include the needs of the child—including health insurance, educational needs, day care, and special needs of the child—the needs of the custodial parent, the payer's ability to pay and the standard of living of the child before divorce.

Needs of the Child

Normally, child support payments are based on two factors—the ability of a parent to provide support and the child's needs.

Relative Income and Assets

When setting child support, a court normally considers the relative income and assets of both spouses. If the custodial parent earns more than the noncustodial parent, child support may be a nominal amount. In the real world, however, the custodial parent is usually the mother and normally has much less income than the noncustodial father. Accordingly, when courts consider the relative assets and income of the parties, they usually end up awarding child support to the custodial parent.

Ability to Pay

Courts always consider a person's ability to pay when setting his child support obligations. A court looks at the payer's gross income from all sources (wages, public benefits, interest and dividends on investments, rents from real property, profits from patents and the like, and any other sources of income), less any mandatory deductions (income taxes, Social Security, health care and mandatory union dues). The result is the payer's net income.

In most states, deductions for credit union payments, wage attachments and the like are not subtracted when calculating net income. Thus, if John makes $2,000 per month, and income tax, Social Security, unemployment insurance benefits and other government deductions reduce his income to $1,500, this is his net income. The fact that $300 more is withheld to pay a credit union loan does not further reduce his net income for the court's purposes. The reason for this rule is that the law accords support payments a higher priority than other types of debts, and would rather see other debts not paid than have a spouse or child go without adequate support.

Also when setting support obligations, in some states the court may take into account the reasonable expenses incurred by the paying spouse for his own basic necessaries of life (such as rent or mortgage, food, clothing and health care). Courts, however, typically do not allow expenses such as school expenses, dining outside the home and entertainment to influence their support determination on the theory that family support should come before these types of personal expenses. And in a growing number of states, the expenses of the paying spouse are irrelevant.

Ability to Earn

When a court computes the amount of child support to be paid by a parent, both parties' ability to earn is usually taken into account. Actual earnings are an important factor in determining a person's ability to earn, but are not conclusive where there is evidence that a person could earn more if she chose to do so.

For example, assume a parent with an obligation to pay child support leaves his current job and enrolls in medical or law school, takes a job with lower pay but good potential for higher pay in the future, or takes a lower paying job that provides better job satisfaction. In each of these situations, a court may base the child support award on the income from the original job (ability to earn) rather than on the new income level (ability to pay). The basis for this decision would be that the children's current needs take priority over the parent's career plans and desires.

Standard of Living

When a court sets child support, it often considers the family's pre-divorce standard of living and attempts to continue this standard for the children, if feasible. Courts, however, are aware of the difficulty of maintaining two households on the income that formerly supported one home. Maintenance of the same standard of living is therefore more of a goal than a guarantee.

ENFORCEMENT OF CHILD SUPPORT PAYMENTS

Each installment of court-ordered child support is owed and to be paid according to the date set out in the order. When a person ordered by a court to pay child support does not comply, the overdue payments are called arrearages or arrears. Courts have become very strict about enforcing child support orders and collecting arrearages, and, to that end, many state and federal laws have been passed to aid in collection.

While the person with arrears can ask a court for a modification of future payments, the court will usually insist that the arrearage be paid in full, either immediately or in installments. For this reason, if a parent with a child support obligation starts falling behind because his income has decreased or his debts have increased, he should immediately seek a temporary modification.

RETROACTIVE MODIFICATION OF CHILD SUPPORT

Courts are supposed to refuse to retroactively modify a child support obligation. This means if a person has been unable to pay support, he may petition the court for a reduction, but even if the court reduces future payments, it should hold him liable for the full amount of support due and owing.

Example: Joe has a child support obligation of $300 per month. Joe is laid off of his job, and six months pass before he finds another one with comparable pay. Although Joe could seek a temporary decrease on the grounds of diminished income, he lets the matter slide and fails to pay any support during the six-month period. Joe's ex-wife later brings Joe into court to collect the $1,800 arrearage; Joe cannot obtain a retroactive ruling excusing him from making the earlier payments.

Child Support Enforcement Act of 1984

Under this law, the district attorneys (or state's attorneys) of every state must offer collection assistance to the recipient parent. Sometimes this means serving the other parent with papers requiring him to meet with the D.A. and arrange a payment schedule, and telling him that if he refuses to meet or pay, he could go to jail. If the nonpaying parent has moved out of state, the D.A. or the recipient parent can use legal procedures to locate him and seek payment. Federal and state parent locator services can also assist in locating missing parents. In addition, federal laws permit the interception of tax refunds to enforce child support orders. Other methods of enforcement include wage attachments and seizing property.

Revised Uniform Reciprocal Enforcement of Support Act (RURESA)

This law (or its predecessor, the Uniform Reciprocal Enforcement of Support Act), has been enacted by every state. It permits a parent who is owed child support to collect it by using the court in her state to enforce her child support order against the other parent living in another state. The court in the state where the recipient parent lives contacts a court in the other parent's state, which in turn requires the parent to pay. This procedure is free for the party seeking support.

As a practical matter, this procedure often falls short of its stated goals. District attorneys commonly give these cases low priority and often have large backlogs of pending RURESA cases. Also, when the party who owes the support is hauled into court halfway across the country, judges often do not order payment of very much support. This is because they have very little information and only one parent before them, who is generally more convincing than the papers in the file which have been forwarded from the court in the state where the parent seeking the support lives.

Uniform Interstate Family Support Act (UIFSA)

This law has been enacted by nearly half of the states. Its purpose is to provide uniform laws for enacting and enforcing child support obligations when one parent lives in one state and the other parent lives in another state. Some terms have been copied verbatim from URESA and RURESA, however, many terms give courts expanded powers to enforce child support orders and improve the efficiency of collecting outstanding support.

For example, under RURESA, a parent owed support has to file two different lawsuits—one in the state where she lives—to get a judgment for the owed support, and then a second in the state where the payer lives—to register that judgment. UIFSA requires that she file only the lawsuit in the state where the payer lives. UIFSA also eases the bureaucracy of trying to modify an order issued by one state when the payer has moved to a different state.

Child Support Recovery Act

This federal law, adopted in 1992, makes it a federal crime to avoid paying child support by fleeing to another state. The law takes effect only if the support has been unpaid for more than one year or is greater than $ 5,000. Punishment upon conviction is as follows:

- first offense—a fine, imprisonment up to six months, or both
- additional convictions—a fine, imprisonment up to two years, or both, and
- all cases—restitution equal to the amount of the past due support.

Parent Locator Service

Parent locator services have been created by state and federal governments to assist a parent in locating her child's other parent in order to enforce child support orders. They also help parents locate missing children who may have been concealed by the other parent. Many parent locator services are associated with district attorney or state's attorney offices.

Wage Attachment

A wage attachment is a court order requiring an employer to deduct a certain amount of money from an employee's paycheck each pay period in order to satisfy a debt. Wage attachments are often used to collect child support arrearages and to secure payment in the future. Under federal law, all states must include some type of automatic wage attachment—actually called a wage withholding—when a parent has been ordered to pay child support. In some states, the payer can get the wage withholding removed if he shows a history of reliable paying.

Example: In Texas, the automatic wage withholding requires that when a judge makes a child support order (or modifies an existing one), he immediately notifies the payer's employer that the payer's wages are being attached to pay her child support. This applies to parents who have a history of non-payment, who have faithfully paid for years without ever missing a payment or who are paying for the first time and have never had an opportunity to make—or miss—a payment. The theory behind the automatic wage withholding law in Texas is that no parent suffers the stigma of a "nonpayer whose wages must be attached" if every parent's wages are withheld.

Miscellaneous Methods

Increasingly, states are enacting laws to seriously punish parents who don't pay child support. Nearly 20 states will revoke or withhold drivers' licenses from delinquent parents. And several states revoke or withhold professional licenses (lawyers', doctors', contractors' and the like). In recent years, parents who don't pay child support are being prosecuted for, and convicted of, failing to support their children. (See, for example, *Indiana v. Taylor*, 625 N.E.2d 1354 (Ind. 1993), *State v. Morovitz*, 867 S.W.2d 506 (Mo. 1993) and *North Dakota v. Mertz*, 514 N.W.2d 662 (N.D. 1994).)

MODIFICATION OF CHILD SUPPORT

After a final decree of divorce is filed with a court, former spouses may agree to modify the child support terms. To be legally enforceable, even an agreed-upon modification for child support must be approved by a judge.

If the parents can't agree on a modification, the parent wanting the change must file a motion requesting a modification of the order from the court that issued it, usually on the ground of changed circumstances.

Cost of Living Adjustment (COLA) Clause

A COLA clause in a child support order means that payments are to increase annually at a rate equal to the annual cost of living increase, as determined by an economic indicator (such as the Consumer Price Index). Some judges include COLAs in their orders when setting child support. This eliminates the need for any requests for modifications from the recipient claiming the cost of living increase as a changed circumstance.

Temporary Modification of Child Support

When the needs of a child change temporarily, or if the payer's ability to pay is temporarily impaired by illness, loss of job or other condition, a court may modify an existing child support order for a specific period of time to account for the temporary condition. At the end of the set period, the temporary modification terminates and the child support reverts to the prior terms unless a modified order for permanent child support is obtained. Although desirable, a temporary modification of child support may not be easy to obtain without a lawyer's help.

Changed Circumstances

When a party files a request for modification of child support, she must show that circumstances have changed substantially since the time of the previously issued order. This rule encourages stability of arrangements and helps prevent the court from becoming overburdened with frequent and repetitive modification requests. Below are several examples of change of circumstances.

Additional financial burden. When a child support obligation is temporarily made more difficult by an additional financial burden (for example, a medical emergency), a court may order a temporary modification of child support, reducing the amount to be paid. Likewise, a person to whom child support is owed may sometimes obtain a temporary increase in support if she faces a temporary additional economic hardship.

Additional income from remarriage. If a parent with child support obligations remarries and has some of his new spouse's income available for living expenses, the parent receiving the support may be able to get an increase by filing a request for modification. This is because the paying parent now has a greater share of his own income available to fund the increase.

In some situations, when a parent receiving child support remarries, the paying parent may be able to obtain a reduction in the amount of court-ordered child support he pays. This usually happens only if the recipient parent and the children have the benefit of the new spouse's income.

Change in law. When a law affecting child support is amended or a new law enacted, this by itself can sometimes constitute the changed circumstance necessary to file a request for modification of a prior child support order.

Change of job. When a person paying child support changes jobs and earns less income, he may be able to obtain a reduction in the child support payments by filing an appropriate request for modification. The change, however, must be in reasonable furtherance of his career development and future increased income opportunities. If the court believes that the decrease in income is for the purpose of lessening or avoiding support obligations, the request for modification will probably be denied.

If a person paying child support changes jobs and receives an increase in pay, the recipient may be able to obtain a corresponding increase in support.

Cost of living increase. When inflation reduces the value of child support payments, the recipient may cite her increased cost of living as a changed circumstance and request an increase.

Decrease in income. When a parent paying child support suffers a temporary decrease in earnings, she may be able to obtain from the court a temporary decrease of child support. If the payer suffers a permanent decrease in income, she should file a request for modification with the court, citing the decrease as the changed circumstance that justifies the request for a reduction.

Disability. A temporary disability suffered by a person paying child support may warrant a temporary decrease of child support. For example, if a construction worker with a child support obligation breaks his leg, a court may suspend his obligation to pay child support until he recovers and goes back to work. A permanent disability may warrant a request for modification of child support based on changed circumstances. Similarly, if a recipient of child support becomes disabled, a court may order an increase if her earnings decreased or her expenses increased (for example, health care or child care) as a result.

Financial emergency. A financial emergency occurs when a person is unexpectedly required to lay out money (for example, to pay sudden medical bills). When a person who pays child support suffers a financial emergency, he may file a request with the court for a temporary decrease of child support. When a person who receives child support suffers a financial emergency, she may ask the court for a temporary increase.

Hardship. If compliance with a legal obligation would cause a hardship on a person or his family, he may be excused from the obligation. For example, a payer's inability to meet a child support obligation without great economic suffering himself is a hardship. If a court finds this hardship substantial, the payer may be relieved of all or a part of his support obligation for a temporary or indefinite period. Because child support is calculated by formula, however, fewer and fewer courts grant hardship reductions.

Increase in income. Child support is based on both parents' financial situations. Thus, when either a paying or recipient parent's income increases, child support may be modified accordingly.

Medical emergencies. Medical emergencies that require large expenditures of money are the kind of temporary and catastrophic circumstances that may support a temporary modification of child support. If the child or the custodial parent suffers the emergency, the noncustodial parent may be required to temporarily increase payments (if he is able). Likewise, if the noncustodial parent is the one with the emergency, his duty to support may temporarily be eased by the court.

Needs of the child. If a child's financial needs decrease after the level of support has been set, a decrease in child support may be ordered if the paying parent files a request for modification to the court. This may occur, for example, if a child changes from private school to public school. If a child inherits a large sum of money, however, a court will not make the modification because state laws generally prohibit inherited money from being used for the child's day-to-day support. (Parents are obligated to support children; children are not required to support themselves.) Conversely, if a child's financial needs increase (for example, a sudden need for tutoring or medical care), an increase in child support may be awarded by a court if the parent who receives the payments can show changed circumstances and submits a request for modification to the court.

New support obligation. A parent paying child support may attempt to reduce his payments after assuming a new legal support obligation. Many courts, however, do not look favorably upon parents who seek to reduce child support obligations in order to support second families.

TAX CONSEQUENCES OF CHILD SUPPORT

For federal income tax purposes, child support is tax-free to the recipient but not deductible by the payer. On the other hand, an alimony payer may deduct payments made pursuant to a court order or written agreement while a recipient must report them as income.

In the past, when ex-spouses had more flexibility in negotiating the amount of child support and alimony, many ex-spouses agreed to greater alimony and less child support because of the resulting tax advantage to the payer. Because all states determine the basic child support obligation by formula, however, shifting the amounts of child support and alimony to take advantage of tax deductions is increasingly difficult.

Children, however, do have plenty of tax consequences—first and foremost, they are considered exemptions. Married couples filing a joint return simply list their children's names, ages and Social Security numbers, and then enter the number of exemptions on their tax return. Divorced parents, unmarried parents and married parents who file separately (this includes separated but not yet divorced parents), however, cannot both claim the same children as tax exemptions. The IRS may audit both returns if it discovers this error on one parent's return.

In the absence of a written agreement, the general IRS rule is that the parent who has the children for the longest part of the year is entitled to the exemption. (26 U.S.C. § 152.) This usually means the mother because she most often gets primary physical custody.

But if the father furnishes over 50% of the child's support, he is entitled to the exemption. He must file with his tax return IRS Form 8332, Release of Claim to Exemption for Child of Divorced or Separated Parents, signed by the mother. (A copy is in the Appendix.) If the father claims the exemption without filing this form, he may have to prove that he furnished over 50% of the support for the kids if the IRS questions his return.

COURT PROCEDURES

The legal system in the U.S. is based on the philosophy that the true facts of a given situation—and hence, justice—will emerge if the parties to a court action act as adversaries rather than as cooperative participants. The theory is that if each side vigorously advances its own version of the facts, an impartial third person or group of persons (judge or jury) will sift out the truth. Critics point out that this system depends on equality of representation (assuming the parties are proceeding through advocates). If one advocate is better than the other, or has more money to prepare the case, the truth may not emerge.

The adversary system's use has been especially criticized in family law cases on the ground that it intensifies divisions within a family rather than ameliorates them. Because cooperation between former spouses is necessary if children are involved, the adversary system seems particularly inappropriate in these instances. In response, a number of innovative procedures are being used to help spouses and domestic partners resolve their disputes without recourse to the traditional adversarial approach. For instance, many states require or encourage parents with children who can't agree on custody and visitation to meet with a mediator. In this meeting, the mediator helps the parties to explore their differences and craft their own solutions. And in many communities, private mediation services are increasingly available for both court referrals and spouses to use before either files for a divorce. Finally, many family law attorneys are themselves becoming mediators and helping divorce-bound parties to resolve their differences without the necessity of each person having an attorney.

Case

A case describes a dispute taken to court. An appellate court decision published in a book of such decisions is also called a case and may be used as guidance or precedent by other courts. A person doing legal research will commonly say that he has to look up a case to see if its ruling on a point should be followed by other courts. The core legal issue in a case is sometimes referred to as the gravaman of the case.

Leading Case

The most important published case in a particular area of law is called the leading case. Such important cases are used as guidance by lawyers and judges who face similar issues later. For example, in the area of abortion, the leading case is *Roe v. Wade*.

Litigation

Litigation is the process of bringing and pursuing a lawsuit. Litigation often proceeds much like trench warfare; initial court papers define the parties' legal positions as trenches define battlefield positions. After the initial activity, lawyers sit back for several months or years and lob legal artillery at each other until they grow tired of the warfare and begin settlement negotiations. If settlement is unsuccessful (90% of all lawsuits are settled without trial), the case goes to trial, and may be followed by a lengthy appeal.

Many states have enacted reforms directed at shortening the time a case takes to get to trial and minimizing the expense traditionally associated with litigation. Among these reforms are:

- "fast track" rules that prohibit delays and require each phase of the case to be completed within a particular period of time
- limits on how much information can be obtained from the opposing party
- requirements that certain types of cases be arbitrated (a simpler procedure) rather than pushed through the court system
- requirements that attorneys inform their clients of alternative dispute resolution procedures such as mediation, and
- court-sponsored techniques such as mini-trials and early neutral evaluation that are designed to get the parties to settle by giving them a realistic assessment of what is likely to happen if the case goes to trial.

Action

Action is another word for lawsuit, case, legal matter or litigation. Cause of action refers to a set of facts that make up the grounds for filing a lawsuit.

Issue

Issue refers to the central point of dispute in a case.

Hearing

A hearing is a legal proceeding (other than a trial) held before a judge or court commissioner. At a trial, disputed questions of fact and law are resolved and the case is concluded (although the parties may appeal). At a hearing, on the other hand, preliminary issues, procedural issues (including granting an uncontested or default divorce) and post-trial modifications and enforcements are heard.

Example 1: Paul has sued Taya for divorce. Their trial is to be held in nine months. Taya needs alimony now, however, so she files a request for temporary alimony. The court schedules a hearing at which Paul and Taya can appear before a judge and orally present their separate sides. After listening to Paul and Taya, the judge will decide if Taya is entitled to the alimony, and if so, how much.

Example 2: Paul receives sporadic royalty payments for a book he wrote seven years ago. He claims that the income is speculative and hopes to keep it from being considered in the upcoming divorce trial where the amount of permanent alimony will be determined. A week before the trial, Paul requests a hearing to determine whether the law requires that the judge consider his royalty income in setting Taya's alimony.

ADMINISTRATIVE HEARING

Administrative law is the body of law governing administrative agencies—that is, those agencies created by Congress or state legislatures, such as the Social Security Administration, state Unemployment Insurance Boards, state Welfare Commissions and the Occupational Safety and Health Administration. The authority these agencies possess is delegated to them by the bodies which created them; the Social Security Administration's power comes from Congress.

Administrative agencies administer law through the creation and enforcement of regulations; most of these regulations pertain to providing some type of benefit to applicants. Frequently, an applicant objects to an agency's decision to deny, limit or terminate the benefits provided and seeks to have the decision reviewed. This review is called an administrative hearing and is held before an administrative law judge (A.L.J.).

Administrative hearings are informal, yet very important. Usually, the A.L.J. meets with representatives from the agency and the applicant seeking benefits. The applicant may choose to be or not be represented by an attorney and in fact, many administrative agencies permit paralegals, law students or law clerks to appear on behalf of applicants. Each side presents its evidence and elicits testimony from its witnesses. The hearing is often tape recorded, as opposed to taken down by a court reporter. The A.L.J. renders a decision called an administrative order, which may be reviewed by either a higher level within the agency or by a court.

Trial

A trial may be before a judge only or before a jury. Virtually all family law trials are held without juries.

Bench Trial

A bench trial is another term for a trial before a judge only. In general, the parties begin with the presentation of evidence, although in some cases they make opening statements. After the plaintiff finishes presenting his evidence, the defendant presents her case. After the defendant concludes her presentation, the plaintiff may rebut the defendant's case. Rarely are closing arguments made. The judge may rule immediately, but more often takes anywhere from a few hours to a few weeks to consider the evidence and reach a decision.

Submission

When a judge does not immediately announce a decision, the judge is said to take the case under submission.

Jury Trial

In a jury trial, the jury is selected by the parties through a process called voir dire, where the judge or parties ask jurors questions in order to determine their biases and opinions. (Each side gets to reject a certain number of potential jurors.) After the jury is chosen and sworn in, the parties give opening arguments, present their evidence and give closing arguments. The jury then deliberates; when it reaches a decision, it returns to the courtroom and announces the verdict.

The roll of the jury is to decide issues of fact. Parties are entitled to a jury trial by the U.S. Constitution in those types of cases, such as breach of contract, which existed in 1789, the effective date of the Constitution. Kinds of cases that have come into existence since then, however, such as divorce (which in 1789 still fell under the religious courts) and actions in juvenile courts, are not guaranteed jury trials. States are free to make jury trials available for such actions, but few have. In fact, only Texas and Georgia permit jury trials for divorces.

HOW LAW IS MADE

There are two major ways in which legal principles are developed in the United States. One is through appellate court decisions in individual cases, called case law. The other is through the passage of laws by voters and legislative bodies, called statutes.

Case Law

Legal principles that are developed by appellate courts when deciding appeals are collectively termed the case law or common law. Since the 12th century, the common law has been England's primary system of law. When the United States became independent, states adopted the English common law as their law. Since that time, decisions by U.S. courts have developed a body of U.S. case law which has superseded English common law in most areas.

PRECEDENT

Precedent is a legal principle, created by a court decision, which provides an example or authority for judges deciding similar issues later. Generally, decisions of higher courts (within a particular system of courts) are mandatory precedent on lower courts within that system—that is, the principle announced by a higher court must be followed in later cases. For example, the California Supreme Court decision that unmarried people who live together may enter into cohabitation agreements (*Marvin v. Marvin*), is binding on all appellate courts and trial courts in California (which are lower courts in relation to the California Supreme Court). Similarly, decisions of the U.S. Supreme Court (the highest court in the country) are generally binding on all other courts in the U.S.

Decisions of lower courts are not binding on higher courts, although from time to time a higher court will adopt the reasoning and conclusion of a lower court. Decisions by courts of the same level (usually appellate courts) are considered persuasive authority. That is, they should always be carefully considered by the later court but need not be followed.

As a practical matter, courts can usually find precedent for any direction they want to go in deciding a particular case. Accordingly, precedent is used as often to justify a particular outcome in a case as it is to guide the decision.

Statute

Under the U.S. and state constitutions, statutes are considered the primary source of law in the U.S.—that is, legislatures make the law (statutes) and courts interpret the law (cases).

Most state statutes are organized by subject matter and published in books referred to as codes. Typically, a state has a family or civil code (where the divorce laws are usually contained), a criminal code (where incest, bigamy and domestic violence laws are often found), welfare code (which contains laws related to public benefits), probate code (where laws about wills, trusts and probate proceedings are collected) and many other codes dealing with a wide variety of topics. Federal statutes are organized into subject matter titles within the United States Code (for example, Title 18 for crimes and Title 11 for bankruptcy).

LEGISLATIVE INTENT

Legislative intent is what a legislature as a whole had in mind when it passed a particular statute. Normally, any given statute is interpreted by looking just at the statute's language. But when the language is ambiguous or unclear, courts try to glean the legislative intent behind words by looking at legislative interpretations (for instance, reports issued by legislative committees) which were relied upon by legislators when voting on the statute.

Statutes are often ambiguous enough to support more than one interpretation, and the material reflecting legislative intent is frequently sparse. This leaves courts free to interpret statutes according to their own predilections. Once a court interprets the legislative intent, however, other courts will usually not go through the exercise again, but rather will enforce the statute as interpreted by the other court.

Uniform Statutes

Uniform laws, such as the Uniform Child Custody Jurisdiction Act, the Uniform Pre-Marital Agreement Act, and others, are model laws proposed by a national group of judges, lawyers and law professors called the Uniform Law Commissioners. The commissioners propose the laws; states are free to enact or reject them.

Topics covered by uniform laws are often ones in which there is much interstate activity, such as marriage, divorce, paternity, custody and child support and in which consistency, predictability and uniformity are desirable. Some uniform laws have been passed by all states (for example, the Uniform Child Custody Jurisdiction Act) whereas others have only been enacted by a few (for instance, the Uniform Divorce Recognition Act). Clearly, the central goal of uniformity is well served only if a significant number of states enact a given uniform law.

Ordinance

An ordinance is a law enacted by a municipal body, such as a city council or county commission (sometimes called county council or county board of supervisors). Ordinances govern matters not already covered by state or federal laws such as zoning, safety and building regulations.

LAWS OF SUBSTANCE AND PROCEDURE

Laws which define legal duties and rights are called the substance of the law, or substantive law. Substantive laws include the standards for custody, the grounds for divorce and the right to have an abortion.

On the other hand, the body of laws which tells how to go to court and get judicial relief is generally called the law of civil procedure. Civil procedure is predominantly made up of statutes and rules issued by individual courts.

PARTIES TO A CASE

A person who sues or defends a lawsuit is called a party. A party has the right to conduct discovery and receive notice of all proceedings connected with the lawsuit.

Pro Per or Pro Se

A party to a lawsuit who represents herself, rather than being represented by a lawyer, is called a party in pro per (or pro se). Both terms mean "for yourself." Pro per and pro se litigants often find it difficult to do their own legal work because the legal system is hostile to self-helpers. Arizona and Colorado, however, have implemented an automated court system that provides people with legal information and helps them complete court documents themselves. Also, self-help law books and paralegals who directly serve the public are increasingly available to help pro per and pro se litigants in many states.

Plaintiff

The person who initiates a lawsuit by filing a complaint is called the plaintiff. When the document that initiates a lawsuit is called a petition rather than a complaint, the initiating person is usually referred to as the petitioner rather than the plaintiff.

Defendant

The person against whom a lawsuit is filed is usually called the defendant. In some states, or in certain types of actions, the defendant is called the respondent. The term respondent is also used to designate the person responding to an appeal.

SPECIAL CONCERNS OF PLAINTIFFS AND DEFENDANTS

In Forma Pauperis. In Forma Pauperis is a Latin term meaning "in the character of a pauper." It refers to a petition filed by a poor person in order to proceed in court without having to pay court costs such as filing fees.

In forma pauperis proceedings are available in every state. A person with a low income (usually eligible for or receiving public assistance) fills out in forma pauperis papers (indicating income and expenses) before filing his first court paper (complaint or answer). The papers request that the court decide whether or not the costs be paid. Although a hearing before a judge is sometimes needed, the more usual practice is for the court to grant or deny the request without a hearing.

Military personnel. A person on active military duty is a person who has enlisted in the armed services and is serving out the term of his enlistment, or is an officer in the armed services who has not transferred to the reserves, resigned, retired or been dismissed. A person on active military duty is prohibited by a federal law (Soldiers and Sailors Civil Relief Act, 50 U.S.C. § 501 et seq.) from being subjected to any civil court action, including a divorce, unless he consents to the power of the court to hear the case. A plaintiff who wants to sue someone on active military duty who won't consent must wait until he leaves active duty. The reasons for this rule are:

- it would not be fair to proceed in court against a serviceperson who is prevented from attending because of his military duty, and
- it would be too disruptive and expensive for the military to have its members coming and going long distances just because they have been sued.

Co-Respondent

The "other man" or "other woman" named in the court papers for a fault divorce alleging adultery is called the co-respondent.

Appellant

The person who objects to the trial court decision and asks the appellate court to review the decision by filing an appeal is called an appellant (also called a petitioner in some states).

Appellee

The party against whom an appeal is filed is called the appellee or the respondent. Sometimes the appellee will also appeal certain aspects of the lower court's decision; he then becomes a cross-appellant as well as an appellee. In this situation, the appellant (the one who filed the appeal) becomes a cross-appellee or cross-respondent.

COURTS

Trial Court

The trial court is the court in which a lawsuit is filed, and where all litigation up to and including the trial is held.

Appellate Court

An appellate court is one which decides appeals of trial court decisions or lower appellate court decisions. A state's highest court—usually called the supreme court—is an appellate court. So is the U.S. Supreme Court.

Family Court

Family courts are special trial courts that hear only family law cases.

COURT PAPERS

All papers filed with a court regarding a lawsuit are called court papers. Court papers typically consist of pleadings (complaint or petition and answer), motions (written requests to the court to take some specific action) and court orders (written orders resulting from a trial or hearing).

The term responsive pleading is used to describe any court paper filed by a defendant in direct response to the complaint or petition filed by the plaintiff. An answer is the typical responsive pleading. Others include various motions, such as a motion to quash service of process or a motion to dismiss the complaint, which is intended to get the complaint or petition dismissed at the outset of the case.

A number of states have developed pre-printed court forms for use in court proceedings involving such matters as divorces, guardianships and temporary restraining orders. These forms are especially helpful to people handling their own cases without lawyers; checking boxes and filling in blanks is usually much easier than figuring out what needs to go into a document that must be typed from scratch. On the other hand, some forms are so confusing that they intimidate all but the most knowledgeable lawyers or paralegals.

Summons

A paper issued by a court informing a person that a complaint has been filed against her (that is, that she has been sued) is called a summons. The summons tells her that she is being sued, by whom, for what, and that she must file a response with the court within a certain time or will lose.

Complaint

The complaint is the first court paper filed in a lawsuit. It briefly states the plaintiff's view of the crux of the legal dispute and asks the court to resolve the dispute. In some types of cases and in certain states, a complaint is called a petition or a libel. Items that typically appear in a complaint include:

Caption. The caption is the heading which appears on all court papers. The caption contains the names of the parties to the lawsuit (for example, Susan Roe, Plaintiff, v. Robert Roe, Defendant), the name of the court (for example, Federal District Court for the Eastern District of Pennsylvania), the case number which has been assigned by the court clerk, and the title of the court paper (for example, Complaint for Annulment).

Allegations. An allegation is a statement made in court papers that sets forth a party's belief as to what the facts are in a given case. Referring to statements made in court papers as allegations serves as a reminder that they may or may *not be true. Thus, when a party has alleged something, she has made charges which remain to be proven.*

Prayer. The prayer is the part of a complaint which requests the court to grant some specific judicial relief (for example, a divorce, possession of the family home, child support or custody).

Answer

An answer is a formal response to allegations made in a complaint (or petition). Normally, the answer either admits or denies the allegations, although some states allow an answer to state a lack of knowledge as to whether a particular allegation is true or false. If the defendant fails to file an answer, the plaintiff usually wins by default. In a divorce, failure to file an answer may result in a default divorce.

Example: Martin is sued for paternity by his former lover, Rhoda. Martin will be served with a complaint (or petition) containing the allegation that Rhoda believes he is the father of her child. He must answer within a certain period of time (usually about 30 days) or lose by default. In his answer, he must either admit or deny each of the complaint's allegations. In some states, Martin may respond that he doesn't know whether or not an allegation is true.

Brief

When a party (either through her lawyer or in pro per) submits a written legal argument to a court—usually to support a motion or a position asserted at a trial—the document is often called a brief. It typically consists of a statement of the facts relevant to the case and arguments supported by references to legal authority (statutes, regulations or earlier court decisions). Many briefs are quite lengthy; the label "brief" is an infamous misnomer celebrated by the writer Franz Kafka, who described a lawyer as "a person who writes a 10,000 word document and calls it a brief."

Points and authorities. A brief usually contains a memorandum of points and authorities. Points and authorities explain why the law authorizes the judge to take the requested action. The term points and authorities comes from the fact that the legal discussion makes certain points, followed by citations to legal authority (usually a court decision or statute) supporting each point.

Citations. The proper reference (as established by the legal profession) to a case, constitution, statute, legal encyclopedia or legal treatise is called a citation. A citation contains the name of the case or other authority, the name of the book in which it is found, the volume in which it appears, its page or section number and the year decided or enacted. Citations allow any reader to find the source and read it.

Example: The proper citation for the case allowing women to have an abortion is *Roe v. Wade*, 410 U.S. 133 (1973). The name of the case includes the name of the plaintiff (Roe) followed by a v. (meaning versus) followed by the defendant's name (Wade). 410 is the volume number where the case is found in the series called United States Reports (abbreviated by U.S.) at page 133. The case was decided in 1973.

Amicus Curiae Brief

Amicus curiae is a Latin term meaning "friend of the court." It is a legal argument filed in a lawsuit by a person or organization not a party to the case, but who has an interest in the outcome. For example, in the Supreme Court abortion case, *Webster v. Reproductive Services*, amicus curiae briefs were filed by hundreds of pro-choice and anti-abortion organizations. The court may give the arguments in the amicus curiae brief as much or as little weight as it chooses.

Affidavit

An affidavit is a written statement made by a person who signs the statement in front of a notary public and swears to its truth. Affidavits are used in place of live testimony in many circumstances (for example, when a motion is filed, a supporting affidavit may be filed with it).

Declaration

A declaration is a written statement submitted to a court in which the writer swears "under penalty of perjury" that the contents are true. That is, the writer acknowledges that if he is lying, he may be prosecuted for perjury. Declarations are normally used in place of live testimony when the court is asked to order temporary provisions for alimony, child support, custody, visitation and property division.

A typical declaration sets forth the factual assertions of the person signing it (called the declarant) and ends with a statement worded like this one: "I declare under penalty of perjury that the foregoing is true and correct, and would be my testimony if I were in a court of law." The date and place of signing are usually included.

Some states allow declarations to be used in the place of affidavits, thus avoiding a trip to the notary public.

Assertion

An assertion is a statement that a thing is true in the mind of the person making the statement, whether or not it has been proven to be true.

Financial Statement

A financial statement (sometimes called an income and expense declaration) is a court paper which requires a party to specify her monthly income and expenses. The court often requires each divorcing spouse to fill out a financial statement so that the court has a complete picture of the parties' financial situations before making a decision on alimony, child support, payment of attorneys' fees or other financial matters.

Habeas Corpus Petition

Habeas corpus is Latin for "you should have the body." In legal terms, it is a petition filed with a court by a person who objects to his own or another's detention or imprisonment. The petition must show that the court ordering the detention or imprisonment made a legal or factual error. Habeas corpus petitions are usually filed by persons serving prison sentences. In family law, a parent who has been denied custody of his child by a trial court may file a habeas corpus petition. Also, a party may file a habeas corpus petition if a judge declares her in contempt of court and jails or threatens to jail her.

TERMS SOMETIMES FOUND IN COURT PAPERS

Above captioned cause. The above captioned cause is a phrase used in court papers meaning the particular case. It allows the writer to refer to the case without restating its name. It is not necessary, however, to use this phrase.

Example: Assume Fred Johnson is representing himself in his divorce and files a request for a modification of child support. In court papers, he may refer to his own case of *Johnson v. Johnson* as "the above captioned cause."

Incorporate by reference. The method of including the contents of a document—such as a letter—in court papers or a contract without actually retyping it is called incorporating by reference. This is done by attaching the document to the back of the court papers or contract and referring to it with convoluted language such as, "the letter is attached to this document as Exhibit A and incorporated by reference as if fully set out within this document."

COURT PERSONNEL

Clerk

Within our judicial system, there are many types of clerks. Court clerks (frequently called county clerks) keep track of documents filed with courts; these clerks may also be called civil or criminal clerks, depending on the court in which they work. Courtroom clerks are assigned to particular judges to handle the paper flow in the courtroom; law clerks (usually law students or lawyers) assist judges (and sometimes attorneys) in legal research and writing. Calendar clerks handle the scheduling of trials and hearings.

Bailiff

A bailiff is a law enforcement officer, usually a sheriff, marshal or constable, assigned to a courtroom to keep peace and assist the judge, courtroom clerks, witnesses and jury.

Judge Pro Tem

A judge pro tem is not a regular judge, but someone (usually a lawyer) who is brought in to serve temporarily as a judge with the consent of the parties. Many courts use pro tem judges because there are too many cases for the regular judges to handle. Although every party has the right to have his case heard by a real judge, judges pro tem are often practitioners in the field in which they are asked to hear cases and have as much, if not more, knowledge than a real judge. Pro tem judges are used often in family law cases, especially in default divorces.

Master

A master (sometimes called a special master) is a court-appointed official who helps the court carry out a variety of special tasks in a specified case. For example, the master may take testimony or permit discovery of evidence. She then prepares a report for the judge. In many family law proceedings, some routine matters, such as uncontested divorces, are conducted by a master.

Court Commissioner

A court commissioner is a person appointed by a judge to assist her in finding facts, hearing testimony from witnesses and resolving issues. Court commissioners are frequently lawyers or retired judges. In many states, court commissioners commonly hear testimony concerning the validity of wills, preside over default divorces and other default hearings, decide alimony and child support modifications, and decide discovery motions.

Court Reporter

A court reporter is a person trained to take down a verbatim account of all proceedings in the courtroom (but usually not in the judge's chambers unless a party requests it). Most court reporters today use special machines that enable them to get down every word. Later, they prepare typed transcripts for use by the parties and the judge on appeal. Court reporters also record and transcribe depositions.

Until recently, court reporters had to manually type out the transcript from their shorthand notes. Now, however, many reporters have machines that read the recording machine tape and create a text file that can be printed out on a standard computer printer.

Notary Public

A notary public is a public official who, depending on the state, has the power to acknowledge signatures, administer oaths and affirmations, take depositions and issue subpoenas in lawsuits. Notaries public are most commonly used to acknowledge signatures, especially on court papers such as affidavits.

Although notaries public are public officials, most are people who work in private industry and take a state-administered test to become notaries public. Often, one or more employees of large institutions which process much paperwork (such as banks, insurance companies and real estate brokers) and large law offices are notaries public. Also, many people who work at courthouses are notaries public.

COURT TERMINOLOGY

Case Number

The number given by the court clerk to a lawsuit when it is filed is called the case number. Each case in a county has a unique number so that it may be distinguished from all other cases in that county.

Case Record

All papers filed with the court during a lawsuit and the transcripts of all hearings and trials (made by a court reporter) become part of the official case record. If a party appeals from a trial court judgment, the appellate court normally considers only information contained in the case record. It is therefore important for a party during the trial to get all of her evidence and objections into the case record in the event she later decides to appeal.

Docket Sheet

A docket sheet is a document kept in a case file at the courthouse. It lists all papers filed and actions taken in a case. The judge may also note on it any action taken during a hearing or trial. Except for juvenile court and certain other types of confidential matters (such as adoptions), case files and docket sheets are public records and can be inspected by anyone.

Calendar

When used as a verb, the word "calendar" is slang for scheduling a trial. (For example, "The Murphy divorce case is calendared for September 3rd.") When used as a noun, it refers to a master list kept by a court, called the civil calendar, which shows cases that are ready for or in trial. Some states do not allow cases to be placed on a court calendar until all preliminary procedures, such as discovery and motions, have been completed. Unless the plaintiff or defendant (or one of their lawyers) requests that a case be placed on this calendar, it will never be scheduled for trial. In fact, many cases are dismissed every year because attorneys fail to take this vitally important step.

Example: Estelle and Ira Green are ordered to return to court in six months for the judge to decide whether Estelle will need alimony any longer. In the courthouse case file for the *Marriage of Green* (the title of the case), Judge Garcia will place a sheet of paper (often a form) on which she has written "Husband to pay wife $250 per month for six months. Parties to return to court in six months for further order."

Court Rule

Every court has rules (often called local rules) governing the procedures specific to that court. Details such as the size and length of the court papers, time limits for filing certain documents, the cost of filing and when a case may be placed on a calendar are dictated by these rules. In most states, statewide court rules govern the amount of alimony and child support to be paid based on the incomes of the spouses and the number of children. Court rules are usually formulated by legislative and administrative judicial bodies, or by the courts themselves.

Bias

Any mental condition that would prevent a judge or juror from being fair and impartial is called bias. It may be grounds for disqualification of the judge or juror in question.

Peremptory Challenge

Most states allow the parties to a case to dismiss the judge assigned to the case without having to prove actual bias. Called a peremptory challenge, this right may usually only be exercised once by a party in any given case.

Bench

The furniture on which the judge sits is called the bench. When something is done from the bench, it means it was done by a trial judge.

Chambers

A judge's office is referred to as her chambers. Settlement conferences and adoptions are usually held in her chambers. During a trial, when the judge wants to examine documents, speak with witnesses or speak with the attorneys outside the jury's presence, the judge presides in camera, the Latin term for "in chambers," and holds a conference either in the chambers or at the bench (where the attorneys and judge whisper so the jury can't hear).

Recusal

Recusal is the process by which a judge voluntarily removes himself from hearing a particular case because of bias, conflict of interest, relation to a party, attorney or witness, or for any other reason.

Continuance

When a court postpones a hearing, trial or other scheduled appointment (such as a settlement conference), it is called a continuance. If one party is not prepared for a hearing or trial, the court may grant a continuance to allow the party to get a lawyer or otherwise prepare so as not to be at a disadvantage. While continuances are often called for on the grounds of fairness, they also are commonly sought by attorneys solely for the purpose of delaying the proceeding or harassing the other side.

SERVICE OF COURT PAPERS

A party to a lawsuit has the right to receive written notice that he is being sued or that a hearing will be held which might affect him in some way. Many rules have been developed to govern what notice needs to be given, and how and when it must be delivered. These are usually contained in court rules and rules of civil procedure.

Service of court papers (also referred to as service of process or service) is the delivery of court papers to a party, witness or other person who has a stake in the case. Every state has detailed laws spelling out just how the papers may be delivered, and by whom. When a person has been provided with formal notice of the filing of a lawsuit (that is, that he has been sued), of a court hearing or trial, or ordering him to attend a hearing, trial or deposition, he is said to have been served.

In most cases, including divorces, the first papers that must be served are the summons and complaint. These documents give the defendant notice that the lawsuit has been filed and what the plaintiff is seeking (for example, a divorce). The court cannot proceed unless the plaintiff properly serves the defendant with these papers. There are five major types of service:

- Personal service—When the person served is physically handed court papers notifying her that she has been sued, she is said to have been personally served. With almost all lawsuits, the complaint and summons must be personally served unless the defendant agrees to accept service. (See below.) If the defendant does not agree to accept service and is not personally served, the court cannot take any action in the case, unless the plaintiff can show that personal service was impossible.

ACCEPTING SERVICE OF COURT PAPERS

The least expensive and most convenient way to satisfy the service requirement is for someone on behalf of the plaintiff to mail the summons and complaint to the defendant and ask her to sign, date and return a form acknowledging that she received them. This voluntary acceptance of court papers is called accepting service or acknowledgment of service, and saves the plaintiff from having to pay someone to locate and hand deliver the papers, which is otherwise required if the defendant doesn't cooperate. In some states, the failure to accept service voluntarily makes the defendant responsible for the cost of service even if he otherwise wins the case.

- Service by mail—Once a party has been properly served with the complaint and summons, most future court papers in the lawsuit may be served on the parties by first-class mail. Most states require that someone other than a party to the action do the actual mailing and file proof of the service with the court.
- Service by publication—When the whereabouts of a defendant are unknown, or personal service within the state is impossible, a court may allow the defendant to be served with notice of the lawsuit by publishing the notice in a newspaper of general circulation. As a general matter, this type of service is only allowed in cases involving property and status (personal relationships affected by the law). Thus divorces and certain adoptions (status) and partition suits (property) may be allowed to proceed after service by publication. But issues such as child custody and support cannot be decided until and unless personal service occurs.

> ### BIFURCATION
>
> In situations where the plaintiff is unable to personally serve the defendant, the parties don't necessarily have to stay married. The court can bifurcate the case—that is, divide it in two. The divorce itself is determined. Only when the defendant is personally served can the court then decide the related issues of custody and visitation, child support, alimony, and property division.

- Nail and mail—Nail and mail service is the posting of the notice on the person's home and then mailing him a copy (hence nailing and mailing).
- Substituted or alternate service—In some states, such as New York, substituted or alternate service is any method of service a court allows when personal service is impossible or impracticable. In other states, such as California, substituted service is leaving the court papers with a responsible person at the defendant's home or business and then mailing the defendant a copy.

In most divorce cases, if a divorce is all that is being sought, service often can be made by mail or publication. If, however, alimony, child support, custody, visitation or a division of property is being sought in addition to the divorce itself, most states require personal service on the defendant. In either case, if the defendant's whereabouts are unknown, service by publication is often the only available method.

Once the defendant has been served with the summons and complaint, service of most subsequent court papers may be done by mailing them, without the need for an acknowledgment of service form. Some papers, however, such as contempt of court hearing notices and temporary restraining orders must still be formally served. The party being served, however, may voluntarily accept these papers.

After the defendant has been served, she usually files an answer or other response. She must serve this on the plaintiff, and usually can serve it by mail because the plaintiff, by initiating the lawsuit, has already appeared in the case and consented to the court's power to hear the case.

Service of court papers on a witness (for example, service of a notice telling the witness that his deposition has been scheduled), must usually be done personally; service by mail or publication is almost never sufficient.

Process and Process Server

Any court document carrying the court seal or clerk's signature, that must be properly served on (that is, given to) the party or witness named in the document, is called a process document or process. A subpoena—a document requiring the appearance of a person or the production of documents at a hearing—and a summons are examples of court process. Rules as to who can serve process and how it must be done vary. Some states allow only sheriffs, marshals and constables to serve process. Other states also authorize registered process servers (often private investigators), and a few states allow service by anyone 18 or over who is not a party to the case.

Proof of Service

A proof of service is a court paper filed by a process server as evidence that she served the witness or party to the lawsuit with the court papers she was instructed to serve.

JURISDICTION AND VENUE—THE POWER OF THE COURT TO DECIDE A CASE

When a court has the authority to decide a case, it is said to have jurisdiction over it. In all states, certain types of courts (often called, depending on the state, superior, circuit, county, district or family courts) are given specific and exclusive jurisdiction to handle family law cases. A family law court cannot, however, hear bankruptcies or criminal cases.

Subject-Matter Jurisdiction

The authority to decide a particular type of case is called subject-matter jurisdiction. The subject-matter jurisdiction of a court is set by the federal or state constitution, or by state statutes.

In order for a court to have subject-matter jurisdiction over a divorce action, at least one spouse must have lived in the county where the court is located for a certain period of time. Some states also require the spouse to have lived within the state for a certain length of time, usually a few months longer than the time in the county. For example, to obtain a divorce in California, a person must have lived in California for at least six months, and in the particular county in which he wants to obtain the divorce for at least three months. In Illinois, a person must have lived in the state for 90 days; in New York and New Jersey, the requirement is one year. In Texas, a person must have lived in the state for six months and in the particular county in which she wants to obtain the divorce for at least 90 days.

Personal Jurisdiction

If the court is being asked to determine alimony, child support, custody, visitation or the division of property, the court must have the power to make orders concerning the individual defendant. This is called personal jurisdiction. Personal jurisdiction is also called "in personam jurisdiction."

For a court to have personal jurisdiction over the defendant, the defendant must have been personally served (or have accepted service of the court papers) and the defendant must have at least some contacts with the state in which the court is located. No set number qualifies as the minimum; each situation must be analyzed case by case. If the defendant lives out of state, the court must look at the defendant's contacts with the state. Going into a state regularly to conduct business is usually sufficient for the court to obtain jurisdiction; sending child support payments to a state, without actually visiting the state, however, is not.

Example: Denise and Walter spent their entire married life in Colorado. Denise moved to New Mexico, established residency and sued for divorce. If Walter has virtually no contacts with New Mexico, the New Mexico court has no personal jurisdiction over him. As a practical matter, this means the court may award Denise a divorce, but cannot make any decisions affecting the division of property, an award of alimony or child support, or a determination of custody and visitation because these matters affect Walter's rights as an individual. If, however, Walter and Denise spent five weeks every summer during their marriage in New Mexico, the court may rule that Walter's contacts with New Mexico are sufficient for there to be personal jurisdiction in New Mexico.

In Rem Jurisdiction

Rem is Latin for "thing." When a court exercises in rem jurisdiction, it exercises authority over a thing, rather than a person. For example, if a divorcing couple asks a court to supervise the sale of their family home, the court exercises in rem jurisdiction over the house. Usually, the property must be located in the same county as the court for it to have in rem jurisdiction.

A court which grants a divorce exercises in rem jurisdiction over the marriage. One spouse must live in the same county as the court (therefore the marriage is in the county) for the court to exercise in rem jurisdiction over the marriage.

Venue

Venue is the legally proper place where a particular case should be filed or handled. Every state has rules determining the proper venue for different types of lawsuits. For example, the venue for a paternity suit might be the county where the mother or the man alleged to be the father lives; the suit couldn't be brought in an unrelated county at the other end of the state. The state, county or district in which a lawsuit is filed or a hearing or trial in that action is conducted is called the forum.

FORUM NON CONVENIENS

Forum non conveniens means "inconvenient forum." Although there are rules which govern where a lawsuit must be filed, sometimes the location is inconvenient for the witnesses or parties. If a party makes an adequate showing of inconvenience, the principle of forum non conveniens allows a judge to decline to hear a case even though the court is an appropriate court for the case.

Example: Vince and Claire's divorce case was decided in Miami, Florida, but both have since moved to Orlando. Any request for modification must first be filed in Miami, but either party could request that the court decline to hear the case, and instead, transfer it to Orlando for the hearing.

ACTIVITIES BEFORE TRIAL

Motions

A motion is a written request to the court. When a party asks the court to take some kind of action in the course of litigation, other than resolving the entire case in a trial, the request is made in the form of a motion. Motions are often made before trials to resolve procedural and preliminary issues, and may be made after trials to enforce or modify judgments. Motions may also be made to resolve legal issues in the case if there is no disagreement about the facts. Usually called a motion for summary judgment or a motion for summary adjudication of the issues, these motions can resolve all or most of the issues in a case without the need for a trial.

Normally, one side submits a motion, the other side submits a written response, and the court holds a hearing at which the parties give brief oral arguments. (Some motions are considered only on the basis of the writings.) Then the court approves or denies the motion.

HEARINGS TO RESOLVE MOTIONS

When a party objects, either in person or in writing, to the other party's motion, the court must hold a hearing on the matter. If the party against whom the motion was filed fails to show up for the hearing, the proceedings usually go forward without her. In these circumstances, usually the party who filed the motion will normally get what he requested.

If a person is served with a subpoena ordering him to appear at a hearing but fails to show up, he may be guilty of contempt of court and subject to arrest, fine or imprisonment. Therefore, a person who has been subpoenaed but who is unable to attend a hearing when it is scheduled should call or write the court clerk in advance and request a continuance.

An in camera hearing is a hearing held in the judge's chambers and is not open to the public. In camera hearings usually take place to protect the privacy of the people involved and are common in cases of guardianships, adoptions and custody disputes alleging child abuse.

A family law case might involve any or all of these motions:

Motion for preliminary orders. When a couple separates or files for divorce, a party often needs the immediate intervention of a court to establish alimony, child support, custody and use of property (for example, the car). Couples who are unable to work out arrangements themselves often request a preliminary hearing (also called a temporary hearing) before the judge.

Order to show cause. An order to show cause is an order issued by a judge, requiring a person to appear in court at a hearing and tell the judge (that is, show cause) why the court shouldn't take a certain action.

Many states allow a spouse or other person victimized by domestic violence to obtain a court order requiring the abuser to appear in court and show cause why the court should not issue a temporary restraining order prohibiting him from further harming the victims. The court can also issue an order requiring an abusive spouse to move out of the family home.

In family law, orders to show cause are also used when a party violates a court order, such as an order to pay alimony or child support. In this situation, the other party will ask the court to hold an order to show cause hearing to determine whether the party who has violated the court order should be held in contempt of court.

FAILING TO SHOW UP AT AN ORDER TO SHOW CAUSE HEARING

If a person fails to appear in court when she has been properly ordered to do so, the judge is authorized to issue a warrant (a court order authorizing a law enforcement officer to arrest someone) for her arrest. A warrant issued this way is called a bench warrant.

Example: Joe has fallen behind on his court-ordered child support. Joe's former wife, Jill, has served Joe with an order to show cause why he should not be held in contempt of court for not complying. Joe failed to appear at the scheduled hearing; the judge issued a bench warrant authorizing the police to arrest Joe and bring him before the judge to answer the charge of contempt.

Motion for a protective order. A protective order is any order issued by a court which is meant to protect a person from harm or harassment. A protective order is commonly used to protect a party or witness from unreasonable or invasive discovery requests (for example, harassing questions in a deposition, or an unnecessary medical examination). Less often, a temporary restraining order issued to prohibit domestic violence is referred to as a protective order.

Motion to quash service of process. When a person who has been served with court papers believes that the service was not made according to law, he can file a motion to invalidate or quash the service. If the motion is successful, service must be tried again. The reasons a court might quash service of process include improper service techniques (such as leaving the papers on a doorstep) or service outside the geographical jurisdiction of the court.

Motion to bifurcate. Bifurcation is the act of dividing a trial into two parts. In family law, bifurcation occurs when the divorce itself is determined separately from the related issues of custody and visitation, child support, alimony, and property division.

Motion to join a party. Joinder is the process of bringing someone into an existing lawsuit as an additional party because his rights or obligations are involved in the case. For example, when a court divides a pension as marital property during a divorce, the pension plan administrator often must be joined as a party to the divorce, so that if the court awards a spouse payments under the other spouse's pension, the plan administrator can make the proper arrangements. This is necessary because most pension plans prohibit the administrators from paying anyone other than the employee or other person named as beneficiary—that is, someone entitled to benefits—of the pension.

Motion to compel discovery. When parties disagree over whether certain information is obtainable through the discovery process, they can request that the court resolve their dispute. They submit their requests in the form of written motions. Normally, a discovery motion asks either for an order compelling the other side to respond to discovery requests or for a protective order limiting the discovery efforts of the other side.

Motion for sanctions. When a court concludes that a party to a lawsuit or an attorney has misused the legal process in some way, a penalty called a sanction may be imposed. Common sanctions are fines (to be paid to the other side or to the court), limitations on a party's ability to make certain arguments or to conduct discovery, and in extreme cases, a finding of contempt of court.

Example: Nate has sued Lois for a breach of their cohabitation agreement. Lois scheduled Nate's deposition, but Nate did not appear, nor did he call to say he needed to reschedule or couldn't attend. As a result, Lois was out the money she paid the court reporter and her attorney. To recover it, she filed a motion asking the court to compel Nate to appear for his deposition and also asking the court to impose sanctions against Nate in the amount of money his non-cooperation cost her.

ORDER

An order is the decision rendered by a judge after a hearing.

Discovery

The formal procedures used by parties to a lawsuit to obtain information before a trial is called discovery. Discovery helps a party find out the other side's version of the facts, what witnesses know, and other evidence. Rules dictating the allowable methods of discovery have been set up by Congress (for federal courts) and by state legislatures (for state courts). Common discovery devices include:

- Deposition—a proceeding in which a witness or party is asked to answer questions orally under oath before a court reporter.
- Interrogatories—written questions sent by one party to the other party for the latter to answer in writing under oath.
- Request for admission—a request to a party that he admit certain facts. One party sends the other a request for admission so that basic issues the parties agree upon can be resolved and not have to be proven if the parties go to trial.
- Request for physical examination—a request to a party that he be examined by a doctor if his health is at issue.
- Request for production of documents—a request to a party to hand over certain defined documents. In family law cases, parties often request from each other bank statements, pay stubs and other documents showing earnings, assets and debts.
- Request for inspection—a request by a party to look at tangible items (other than writings) in the possession or control of the other party. Items to be inspected include houses, cars, appliances and virtually any other physical item.
- Subpoena—an order telling a witness to appear in court or at a deposition. A subpoena is issued by the court, and if the witness fails to comply, he can be held in contempt of court.
- Subpoena duces tecum—an order telling a witness to turn over certain documents to a specific party or to bring them to a scheduled deposition. A

subpoena duces tecum is issued by the court, and if the witness fails to comply, he can be held in contempt.

The scope of information obtainable through discovery is quite broad and not limited to what can be used in a trial. Federal courts and most state courts allow a party to discover any information "reasonably calculated to lead to the discovery of admissible evidence." Because of this broad standard, parties often disagree about what information must be exchanged and what may be kept confidential. These disputes are resolved through court rulings on discovery motions.

Example 1: Ellen and Amy have been living together for seven years and have purchased a car, some furniture and many household goods. They're going separate ways, but cannot agree on how to divide their property. Their dispute becomes nastier as the days progress, and Ellen sues Amy, claiming Amy has breached an oral agreement. Amy's lawyer wants to know Ellen's understanding of how they owned their property, so he schedules Ellen's deposition. He will ask Ellen what she understood to be the arrangement and further will ask her to identify any documents supporting her position, such as agreements, receipts or bank statements.

Example 2: Bill and Bernice are divorcing. The court ordered Bill out of the family home to allow Bernice to stay there with the children. Bill and Bernice have decided to sell the house, but don't agree on the value, and therefore each plans to have an appraiser submit an appraisal. If Bernice refuses to allow Bill's appraiser access to the house, Bill will have to request an inspection.

Stipulations

A stipulation is an agreement between parties to a lawsuit that a certain fact may be considered true or that a certain procedure may be followed in court. Most stipulations are put in writing, but this is usually not a requirement.

Example: Pedro and Maria are divorcing. During their marriage they bought a house, which they now agree is worth $140,000. They disagree, however, as to what portion is Maria's separate property, what portion is Pedro's separate property and what portion is marital property. Before their trial, Pedro and Maria will stipulate that the house's value is $140,000.

Settlement Conference

Many states now require parties to family law disputes and their attorneys to meet before trial with a judge to see if the matter can be settled. At these settlement conferences, each side makes offers and the judge comments on their validity and fairness. The judge has no official power to make the parties settle at this stage, but usually strongly encourages settlement by bluntly critiquing the parties' trial positions and indicating how she is likely to rule on disputed issues during the trial.

Mini-Trials and Early Neutral Evaluations

Many courts encourage the parties to settle without the need for a formal trial by holding a mini-trial in which the parties present their evidence and the court decides the outcome. While either party is free to proceed to a formal trial, regardless of the mini-trial's outcome, few do.

Another device to get the parties to settle—called early neutral evaluation—is to have them present their case to an impartial person (often a retired judge or experienced lawyer) and receive from that person an honest assessment of who is likely to prevail in trial.

DEFINING JUDICIAL FAIRNESS

Due Process

Due process is best defined in one word—fairness. Throughout the U.S.'s history, its constitutions, statutes and case law have provided standards for fair treatment of citizens by federal, state and local governments. These standards are known as due process. When a person is treated unfairly by the government, including the courts, he is said to have been deprived of or denied due process.

Example: Ezra and Sharon married in New York and had a son, Darwin. They divorced and Sharon moved to California; Darwin stayed with Ezra. Darwin later moved to California to live with Sharon; Sharon sued Ezra for child support in California. Ezra claimed that because he didn't live in California and had never been to California it would be unfair (a denial of due process) for him to defend the child support lawsuit in California. The U.S. Supreme Court agreed, saying that Sharon should bring her child support request in New York. (This example is based on a case called *Kulko v. Superior Court*, 436 U.S. 84 (1978).)

Retroactive Application of Laws

A statute passed by a legislature usually states that it shall only apply after a certain date. Occasionally, though, laws are made retroactive—that is, they apply to events that happened before the law was passed. (Criminal laws are never retroactive—the legislature cannot make a past act a crime.) If the statute itself doesn't indicate the date it is to become effective, courts normally interpret it to have future effect only.

Example: Assume that the Minnesota legislature passes a law requiring a couple to undergo a blood test as a requirement of being married. The legislature intends that it apply to couples both planning to marry and already married. (Currently, Minnesota does not require blood tests before marriage.) Applying the law to already married couples is a retroactive application of the law. A married Minnesotan might challenge the law arguing that applying it to her is unconstitutional because she had no expectation of ever having to undergo a blood test as a requirement of being married in Minnesota.

Estoppel

In certain situations, the law refuses to allow a person to deny facts when another person has relied on and acted in accordance with the facts on the basis of the first person's behavior. This is called estoppel.

There are two kinds of estoppel.

Collateral estoppel prevents a party to a lawsuit from raising a fact or issue which was already decided against him in another lawsuit. For example, if Donna obtained a paternity judgment against Leroy and then sued him for child support, Leroy would be collaterally estopped from claiming he isn't the father.

Equitable estoppel prevents one party from taking a different position at trial than she did at an earlier time if the other party would be harmed by the change. For example, if after obtaining the paternity judgment, Leroy sues Donna for custody, Donna is now equitably estopped from claiming in the custody suit that Leroy is not the father.

Res Judicata

Res judicata is Latin for "a thing adjudicated." This means that once a matter has been decided by a court, it won't be disturbed. Res judicata usually applies when a conflict arises between the same parties over the same facts that were resolved in an earlier case. The court refuses to hear the matter a second time, citing res judicata.

Collateral Attack

When a separate and new lawsuit is filed to challenge some aspect of an earlier and separate case, it is called a collateral attack on the earlier case. This is different than an appeal, which is a challenge to some aspect of a decision made in the same case.

Example: Sam obtains a divorce in Nevada without properly notifying his wife, Laurie. Laurie files a later lawsuit seeking to set aside the divorce and start the divorce proceedings over. Laurie's case is a collateral attack on the divorce.

The law wants judgments to be final whenever possible, and thus collateral attacks are discouraged. Many are filed, but usually only succeed when an obvious injustice or unconstitutional treatment occurred in the earlier case.

Ex Parte

Ex parte means "by one side." Although a judge is normally required to meet with all parties in a case and not with just one, there are circumstances where this rule does not apply and the judge is allowed to meet with just one side (ex parte). In addition, sometimes judges will issue temporary orders ex parte (that is, based on one party's request without hearing from the other side) when time is limited or it would do no apparent good to hear the other side of the dispute. For example, if a wife claims domestic violence, a court may immediately issue an ex parte order telling her husband to stay away. Once he's out of the house, the court holds a hearing, where he can tell his side and the court can decide whether the ex parte order should be made permanent.

Equitable Power

If strict application of the law would be unfair to a person, most courts have the authority, called equitable power, to bend the rules to prevent such an outcome. English Courts of Equity were established hundreds of years ago to temper the legalistic rigors of English common law. Equity principles were adopted by U.S. courts when this country was formed. Today, when a court exercises equitable powers, it often does so to prevent one party from taking unfair advantage of another or from profiting by her own wrongdoing.

Clean Hands Doctrine

Under the clean hands doctrine, a person who has acted wrongly, either morally or legally—that is, who has "unclean hands"—will not be helped by a court when complaining about the actions of someone else.

In family law, the doctrine is invoked most often in two situations. First, a parent who kidnaps and then later requests custody will often be denied custody unless the child is in danger of harm from the other parent. Second, a spouse who conceals assets or otherwise misappropriates marital property during the marriage or separation will often be penalized in the division of property at the divorce by being awarded less than her fair share. This, of course, requires that the innocent spouse learn of the concealment or misappropriation.

Statute of Limitation

A statute of limitation is a law that sets the deadline for filing a lawsuit in a particular kind of dispute. These deadlines vary depending on the state, the type of issue and the circumstances of the case. A lawsuit filed after the deadline will be thrown out of court.

In California and Texas, for example, when one person breaches a written contract, the other person has four years to sue; this is called a four-year statute of limitation. A personal injury suit, such as an assault and battery case brought by the victim of domestic violence, must be brought within one year from the date of the injury in California and within two years in Texas.

There are no statutes of limitation for filing a no-fault divorce. Filing a fault divorce, however, usually involves a time limitation; for example, an innocent spouse has only a set period of time after learning of her spouse's adultery (or desertion or cruelty) to file for divorce on this ground. Failure of one spouse to file the fault divorce within the time period may provide the other spouse with a defense to the divorce.

Presumption

A fact assumed to be true under the law is called a presumption. For example, a criminal defendant is presumed to be innocent until the prosecuting attorney proves beyond a reasonable doubt that she is guilty. Presumptions are used to relieve a party from having to actually prove the truth of the fact being presumed. Once a presumption is relied on by one party, however, the other party is normally allowed to offer evidence to disprove (rebut) the presumption. The presumption is known as a rebuttable presumption. In essence, then, what a presumption really does is place the obligation of presenting evidence concerning a particular fact on a particular party.

Conclusive Presumption

The law does not allow some presumptions to be disproved, no matter how strong the evidence to the contrary. These are called conclusive presumptions. The presumption that a child born to a married couple is considered the child of the husband is often irrebuttable (that is, you can't argue with it even if you can prove the husband isn't the father). A growing number of courts, however, have held conclusive presumptions to be unconstitutional (too unfair, and thus a denial of due process), especially in the area of paternity, because of blood tests which can exclude paternity with 100% accuracy.

Full Faith and Credit

Full faith and credit is a legal principle requiring judges to recognize and enforce valid decrees and judgments issued by courts in other states. Thus, a Wisconsin judgment for back alimony can be enforced in Idaho, if the recipient takes the steps necessary to convert it to an Idaho judgment.

In the past, states often did not afford full faith and credit to custody decisions of courts in other states, preferring instead to decide the issues on the evidence before them. This often led to contradictory custody orders and sometimes children were kidnapped and thrown back and forth. Now, however, the Parental Kidnapping Prevention Act and the Uniform Child Custody Jurisdiction Act require states to give full faith and credit to custody decisions rendered in other states.

Comity

Comity is the legal doctrine under which countries recognize and enforce each others' legal decrees. Comity usually arises in two situations in family law. The first is where a divorce is granted by another country. If both parties were present and consented to the divorce, there is usually no problem with the U.S. recognizing the foreign divorce decree. The second situation arises in child custody cases. The Uniform Child Custody Jurisdiction Act requires that state courts recognize properly entered custody decrees of other nations; in turn, many other countries are beginning to recognize U.S. custody orders.

COURT PROCEDURES

WEIGHING THE EVIDENCE

Witnesses who testify at a trial or hearing are questioned by two basic techniques—direct examination and cross-examination. Lawyers, or the parties themselves if they aren't represented by lawyers, do the examining (questioning).

Direct Examination

Direct examination consists of questions asked in a direct form, that is, a form which does not suggest the answer, such as "Where were you on July 18th?" Direct examination is conducted of witnesses who are friendly to the questioner.

Cross-Examination

A question that suggests the answer—for example, "You were at the shop on July 18th, weren't you?"—is called a leading question and can be used only on cross-examination. Cross-examination questions are asked by the party whose position is opposed by the witness.

Sometimes, when parties aren't represented by lawyers, these formal rules of questioning are not used. Instead, witnesses use narrative formats and simply tell their stories.

> ### EXPERT WITNESS
>
> An expert witness is a person who testifies at a trial because she has special knowledge in a particular field. This entitles her to testify about her opinion on the meaning of facts. Non-expert witnesses are only permitted to testify about facts they observed and not their opinions about these facts. In family law trials, common expert witnesses include:
> - actuaries, who testify about values of spouses' pension plans for the purpose of dividing them at divorce
> - child psychologists or development specialists, who testify about the best interests of the child when custody or visitation is in dispute
> - appraisers, who testify about property values when the parties cannot agree, and
> - career counselors, who testify about a homemaker's ability to return to the work force for the purpose of determining the amount and duration of alimony.

Burden of Proof

The burden of proof refers to the obligation of a party to prove his allegations during a trial. Typically, the plaintiff must prove whatever allegations he included in his complaint in order to win his case. The defendant is given the opportunity to submit evidence to rebut the plaintiff's case. To rebut generally means to contest a statement or evidence presented by another.

Standard of Proof

The amount of evidence which a plaintiff (or prosecuting attorney, in a criminal case) must present in a trial in order to win is called the standard of proof. Different cases require different standards of proof depending on what is at stake. The common standards are:

- Beyond a reasonable doubt (criminal cases)—for a criminal defendant to be convicted of a crime, the prosecutor must prove her case to the point that the jurors have no reasonable doubts in their minds that the defendant did whatever he is charged with having done.
- Clear and convincing evidence (civil cases involving the potential loss of important interests such as the termination of parental rights)—for a party to prove a case under this standard, she must show something more than it is more likely than not, but not as much as beyond a reasonable doubt. No legal scholar has ever been able to define clear and convincing evidence more precisely than that.
- Preponderance of the evidence (most civil cases, including fault divorces)—preponderance of the evidence generally means that a party will win if she can show that it is more likely than not that her contention is true.

Rules of Evidence

Rules of evidence (found in the statutes and court rules of each state) determine what evidence may be admitted into a trial or hearing and under what circumstances.

Admissible Evidence

Anything a judge allows a jury (or himself) to consider in reaching a decision during the trial is called admissible evidence because it is "admitted" into evidence. Many types of evidence are not admissible because they don't satisfy legal standards of reliability or fairness. These standards have developed over hundreds of years and are constantly subject to change.

Example: Laura is six years old, and there is evidence that she has been abused by her father. Under traditional evidence rules, any statements Laura made outside of the courtroom to a counselor, parent or other person concerning the abuse would be considered inadmissible evidence. Only her statements made in court in front of her father would be admissible. Because of the difficulty in having a child speak freely in a court, many states are now experimenting with allowing children to testify on videotape outside the courtroom and then showing the tape in court.

The following are types of admissible evidence:

Admissions. An admission is any statement made by a party to a lawsuit (either before a court action or during it) which tends to support the position of the other side or diminish his own position. For example, if a husband sues his wife for divorce on the grounds of adultery, and she states out of court that she has had affairs, her statement is an admission. Any admission made by a party is admissible evidence in a court proceeding, even though it is technically considered hearsay (which is normally inadmissible). Attorneys tell their clients not to talk to anyone about their case or about the events leading up to it in order to prevent their clients from making admissions.

Character evidence. Evidence introduced in a trial which bears on the truth and honesty of a witness or party is termed character evidence. Character evidence includes criminal convictions and reputation in the community for honesty. Character evidence is usually permitted when a person's honesty is an issue, such as when a criminal defendant testifies or has been charged with perjury or fraud. It is not permitted when the defendant does not testify and the crime he is charged with doesn't involve the defendant's truthfulness (for example, the defendant is charged with illegal possession of drugs). Although used infrequently in civil cases, character evidence may be given in custody cases where the honesty of a party arguably affects her ability to be a good parent (for example, in the case of a habitual liar), or in cases of fault divorce.

Circumstantial evidence. Circumstantial evidence is best explained by saying what it is not—it is not direct evidence from a witness who saw or heard something. Circumstantial evidence is a fact that can be used to infer another fact.

Example: Bart is suing his wife, Pam, for a divorce, claiming she is having an affair with Tony. Tony's fingerprints are found on a book in Bart and Pam's bedroom. A judge or jury may infer that Tony was in the bedroom. The fingerprints are circumstantial evidence of Tony's presence in the bedroom. Circumstantial evidence is usually not as good as direct evidence (an eyewitness saw Tony in the bedroom) because it is easy to make the wrong inference—Pam may have loaned Tony the book and then carried it back to the bedroom herself after getting it back.

Circumstantial evidence is generally admissible in court unless the connection between the fact and the inference is too weak to be of help in deciding the case.

SUPPORTING THE EVIDENCE

Authentication of evidence. When a document or other physical item is offered into evidence at trial, it is necessary to show that the item is genuine. This process is called authentication. One way to authenticate a document is by the testimony of the person who wrote or signed it; another is by the testimony of an expert witness such as a document examiner or handwriting analyst.

Corroboration. Corroboration is additional evidence that supports an accusation or item of circumstantial evidence. For instance, in the case of alleged adultery, corroboration might consist of a love letter or a hotel clerk's testimony that the spouse and the co-respondent rented a room together.

Evidence rules are more often than not defined by what is not admissible. Here are examples of some often inadmissible evidence:

Immaterial evidence. Evidence deemed too unconnected with the main issues of a case is considered immaterial and will be excluded from a trial.

Incompetent evidence. Evidence considered inherently unreliable is called incompetent and is not admissible in a trial. Examples of incompetent evidence include secondhand information, observations made while the witness was drunk or under the influence of drugs, and self-serving statements.

Irrelevant evidence. Relevancy is the logical connection between facts or statements, especially those offered as evidence in court. Before evidence is admitted during a trial or hearing, it must be shown to be relevant to the issues in the case. Thus, the fact that a spouse has three bank accounts is irrelevant to the issues in a custody hearing, but may be quite relevant in one distributing the marital property.

Example: Grace and Ian are divorcing in Michigan, an equitable distribution state. Grace and Ian have sold their marital home, and the only issue in their case is the division of the proceeds. The house was purchased with a combination of Grace's pre-marital savings (her separate property), Ian's pre-marital savings (his separate property), and their earnings during marriage. At the trial, Ian asks his friend Walter to testify that Grace didn't like the house and never wanted to buy it. Because Walter's testimony is irrelevant to dividing the proceeds, the judge will not let Walter testify.

Privileged communications. In judicial proceedings, the law allows people to refuse to disclose the contents of certain privileged conversations and writings. Communications between an attorney and client, husband and wife, clergyperson and penitent, and doctor and patient are all privileged. In a few states, the privilege extends to a psychotherapist and client.

To qualify for privileged status, communications must generally be made in a private setting (that is, in a context where confidentiality could reasonably be expected). The privilege is lost (waived) when all or part of the communication is disclosed to a third person.

These privileges are held by the client (but not the lawyer), the patient (but not the doctor or psychotherapist), the speaking (but not the spoken-to) spouse and both the clergyperson and the penitent. The lawyer, doctor, psychotherapist and spoken-to spouse, however, cannot reveal the communication without the other person's consent. The client, patient, speaking spouse, clergyperson and penitent may waive the privilege (that is, testify about the conversation) and also may prevent the other person from disclosing the information.

Example: Sue and Martin are divorcing. When Martin first left Sue, he emptied out a joint bank account and placed that money in a separate account in another state. He refuses to tell Sue where the money is, but he has told his lawyer, Ann. The discussion between Martin and Ann is privileged, and unless Martin authorizes Ann to tell Sue where the money is, or unless Martin himself tells another person about his conversation with Ann, Ann cannot be forced to disclose the information.

Marital communications privilege. Courts cannot force husbands and wives to disclose the contents of confidential communications made during marriage. The purpose of the privilege is to protect and promote honesty and confidence within marriages.

Example: Sandy has a budding marijuana brownie business which she operates out of her home. Sandy has told her husband, Doug, about her endeavors. All private conversations between them are privileged; that is, if Sandy is ever prosecuted for her business, she can prevent Doug from disclosing what he knows.

Spousal privilege. Courts cannot force husbands and wives to testify against each other. For example, when a former husband trying to gain custody of his child called his ex-wife's new husband as a witness to testify about her treatment of the child, the court refused to force him to testify on the grounds that it could jeopardize an existing marriage.

HEARSAY—ADMISSIBLE OR INADMISSIBLE?

Hearsay is any statement made outside a hearing or trial which is presented at the hearing or trial to prove the truth of the contents of the statement. All evidence rules begin with the premise that hearsay cannot be used in court because secondhand testimony is considered unreliable and because the person who made the original statement is often unavailable for cross-examination. Statements in the forms of letters, affidavits, declarations, diaries, memos, oral statements, notes, computer files, legal documents, purchase receipts and contracts all constitute hearsay when they are offered to prove that their contents are true.

Testimony during a hearing or trial is not hearsay unless the witness tries to repeat something someone else said or wrote. In addition, a statement introduced to prove something other than its truth is not hearsay. For example, testimony may be offered to show the speaker's state of mind.

Example: Dana and Bruce were fighting, and Dana shouted "Bruce, you are a lousy bastard." Marla heard the argument and was asked to testify at Dana and Bruce's divorce trial. Marla was permitted to repeat the statement "Bruce, you are a lousy bastard," because it is not hearsay. It was not introduced at the trial to prove that Bruce has lice or is an illegitimate child, but rather to show that Dana was angry.

A witness's earlier out-of-court statement may be presented at a trial or hearing if it contradicts his in-court testimony, because the statement is being used to cast doubt on the witness's credibility, rather than prove the statement's truth or falsity.

A great many exceptions to the hearsay rule exist and much hearsay tends to be admitted under these exceptions. Evidence which qualifies as exceptions is usually statements which are reliable and believed to be unfabricated. Some common exceptions are:

- utterances made at the time of a startling event which provoked the observer into speaking (for example, seeing one's spouse in bed with someone else)
- statements describing a current condition (for example, "I feel sick.")
- prior testimony from a hearing, trial or deposition
- religious records, family records and marriage certificates
- property documents (for example, deeds)
- statements made against one's own monetary or penal interest (that is, an admission of a crime)
- declarations made by someone who believes his death is imminent
- business records made in the regular course of business
- official records
- ancient documents, and
- court judgments.

JUDGES' DECISIONS

Interlocutory and Final Judgment

Interlocutory means interim, provisional or not final. In some states, a divorce occurs in two phases. The first is often called the interlocutory stage, where all the issues (for example, division of property, alimony, child support, custody and visitation) get decided either by agreement of the spouses or by a judge after a hearing or trial.

The second phase, when the judgment of divorce becomes final, doesn't occur until after a waiting period—usually two to six months. The waiting period (sometimes referred to as the cooling-off period) is designed to give the divorcing couple every opportunity for reconciliation. It begins on the date the interlocutory judgment is entered. When the time period passes, if no appeal is pending and if the appropriate papers have been filed with the court, the final judgment is entered.

In some states, a party who is eager to remarry as soon as possible can get the waiting period shortened or set aside entirely, if the judge is convinced that the reasons are good.

NUNC PRO TUNC

Nunc pro tunc literally means "now for then." Occasionally, a court or party to a divorce forgets to file the papers necessary to obtain the final decree (after the interlocutory judgment has been granted), and the result is that the divorce never becomes final. If the oversight presents a problem (for example, one party has already remarried, or there is a tax advantage to being divorced earlier), the court may agree to issue a nunc pro tunc order, which grants the final divorce retroactive to the earlier date.

Pendente Lite

Pendente lite means "pending the litigation." When the court makes an order, for example, for temporary alimony or child support, which lasts only until the date of a divorce trial or until the parties to a lawsuit work out a settlement, it is a pendente lite order.

Pendente lite should not be confused with lis pendens. Lis pendens also means pending lawsuit. But lis pendens is a document filed in the public records of the county where particular real property is located stating that a pending lawsuit may affect the title to the property. Because nobody wants to buy real estate if its ownership is in dispute, a lis pendens notice effectively ties up the property until the case is resolved. Lis pendens notices are often filed in divorce actions when there is disagreement about selling or dividing the family home.

Ruling

Any decision made by a judge during the course of litigation is called a ruling. For example, if a court grants a father custody after a trial on the custody issue, that is a ruling. Also, if a court sustains or overrules an objection to evidence raised during a trial, that is a ruling.

Judgment

A final decision made by a judge on a material issue during a case is termed a judgment. A judgment can provide all or a portion of the relief sought in a case, including property division, alimony, child support, custody or an injunction.

In most states, the court order granting a divorce and ruling on the issues associated with the divorce (alimony, child support, custody, visitation and division of property) is called a decree. Decrees can be temporary, interlocutory (semi-permanent) or permanent. For all practical purposes, a decree is the same thing as a judgment.

Judgment Nisi

Nisi is Latin for "unless." A judgment nisi is an intermediate judgment which will become final unless a party appeals or formally requests the court to set it aside. An interlocutory decree is properly referred to as a judgment nisi.

Entry of Judgment

When a court judgment (such as a judgment of divorce) is actually written into the official court records by the court clerk, the judgment is "entered." The court clerk sends a notice of the entry to each party. The date the judgment is entered can be important. For example, if one party wants to appeal, he usually has ten to 30 days from the date of entry of judgment to file a paper indicating his intent to appeal. Also, some states require an individual to wait a period of time (20 days to 18 months) after the entry of judgment of divorce before remarrying.

Findings of Fact and Conclusions of Law

After trial of a family law case, the judge often will issue findings of fact and conclusions of law, especially if requested to do so by a party. These set forth the facts the judge found to be true and the conclusions of law he reached regarding those facts. This allows a losing party to know how and why the judge reached his decision and whether an appeal is warranted. If the losing party appeals, the appellate court will determine whether the factual findings are supported by the evidence and whether the legal conclusions are correct. If the court answers either question in the negative, the case will usually be reversed and sent back to the trial court for a new trial.

Award

Award means the amount and/or form of a judgment a judge or jury gives the successful party in a lawsuit. It is often, but not always, an amount of money.

Example: In a divorce case, one party might be awarded the divorce, $300 per month in alimony, custody of the children, $600 per month in child support and the family home. The other party might be awarded the family business.

Actual Damages

When damages, which have been suffered by someone as a result of another's wrongdoing, can be precisely measured, they are called actual damages. Examples of actual damages are:
- loss of income because of an injury
- medical expenses
- costs of repairing damaged property, and
- specific business losses occurring because of a breach of a contract.

Actual damages are rarely awarded in family law cases, although some states now allow a parent to recover from his child's other parent the actual damages suffered if thwarted when trying to exercise visitation rights. An example is the visiting parent who buys a non-refundable plane ticket to have his child visit him, only to find out that the child has suddenly been shipped off to his grandmother's.

Punitive Damages

Punitive damages are damages (money) awarded by a court to the prevailing party in a lawsuit to punish the other party for her behavior and set an example for others. Actual damages are awarded to compensate a party for loss he has suffered. Most family law cases do not include punitive damages because these cases mainly involve dividing property, deciding child support and alimony, awarding custody or granting adoptions. A few family law cases, however, especially those for monetary compensation where there has been domestic violence or where one party has committed fraud against the other concerning marital property, may include punitive damage awards.

Equitable Relief

In many situations, a court cannot achieve a fair result simply by awarding the winner a sum of money. A non-monetary award by a court is called equitable relief. For example, if a woman is the victim of domestic violence, a later award of money may compensate her for her medical costs, but will not prevent her from being further injured. In this situation a court may grant equitable relief in the form of a temporary restraining order (TRO), ordering the abuser to stop the abuse and leave the family home. Violation of the TRO (called contempt) can be punished by a jail sentence.

Other examples of equitable relief include:

- Ordering property returned to its owner. This may arise if one spouse locks the other out of the family home and refuses to turn over his belongings.
- Rewriting a divorce agreement (or any other contract) to reflect the actual intentions of the parties if a mistake was made in drafting.
- Ordering an agreement, such as a contract for sale of a house, to be carried out.

Injunction

A court order requiring a person to do (or preventing a person from doing) a certain action is called an injunction. For example, if a party has threatened to remove marital property, or has threatened to kidnap, a court might prohibit the party from touching any marital property or removing the child from the county.

Emergency injunctions that are in effect only a short time are called temporary restraining orders. Courts also issue permanent injunctions which stay in effect indefinitely.

APPEALING

When one or both parties to a lawsuit disagree with the result in the trial court, it is usually possible to get a higher court (called an appellate court) to review the decision. Normally, an appellate court reviews only whether the trial court followed the correct law and procedures, and no evidence is presented. Some states have two levels of appeals courts; an appeal is usually first considered by an intermediate court (often called a court of appeals). If a party is still unhappy with the result, it is sometimes possible to get the state's highest court (usually called the supreme court) to review the case.

To appeal the trial court's decision, a notice must usually be filed with the trial court within a short period of time (usually about 30 days) after the entry of judgment by the court clerk.

The appellate court will require that both sides submit briefs and may also require the parties to orally argue before the court. After weighing the evidence submitted, the court makes its ruling, called a holding. The likely outcome of the appeal will be one of the following:

Affirm. The act of an appellate court upholding a decision of a trial court or a lower appellate court is called affirming the decision.

Remand. When an appellate court sends an appealed case back to the trial court for further action, the case is said to be remanded. This usually happens if the trial judge has made an error which requires a new trial or hearing. For example, assume that a trial court refuses to allow a party to introduce certain evidence (believing it to be inadmissible under the hearsay rule). If the appellate court decides that the evidence should have been admitted and that the exclusion of the evidence was prejudicial to the party offering it, the appellate court would likely remand the case for new trial and order the evidence introduced.

Vacated judgment or opinion. When an appellate court replaces a decision issued by a trial court or lower appellate court with its own opinion or judgment, the higher court usually declares the lower court's opinion or judgment vacated. A vacated opinion or judgment is considered to have never existed and cannot be used as authority when deciding similar future cases.

Reversal. If an appellate court rules that a trial court or lower appellate court made errors that may have caused an incorrect outcome in a case, the appellate court can do a number of things, including:

- reverse (wipe out) the outcome and send the case back for a new trial, if the error occurred during trial
- substitute a new decision, if the error occurred at the first appeal, or
- modify the outcome, for example, reduce the amount of damages.

In deciding an appeal, the court applies the following standards to the behavior of the trial judge:

Abuse of discretion. When judges make decisions on questions of child custody, alimony and property division, they must, of course, follow the standards set out by state law. These standards, though, often allow judges a lot of leeway (which is called discretion). Judges are given this discretion so they can make decisions that are fair in a particular case, instead of being locked into a formula that may not suit every situation.

The exercise of judicial discretion is difficult to attack on appeal, because the decision, by law, was left to the judge in the first place. Nevertheless, judicial discretion must be exercised fairly and impartially, and a showing to the contrary may result in the ruling being reversed as an abuse of discretion.

Erroneous. When a trial court makes a mistake about the law or finds certain facts to be true without adequate evidence, the court is in error. If the error affects the outcome of the case, it is called a prejudicial error, and the decision may be reversed on appeal. If this happens, the case is usually returned to the trial court for new trial. If, however, the error made in the course of a trial does not affect the outcome of the case (called a harmless error), an appellate court will not reverse the trial court decision.

Arbitrary and capricious. When a judge makes a decision without reasonable grounds or adequate consideration of the circumstances, it is said to be arbitrary and capricious and can be invalidated by an appellate court on that ground. There is, however, no set standard for what constitutes an arbitrary and capricious decision; what appears arbitrary to one judge may seem perfectly reasonable to another.

Example: Paul and Myra, both in their mid-30s, are involved in a disputed custody case. Both parents are fit to have custody of the child, so the judge must review all relevant information and decide what is in the best interest of the child. Myra raised the fact that when Paul was 16, he pleaded guilty to possessing marijuana. Based solely on Paul's previous conviction, the judge awarded custody to Myra. Paul appealed, arguing that the judge's decision was arbitrary and capricious, that his conviction nearly 20 years earlier was irrelevant, and that there is no reasonable basis to support the decision. The appellate court judges will make the decision.

> **FRIVOLOUS APPEAL**
>
> An appeal without any arguable legal basis is called a frivolous appeal and can be dismissed (thrown out) by the appellate court. Because lawyers can create a plausible legal basis for almost any argument imaginable, however, few appeals are ever ruled frivolous. The most outrageous time-waster is usually only said to "border on the frivolous."

ALTERNATIVES TO GOING TO COURT

Any process that helps people put an end to their disputes is called dispute resolution. While courts have been a central feature of our public dispute resolution system for a long while, most disputes have traditionally been solved by consensus (agreement of the disputants) with the help of community and religious leaders, with no government intervention being necessary.

In recent years, as the courts have become more and more crowded, a number of alternative dispute resolution techniques (ADR) have arisen to aid people in solving their disagreements and getting on with their lives. And the courts themselves are increasingly relying on these techniques to clear their crowded calendars and help parties to solve their own problems.

The most common forms of alternative dispute resolution (sometimes referred to as appropriate dispute resolution) are mediation, arbitration, conciliation and a combination of mediation and arbitration called med-arb (in which the mediator will decide the issues for the parties if they fail to reach agreement in the mediation).

Mediation. Mediation is a non-adversarial process where a neutral person (a mediator) meets with disputing persons to help them settle the dispute. The mediator, however, does not have the power to impose a solution on the parties.

Mediation is often used to help a divorcing or divorced couple work out their differences concerning alimony, child support, custody, visitation and division of property. Some lawyers and mental health professionals employ mediation as part of their practice. Sixteen states require mediation in custody and visitation disputes. Thirty-one states allow courts to order mediation while one state permits voluntary mediation. (These states are listed in Table 5.2 in the appendix.) A few states have started using mediation to resolve financial issues as well.

Conciliation. In conciliation, the parties meet unantagonistically with a third party who helps them reach an agreement. It is very similar to mediation.

Arbitration. Arbitration is the submission of a dispute to an impartial third person or persons. The arbitrator or arbitrators are selected directly by the parties or are chosen in accordance with the terms of a contract in which the parties have agreed to use a court-ordered arbitrator or an arbitrator from the American Arbitration Association. If there is no contract, usually each party chooses an arbitrator and the two arbitrators select a third. When parties submit to arbitration, they agree to be bound by and comply with the arbitrators' decision. The arbitrators' decision is given after an informal proceeding where each side presents evidence and witnesses.

Some arbitration proceedings are mandatory (enforced by statute), such as many labor disputes. Other arbitration proceedings are selected in advance and written into contracts. In fact, many couples who sign cohabitation agreements or divorce agreements include a clause agreeing to go to arbitration if any dispute should arise, thereby avoiding the delay, expense, bitterness and formality of litigation. Other arbitration proceedings are chosen by the disputing parties after the conflict arises, but are also to avoid the delay, expense, bitterness and formality of courts.

CIVIL AND CRIMINAL WRONGDOING

Tort

A tort is an act that injures someone in some way, and for which the injured person may sue the wrongdoer for damages. Legally, torts are called civil wrongs, as opposed to criminal ones. (Some acts like battery, however, may be both torts and crimes; the wrongdoer may face both civil and criminal penalties.)

Under traditional law, family members were prohibited from suing each other for torts. The justification was that allowing family members to sue each other would lead to a breakdown of the family. Today, however, many states recognize that if family members have committed torts against each other, there often already is a breakdown in family relationships. Thus, they no longer bar members from suing each other. In these states, spouses may sue each other either during the marriage or after they have separated.

Normally, tort lawsuits against a spouse are brought separate and apart from any divorce, annulment or other family law case. Alabama, Georgia, Nevada, New York and Tennessee, however, allow or encourage combining the tort case with the family law case; New Jersey requires it.

The jurisdictions that still prohibit one family member from suing another include Arizona, Delaware, Hawaii, Illinois, Iowa, Louisiana, Missouri, Ohio, Texas, Utah, Wyoming and Washington, DC. These places may make an exception when the tort is intentional. See, for example, *Bounds v. Candle*, 611 S.W.2d 685 (Texas 1980); *Townsend v. Townsend*, 708 S.W.2d 646 (Missouri 1986) and *Green v. Green*, 446 N.E.2d 837 (Ohio 1982).

Crime

A crime is a wrongdoing classified by the state or Congress as a felony or misdemeanor.

Felony. A felony is a serious crime punishable by at least one year in prison. Some family law felonies include kidnapping and custodial interference (in some states).

People convicted of felonies lose certain rights, such as the right to vote or hold public office. During the term of sentence, the convicted person may also be prohibited from making contracts, marrying, suing or keeping certain professional licenses. Upon release from prison, the convict may also be required to register with the police.

Misdemeanor. A misdemeanor is a crime for which the punishment is usually a fine and/or up to one year in a county jail. Often a crime which is a misdemeanor for the first offense becomes a felony for repeated offenses. All crimes that are not felonies are misdemeanors.

CONTEMPT OF COURT—CIVIL OR CRIMINAL

A judge who feels someone is improperly challenging or ignoring the court's authority has the power to declare the defiant person (called the contemnor) in contempt of court. There are two types of contempt—criminal and civil. Criminal contempt occurs when the contemnor actually interferes with the ability of the court to function properly—for example, by yelling at the judge. This is also called direct contempt because it occurs directly in front of the judge. A criminal contemnor may be fined, jailed or both as punishment for his act.

Civil contempt occurs when the contemnor willfully disobeys a court order. This is also called indirect contempt because it occurs outside the judge's immediate realm and evidence must be presented to the judge to prove the contempt. A civil contemnor, too, may be fined, jailed or both. The fine or jailing is meant to coerce the contemnor into obeying the court, not to punish him, and the contemnor will be released from jail just as soon as he complies with the court order. In family law, civil contempt is one way a court enforces alimony, child support, custody and visitation orders which have been violated.

CUSTODY AND VISITATION

TOPICS

WHO ARE THE PARENTS?
TYPES OF CUSTODY
TYPES OF VISITATION
TEMPORARY AND PERMANENT CUSTODY AND
VISITATION ORDERS
REPRESENTING THE CHILD'S INTEREST
MEDIATION
PARENTING AGREEMENTS
HOW CUSTODY AND VISITATION ARE DECIDED
INTERFERENCE WITH CUSTODY OR VISITATION
MODIFICATION OF CUSTODY OR VISITATION
WHEN A PARENT HAS MOVED OUT OF STATE
CUSTODY AND THE IRS

Custody and visitation issues arise only when a married couple with minor children separate or divorce, when an unmarried couple splits up, or when parents who never married each other or lived with each other both seek parental time with the child. In recent years, custody disputes have also arisen over frozen embryos. In these cases, the couple has decided to postpone parenting, but for medical reasons have already used the man's semen to fertilize an egg from the woman, creating an embryo. The couple had the embryo frozen, intending for it to be implanted in the woman at a later time.

This chapter covers custody and visitation as they relate to existing children. See the *Reproductive Rights and Reproductive Technology* chapter for a discussion of custody disputes over frozen embryos.

Custody generally refers to the legal authority to make decisions about a child (legal custody) and to maintain physical control over a child (physical custody). When one parent is awarded sole physical custody of the child, the other parent is awarded the right to see the child regularly, called visitation rights. The only time the court denies a parent visitation rights is if the court believes visitation would be so detrimental to the child that the parent should be prohibited from seeing the child.

Traditionally, legal and physical custody were granted to the mother and visitation rights to the father. This arrangement is still the norm in many states. Some states, however, have laws which allow divorced parents to share physical custody, legal custody or both.

Custody should not be confused with child support. Every parent has an obligation to support his children. When one parent has physical custody and the other visitation rights, the parent with visitation rights is usually ordered to pay some child support to the other parent, while the other parent is deemed to meet her obligation through the custody itself.

Although child support is a separate legal obligation, studies have shown that the more closely involved a non-custodial parent is with the raising of the children, the more likely it is that the child support obligation will be met in full.

WHO ARE THE PARENTS?

The days are long over when a child had at most two parents—one mother and one father—and everyone knew exactly who those people were.

Custodial Parent

The parent who has physical custody of a child is called the custodial parent. The other parent is termed the noncustodial parent. This is true even if the parents share legal custody. Some states now grant joint physical custody, where the parents share the physical custody of their child (for example, alternate months or years, or three days a week in one home and four in the other). In joint physical custody arrangements, a parent is considered the custodial parent when she actually has the child.

Noncustodial Parent

When one parent is awarded sole physical custody of a child, the other parent is referred to as the noncustodial parent. When the parents share the physical custody of their child, sometimes the parent with whom the child is *not* living is considered the noncustodial parent. Noncustodial parents almost always have some sort of visitation arrangement with the child.

Psychological Parent

An adult who is not legally responsible for the care, custody and support of a child, but who has established a significant emotional bond with the child such that termination of the contact between them would be detrimental to the child, is sometimes referred to as the child's psychological parent. A few courts give psychological parents visitation rights with the children.

Equitable Parent

In Michigan (*Atkinson v. Atkinson*, 408 N.W.2d 516 (1987)) and Wisconsin (*In re Paternity of D.L.H.*, 419 N.W.2d 283 (1987)), a spouse who is not a legal parent (biological or adoptive) may be granted custody or visitation under the notion of equitable parent. Courts apply it when a spouse and child have a close relationship and consider themselves parent and child, or when the legal parent encouraged this relationship. If the court grants an equitable parent custody or visitation, then the parent will also be required to pay child support.

Equitable parenthood arose to protect husbands who discover, in the course of a divorce, that they are not the biological fathers. It could also protect a stepparent who is divorcing a biological parent when the other biological parent is either deceased or absent.

Adoptive Parent

An adoptive parent is an adult who has legally adopted a child. In this situation, the biological parents' rights and obligations are terminated (meaning that they are not entitled to custody of or visitation with the child, nor are they obligated to support the child) and the adoptive parents gain these rights and obligations. If the parents of an adopted child split up, they (assuming they both legally adopted the child) are both entitled to seek custody of or visitation with the child.

Biological Parent

A biological parent is someone whose sperm or egg has been used to create a child. In most situations, biological parents are also the legal parents of the child—if they divorce or otherwise decide not to live together, they are both entitled to seek custody of or visitation with the child. Sometimes, however, a biological parent relinquishes a child or has a child taken away and placed for adoption. These parents no longer have the right to seek custody of or visitation with the child.

Sometimes, a biological parent may not be considered the legal parent of a child. In certain states, including California, for example, a man who donates his sperm to a physician to be used to artificially inseminate a woman may not be legally considered the father of the child. (California Family Code § 7613.) In states that permit surrogate mother contracts (see *Reproductive Rights and Reproductive Technology* chapter) often a man's semen is used to inseminate another woman who acts as the surrogate mother. After the child is born, the biological mother—the surrogate mother—relinquishes her rights to custody and visitation. The man may raise the child himself, with his male partner, or most commonly, with his wife who formally adopts the child.

Natural Parent

Natural parent is a term sometimes used to describe a biological parent.

Stepparent

A stepparent is a person married to a man or woman who has a child. In general, the stepparent and stepchild have no legal relationship. This means, in most states, that there is no right of inheritance between a stepparent and a stepchild (absent a will) and no obligation to support nor any rights of visitation if the legal parent and the stepparent divorce.

In a few states, however, a stepparent may be considered to have a legal relationship with a child for purposes of inheritance if the stepparent tried to adopt the child but was prevented from doing so because of a legal obstacle.

If a stepparent has adopted his or her spouse's child (see *Adoption* chapter) and then later divorces the biological parent, the stepparent and biological parent have equal rights to seek custody of or visitation with the child. If a stepparent has not adopted the child and the couple divorces, the stepparent, in many states, may seek visitation with the child as a psychological parent.

TYPES OF CUSTODY

Legal Custody

Legal custody of a child is the right and obligation to make decisions about a child's upbringing. Decisions regarding schooling, and medical and dental care, for example, are made by a parent with legal custody. In many states, courts now award joint legal custody to the parents, which means that the decision-making is shared.

Physical Custody

Physical custody is the right of a parent to have a child live with him. Some states recognize the concept of joint physical custody where the child spends approximately half the time in each parent's home.

Sole Custody

Sole custody means that only the custodial parent has physical custody and legal custody of a child, and that the noncustodial parent has visitation rights. In most states, one parent is awarded sole custody of the children, although, if there is more than one child, one parent may have sole custody of one child and the other parent sole custody of the other. (This is unusual, however, as most judges are reluctant to separate siblings.) In some situations, one parent is given sole physical custody, but legal custody is exercised jointly by the parents.

> ### TENDER YEARS DOCTRINE
>
> In the past, most states provided that custody of children of tender years (about five and under), had to be awarded to the mother when parents divorced. This rule has been rejected in most states, or relegated to the role of tie-breaker when both parents request custody, are fit to have custody and the children are pre-school age.

Joint Custody

Parents who don't live together have joint custody (also called shared custody) when they agree, or a court orders them, to share the decision-making responsibilities for, and/or physical control and custody of, their children. Joint custody can exist if the parents are divorced, separated, no longer cohabiting or even if they never lived together. Joint custody may be joint legal custody, joint physical custody (where the children spend a significant portion of time with each parent) or both. It is common for couples who share physical custody to also share legal custody, but not necessarily the other way around.

Table 5.1 in the Appendix summarizes each state's joint custody law.

Usually, when parents share joint custody, they work out joint physical custody according to their schedules and housing arrangements. If the parents cannot agree, the court will impose an arrangement. A common pattern is for children to split weeks between each parent's house. Other joint physical custody arrangements include alternating years or six-month periods, or spending weekends and holidays with one parent while spending weekdays with the other.

Joint custody has the advantages of assuring the children continuing contact and involvement with both parents, and alleviating some of the burdens of parenting for each parent. There are, of course, disadvantages—children must be shuttled around, parental non-cooperation can have seriously devastating effects on children and maintaining two homes for the children can be expensive.

Example 1: LeMar and Shirley are divorced. LeMar lives in Kansas City, and Shirley lives in St. Louis. Joint physical custody is impossible because of the distance between them, but they speak at least once a week concerning the children's upbringing and share in the decision-making responsibility. This is joint legal custody.

Example 2: Ted and Dorothy had two children during their marriage. They are now divorced, but live in the same county and have joint physical and legal custody of the children. The children live with Ted Sunday through Wednesday morning, and live with Dorothy Wednesday after school through Saturday. Ted and Dorothy also share the decision-making responsibility.

Bird's Nest Custody

Bird's nest custody is a joint custody arrangement where the children remain in the family home and the parents take turns moving in and out.

TYPES OF VISITATION

Reasonable Visitation

When a court determines the visitation rights of a noncustodial parent, it usually orders visitation at reasonable times and places, leaving it to the parents to work out a more precise schedule. Reasonable times and places allow the parents to exercise flexibility by taking into consideration both the parents' and the child's schedules. For the reasonable visitation approach to succeed, however, the parents must cooperate and communicate with each other frequently.

Fixed Visitation Schedule

Sometimes courts ordering custody and visitation for children set up schedules, including the times and places for visitation with the noncustodial parent, such as every other weekend or Tuesday and Thursday evenings. A court will be inclined to order a fixed schedule especially if the hostility between the parents is so severe that the constant contact between them may be detrimental to the child.

Supervised Visitation

When a noncustodial parent has a history of violent or destructive behavior, especially toward the child, the court often requires that visitation between that parent and the child be supervised. This means that an adult (other than the custodial parent) must be present at all times during the visit. The adult may be known or unknown to the child, and may be someone agreed upon by the parents or appointed by the court. No matter how the adult is chosen, he must be approved by the court ordering the supervised visitation.

Grandparents' Visitation

When parents separate or divorce, grandparents' relationships with their grandchildren are often at risk. To minimize the risk, all states have laws which allow grandparents to seek visitation rights with their grandchildren after divorce or separation. This right may be enforced even when both parents of the child object to the visitation or when the child's family is still intact. For example, the Supreme Court of Missouri decided that a statute authorizing a court to grant reasonable visitation rights to the grandparents was constitutional even though the parents claimed that such visitation would interfere with their constitutional right to raise their child as they saw fit. (*Herndon v. Tuhey*, 857 S.W.2d 203 (1993).) A New York couple won visitation rights with their grandson even though their grandson's family was still intact. (*Emanuel S. v. Joseph E.*, 78 N.Y.2d 178 (1992).)

TEMPORARY AND PERMANENT CUSTODY AND VISITATION ORDERS

Temporary Custody or Visitation

When a couple separates or files for divorce, the spouses often need the immediate intervention of a court to establish custody and visitation. Either spouse may request a preliminary hearing before the judge to have these issues resolved. The orders made in these preliminary hearings are often, but not necessarily, what the final judgment will include.

Example: Ken and Kim have separated; they have three teen-aged children. Ken is a psychotherapist who works out of the home and Kim is a television reporter. Because Ken's practice is in the home, he stayed there with the kids and Kim moved in temporarily with a friend. Kim filed a motion with the court requesting a preliminary hearing on the issues of use of the house and custody. At the hearing, the court is likely to grant Ken use of the home because of his professional needs and because he's got the kids. If the kids were younger, or if Kim worked part-time, the court might have been more inclined to grant her use of the home and custody and to order Ken to set up his practice elsewhere. When the court later makes the permanent orders (at the trial or when asked to review the couple's divorce agreement), it is likely to make these temporary provisions permanent unless the situation has changed or the parties agree to something different.

Permanent Custody or Visitation

A permanent custody or visitation order is permanent because it is from a final court order. It is intended to remain as ordered until the child reaches the age of majority. In reality, however, permanent custody or visitation may be modified if the parents agree or if the parent wanting the change petitions the court, shows a change of circumstance and the court issues a new order.

REPRESENTING THE CHILD'S INTEREST

Parens Patriae

Parens patriae is a Latin phrase meaning "parent of the country," which means that a state may act as the guardian of any child within its borders. The concept was used by courts under traditional common law to provide their authority for making custody decisions and other decisions affecting minors and adults legally unable to care for themselves. Today, every state has laws explicitly defining the court's power in the area of child custody. Thus, courts today never use parens patriae power to make custody rulings.

Guardian Ad Litem

If a party in a lawsuit is a minor, the court must appoint a person to protect and manage the minor's interests. That person is called a guardian ad litem and is often, although not always, a parent or close relative, or an attorney. Twenty-five states also authorize the appointment of a guardian ad litem to represent the child's interests, without the child actually becoming a party to the case, when custody is an issue.

Custody When a Parent Dies

When parents are living together and one of them dies, the other parent typically will assume sole custody of the children without further inquiry. Similarly, if a divorced parent with sole custody of the children dies, the other parent will usually take over custody—assuming he or she is willing or able. If, however, it appears that placing the children in the custody of the other parent would be harmful to them, a court may step in and designate another person to assume custody of the children—as their personal guardian.

Many people with young children use their will to designate their choice for a personal guardian—in case the other parent is not available. Although some divorced parents with sole custody try to use their will to prevent the other parent from assuming custody, this only works if the other parent clearly is not fit.

MEDIATION

Mediation is a non-adversarial process where a neutral person (a mediator) meets with disputing persons to help them settle the dispute. The mediator, however, does not have the power to impose a solution on the parties.

Mediation is often used to help a divorcing or divorced couple work out their differences, especially custody and visitation. Some lawyers and mental health professionals employ mediation as part of their practice. Sixteen states require mediation in custody and visitation disputes. Thirty-one states allow courts to order mediation and one state permits voluntary mediation. See Table 5.2 in the Appendix.

PARENTING AGREEMENTS

Traditionally, a divorce decree would award sole custody to one parent and reasonable visitation to the other—without spelling out how this would work in practice. In recent years, many parents have negotiated a detailed agreement—commonly referred to as a parenting agreement or parenting plan—about how they will raise their children separately. Not only do parenting agreements provide an intelligent parenting framework, but they also provide a basis for the part of any final divorce or separation order that governs custody and visitation. While a court can reject the agreement, it usually follows the agreement unless it appears unrealistic or not in the children's best interests.

A typical parenting plan addresses issues such as:

- the custody label for the overall plan (for example, sole custody or joint custody)
- where the children will live and maintaining contact when the children are with the other parent
- when the parents will spend time with the children
- handling holidays, vacations, special occasions and family events
- the role of each parent in the children's education
- the role of each parent in the children's health care
- the children's surname
- the children's religious training
- when the children may travel out of the country
- whether the children may own a motor vehicle
- whether the parents will give permission for an underage child to get married or join the military
- maintaining and paying for insurance for the children
- making decisions and resolving disputes when making decisions together
- exchanging information between the parents
- handling histories of domestic violence, child abuse or substance abuse
- child care

- if a parent needs to move far away
- new partners, and
- modifying the agreement when circumstances change.

While some parents can decide these issues on their own, without outside help, many others turn to mediators or family law counselors to help them resolve one or more problem areas.

HOW CUSTODY AND VISITATION ARE DECIDED

Best Interests of the Child

When deciding custody and visitation rights, a court gives the best interests of the child the highest priority. What the best interests of the child are in a given situation depends upon many factors, including:

- age and sex of the child
- mental and physical health of the child
- mental and physical health of the parents, including whether the child is exposed to secondhand smoke and any history of child abuse
- lifestyle and other social factors of the parents
- the love and emotional ties between the parent and the child
- the ability of the parent to give the child love and guidance
- the ability of the parent to provide the child with food, shelter, clothing and medical care
- established living pattern for the child concerning school, home, community, religious institution
- school quality—particularly when one parent wishes to move
- the child's preference, if the child is above a certain age, usually about 12, and
- the ability of the parent to foster healthy communication and contact between the child and the other parent.

Established Living Pattern

When a parent seeks custody of, or more visitation with, a child, the court's decision will normally favor the parent who will best maintain stability in the child's surroundings. There is no set standard as to what constitutes stability, but a judge looks for continuity in a child's life. It is important that the child, to the degree possible, keep the same school, community and religious ties. If maintaining the same contacts is not possible, the judge looks to which parent is best able to create a stable environment for the child.

Example 1: Larry and Tanya divorced after 15 years of marriage and two children. Both requested custody. The judge was faced with a hard decision because both Larry and Tanya were able, loving parents. After the divorce, however, Larry moved 100 miles from where the family lived; Tanya stayed in the same town. Because both parents would provide the children with love, guidance and financial support, the judge awarded custody to Tanya, emphasizing that the children's home, school and community ties were established and that there was no reason to disrupt them.

Example 2: Byron is eight years old. He's in the third grade and a member of the school band, and takes kiddie cooking classes once a week. Byron's parents have recently separated, and both want custody. Byron's family has moved every other year due to his father's business obligations. Byron's father argued to the judge that frequent moving is not harmful to Byron, and gives him an opportunity to experience different places and people while growing up. Byron's mother emphasized that she has no plans to move and that she feels Byron needs to settle in one place. The judge agreed with the mother, ruling that stability in Byron's life was more important than the opportunity to live in many places and meet many people.

Lifestyle and Social Factors

The way each parent lives can be an important factor when a court decides which parent is entitled to physical custody and what visitation rights are appropriate. In any given case, the judge may consider one parent's lifestyle more in the best interest of the child than the other's. The main elements courts tend to consider when examining a parent's lifestyle are family stability, occupation, type of home maintained, interests and hobbies, sexual history, religious practices and income.

GAY OR LESBIAN PARENT

If a parent is gay or lesbian, many courts deny or strictly limit the parent's custody of or visitation with his or her children. In a few states, however, a parent's sexual orientation cannot in and of itself prevent a parent from being given custody of her child. As a practical matter, however, lesbian and gay parents in those states may still be denied custody. This is because judges, when considering the best interests of the child, may be motivated by their own prejudices as well as by the prejudices of the community and may find reasons other than the parent's sexual orientation to deny the lesbian or gay parent custody.

Child's Preference

Over 30 states have laws authorizing courts to consider a child's preference concerning which parent she wants to live with following a divorce or separation, provided the child is over a certain age (about ten). Generally, the older the child, the more weight the desire is given. In a few states, the court must grant the child's wish if the child is at least a certain age (usually 12 to 14).

Child Abuse

Physical, emotional or sexual mistreatment of a child is child abuse. Physical abuse generally consists of causing physical harm to a child, even if the injury is temporary. Thus, corporal punishment that causes bruising or burning, and deprivations of food, water or needed medical treatment are all examples of physical abuse. While some parents who rely on force to discipline their children may be unable to tell the difference between child abuse and proper parental treatment, most parents know where the line is, even if it can't be defined.

Emotional abuse includes speech and conduct calculated to deprive the child of dignity and self-esteem, such as humiliating the child in front of family or friends, isolating the child from other persons for long periods of time and habitually directing language or gestures at the child that are designed to punish rather than instruct.

Sexual mistreatment includes virtually all behavior toward the child that is designed to lead to sexual gratification of either the adult or the child. While the most common forms of sexual mistreatment are outright sexual acts such as fondling or sexual intercourse, sexual mistreatment may also consist of placing the child in compromising situations such as nudity, inappropriate clothing, and methods of discipline that are commonly associated with sexual gratification.

Transportation of Children

One issue which must be decided when arranging custody and visitation is who will be responsible for transporting the children to and from the noncustodial parent. Often, the time and cost involved is shared, or if the parents live far from each other, the parent in better economic condition may be required to pay more of the cost. Transportation of children for visitation purposes is a commonly disputed issue after the divorce and should not be overlooked when the parents draft their divorce agreement.

INTERFERENCE WITH CUSTODY OR VISITATION

Custodial interference occurs when a parent (guardian or other relative) keeps a child away from a person who has a legal right to custody. In most states, it's a crime to take a child from his parent or legal guardian intending to deprive that person of custody, even if the taker also has custody rights. In many states, depriving a parent or guardian of custody is a felony if the child is taken out of state. Many states, however, recognize good-cause defenses, such as the taker acted to prevent imminent bodily harm to herself or the child. In addition, some states let the taker take the child if the taker is requesting custody in court and has notified the court or police of the child's location. In most states, the parent or guardian deprived of custody may sue the taker for damages. See Table 5.3 in the Appendix.

Visitation interference occurs when the custodial parent makes the visitation of the child by the noncustodial parent impossible or irregular.

Kidnapping or Child Concealment

When a parent without physical custody (who may or may not have visitation rights) removes a child from, or refuses to return a child to, the parent with physical custody, in addition to being custodial interference, it is considered kidnapping or child concealment. Federal and state laws have been passed to prosecute and punish parents guilty of kidnapping, which is a felony in over 40 states.

PARENTAL KIDNAPPING PREVENTION ACT (PKPA)

The Parental Kidnapping Prevention Act (28 U.S.C. § 1738A and 42 U.S.C. §§ 654, 663) is a federal statute enacted in 1980 to address kidnapping by noncustodial parents and inconsistent child custody decisions made by state courts. The law provides for penalties for kidnapping and requires states to recognize and enforce the custody decisions of courts in other states, rather than make a second, and possibly inconsistent, decision.

Federal Parent Locator Service

Parent locator services have been created by state and federal governments to assist a parent in locating her child's other parent in order to enforce child support orders. They also help parents locate missing children who may have been kidnapped by the other parent. Many parent locator services are associated with district attorney or state's attorney offices.

INTERNATIONAL CHILD ABDUCTION REMEDIES ACT

The International Child Abduction Remedies Act (12 U.S.C. §§ 11.601 through 11.610) is a federal statute that enables the Hague Convention on the Civil Aspects of International Child Abduction to be followed in the U.S. This Hague Convention is an international agreement among the U.S. and around 40 other countries that has the purpose of providing the prompt return of children wrongfully removed or retained in any participating country and ensuring that the rights of custody and access under the law of one country are effectively respected in another country. It addresses jurisdictional questions and provides common rules and procedures to determine child custody in a dispute that crosses international borders.

U.S. State Department Office of Citizen and Counselor Services

The federal government office that provides assistance both when a child is abducted from the U.S. to another country and when a child is abducted from another country to the U.S. is the U.S. State Department Office of Citizen and Counselor Services.

MODIFICATION OF CUSTODY OR VISITATION

After a final decree of divorce is filed with a court, former spouses may agree to modify the custody or visitation terms. This modified agreement (also called a stipulated modification) may be made without court approval. If one person, however, later reneges on the agreement, the other person may not be able to enforce it unless the court has approved the modification. Thus, it is advisable in most situations to obtain court approval before relying on such agreements. Courts usually approve modification agreements unless it appears that they are not in the best interest of the child.

If a parent wants to change an existing court order affecting custody or visitation and the other parent won't agree to the change, he must file a motion requesting a modification of the order from the court that issued it, usually on the ground of changed circumstances.

Changed Circumstances

When a party files a request for modification of custody or visitation, she must usually show that circumstances have changed substantially since the time of the previously issued order. This rule encourages stability of arrangements and helps prevent the court from becoming overburdened with frequent and repetitive modification requests. What follows are a couple of examples of change of circumstances:

Change in lifestyle. Changes in custody or visitation orders may be obtained if substantial changes in a parent's lifestyle threaten or harm the child. If, for example, a custodial parent begins working at night and leaving a nine-year-old child alone, the other parent may request a change in custody. Similarly, if a noncustodial parent begins drinking heavily or taking drugs, the custodial parent may file a request for modification of the visitation order (asking, for example, that visits occur when the parent is sober, or in the presence of another adult).

What constitutes a lifestyle sufficiently detrimental to warrant a change in custody or visitation rights varies tremendously depending on the state and the particular judge deciding the case. For instance, cohabitation by a parent may be ignored in one place, but not another.

RACE

Palmore v. Sidoti, 466 U.S. 429 (1984) is a U.S. Supreme Court decision in which the court ruled that it was unconstitutional for a court to consider race when a noncustodial parent petitions a court for a change of custody. In the case, a white couple had divorced, and the mother had been awarded custody of their son. She remarried an African-American man and moved to a predominantly African-American neighborhood. The father filed a request for modification of custody based on the changed circumstance that the boy was now living with an African-American man in an African-American neighborhood. A Florida court granted the modification. The U.S. Supreme Court reversed, ruling that societal stigma, especially a racial one, cannot be the basis for a custody decision.

Destabilized household. A home in which a devastating event has occurred may be referred to as a destabilized household. Examples of such events include the arrest of a parent for a violent crime, the death or desertion of a parent, or an allegation that a parent has sexually abused his child. If a noncustodial parent can prove to a judge that the custodial parent's home has become destabilized and that the event is devastating to the child, a request for modification of custody may be granted.

Geographic move. If a custodial parent geographically relocates a substantial distance, the move may constitute a changed circumstance that justifies the court's modification of a custody or visitation order in order to accommodate the needs of the noncustodial parent. Some courts switch custody from one parent to the other. Other courts require that the relocating parent pay transportation costs for visits with the noncustodial parent. To discourage moves, some courts forbid parents to remove the children from the state of the divorce without first giving written notice to the other parent. This notice gives the noncustodial parent the opportunity to go to court and ask for a custody or visitation modification.

Temporary Modification of Custody

When a custodial parent will be temporarily out of state, hospitalized, or otherwise unable to care for the child, she may request that a court make a temporary modification of custody, giving the other parent custody for the time of the incapacity, but restoring custody to her when the incapacity ends.

Where the custodial parent will be temporarily unavailable to care for the child, and there is no other parent to have custody, the custodial parent should name someone to act as guardian of the child for the temporary period.

WHEN A PARENT HAS MOVED OUT OF STATE

Uniform Child Custody Jurisdiction Act (UCCJA)

All states and the District of Columbia have enacted a statute called the Uniform Child Custody Jurisdiction Act, which sets standards for when a court may make a custody determination and when a court must defer to an existing determination from another state. In general, a state may make a custody decision about a child if (in order of preference):

- The state is the child's home state—this means the child has resided in the state for the six previous months, or was residing in the state but is absent because a parent has removed the child from or retained the child outside of the state.
- There are significant connections with people—such as teachers, doctors and grandparents—and substantial evidence in the state, concerning the child's care, protection, training and personal relationships.
- The child is in the state and either has been abandoned or is in danger of being abused or neglected if sent back to the other state.
- No other state can meet one of the above three tests, or a state can meet at least one of the tests but has declined to make a custody decision.

If a state cannot meet one of these tests, even if the child is present in the state, the courts of that state cannot make a custody award. Also, a parent who has wrongfully removed or retained a child in order to create a home state or significant connections will be denied custody. In the event more than one state meets the above standards, the law requires that only one state award custody. This means that once the first state makes a custody award, another state can neither make another "initial" award nor modify the existing order.

Having the same law in all states helps achieve consistency in the treatment of custody decrees. It also helps solve many of the problems created by kidnapping or disagreements over custody between parents living in different states.

Example: Sam and Diane met and married in Missouri. They moved to Delaware where their child (Sam Jr.) was born. Sam, Diane and Junior lived in Delaware until Junior was ten. At that time, Sam took Junior to Missouri in an effort to divorce Diane and raise Junior himself. When Sam went to court in Missouri and requested custody, his request was denied because Delaware is Junior's home state, the state with which he has significant connections, and Sam removed Junior from Delaware in an effort to create home state jurisdiction in Missouri. (Diane should go to court in Delaware and request custody, even though Junior is in Missouri.)

Despite the success of the UCCJA, parents still find difficulty in enforcing custody orders across state lines. The Uniform Law Commissioners have taken on the task of strengthening the UCCJA, and are likely to propose the Uniform Interstate Child Visitation Act sometime in the late 1990s.

CUSTODY AND VISITATION

FULL FAITH AND CREDIT

Full faith and credit is a legal principle requiring judges to recognize and enforce valid decrees and judgments issued by courts in other states.

In the past, states often did not afford full faith and credit to custody decisions of courts in other states, preferring instead to decide the issues on the evidence before them. This often led to contradictory custody orders and sometimes children were kidnapped and thrown back and forth. Now, however, the Uniform Child Custody Jurisdiction Act requires states to give full faith and credit to custody decisions rendered in other states.

CUSTODY AND THE IRS

The following tax benefits are available to parents to offset the cost of raising children:

- the earned income credit
- the child care credit
- medical expense deductions, and
- the head of household filing status.

Only a custodial parent is entitled to claim the child care tax credit. In general, employed custodial parents of a dependent child under the age of 13 are eligible for the credit for child care expenses incurred so that the parent can earn an income. As the custodial parent's income increases, however, the credit phases out.

Both parents can claim a deduction for medical expenses actually paid, but only if those medical expenses exceed 7.5% of their adjusted gross income. If your total medical expenses are high enough, you may want to allocate them to the lower wage earner so that that parent can take the deduction.

Only a parent with physical custody (meaning custody more than half of the time) can file as head of household. If the parents have joint legal and physical custody (and physical custody is divided 50–50), neither can file as head of household because the dependent child resides with neither parent for more than 50% of the year.

If you have more than one minor child and share physical custody, you can specify your arrangement as 51% for one child with one parent and 51% for the other child with the other parent. Because each parent has a dependent child in the home more than 50% of the year, each parent can file as head of household.

DIVORCE

TOPICS

SEPARATION
TYPES OF DIVORCE
GROUNDS FOR DIVORCE
DEFENSES TO DIVORCE
DIVORCE REQUIREMENTS
DIVORCE AGREEMENTS
RECONCILIATION AND MEDIATION
CONSEQUENCES OF DIVORCE
UNIFORM DIVORCE LAWS

Divorce is the legal termination of a marriage. In some states, divorce is called dissolution or dissolution of marriage. A divorce or dissolution severs (ends) a marriage.

This discussion refers to civil annulments; within the Roman Catholic Church, a couple may obtain a religious annulment after obtaining a civil divorce, in order for one or both spouses to remarry.

ANNULMENT

Annulment is a court procedure that dissolves a marriage and treats it as though it never happened. Annulments may be obtained for one of the following reasons:

- misrepresentation (for example, a spouse lied about the capacity to have children, stated that she had reached the age of consent or failed to say that she was still married to someone else)
- concealment (for example, concealing an addiction to alcohol or drugs, conviction of a felony, children from a prior relationship, a sexually transmitted disease or impotency)
- refusal or inability to consummate the marriage—that is, refusal or inability of a spouse to have sexual intercourse with the other spouse, or
- misunderstanding (for example, one person wanted children and the other did not).

In the past, when divorces were difficult to obtain because fault had to be proved—until 1966, adultery was the only ground for divorce in New York—judges often interpreted annulment statutes liberally in order to make annulments readily available. Today, however, it is relatively easy to obtain a divorce in most states and annulments are rare. Where an annulment occurs after children have been born, those children are not considered illegitimate, even though the parents were "never married."

SEPARATION

There are four types of separation:

Trial Separation

When a couple lives apart for a test period—that is, to decide whether to permanently go separate ways or to get back together (called reconciliation)—it's called a trial separation.

Living Apart

When spouses no longer reside in the same dwelling, they are said to be living apart even if they occasionally have sexual relations with each other. In some states, living apart without intending to reunite changes the spouses' property rights. For example, some states consider property accumulated and debts incurred between living apart and divorce to be the separate property or debt of the person who accumulated or incurred it. If the couple lives apart for a trial period with the hope of reconciliation, however, even if they don't get back together, the assets and debts they accumulate or incur during the trial period remain jointly owned until they decide to permanently live apart or obtain a divorce or legal separation.

Permanent Separation

When a couple decides to split up, it's often called a permanent separation. It may follow a trial separation, or may begin immediately when the couple starts living apart. In many states, all assets received and most debts incurred after permanent separation are the separate property or responsibility of the spouse incurring them.

Legal Separation

A legal separation results when the parties separate and a court rules on the division of property, alimony, child support, custody and visitation—but does not grant a divorce. This separation is also called a separation from bed and board. The money awarded for support of the spouse and children under these circumstances is often called separate maintenance (as opposed to alimony and child support).

Legal separation is usually a substitute for, and not a step toward, divorce. It often occurs when there is a religious objection to divorce, or if a dependent spouse needs medical care and will not qualify for it on her own—but will maintain coverage under her spouse's plan if they stay married. Most couples who intend to divorce begin living apart without going through formal separation procedures. Prior to no-fault divorces, however, legal separations were often obtained by couples wishing to live apart (who needed to get legal permission from the court to do so).

IT WOULDN'T BE LAW IF WE COULDN'T SAY IT IN LATIN

Vinculo matrimonii. Vinculo matrimonii is a Latin term literally meaning "from the chains of matrimony," and which has come to mean a complete divorce, as opposed to a legal separation.

A mensa et thoro. A mensa et thoro is a Latin term meaning "from table and bed" which became used in English as "from bed and board." A separation a mensa et thoro—that is, a separation from bed and board—is another term for a legal separation.

In a few states, a legal separation serves another purpose. If a couple legally separates for a set period of time—between six months and five years—they will have established a ground for a no-fault divorce.

SEPARATION AGREEMENT

If a couple agrees to all the terms of a legal separation, or agrees to live apart for a lengthy period of time in contemplation of divorce, the parties often write and sign a separation agreement which settles the property, custody, alimony and child support issues between them. The agreement should be presented to the court for approval if it is part of a legal separation. The agreement becomes part of the legal separation order and does away with the necessity of having a trial on the issues covered by the agreement. It serves the same purpose as a divorce agreement except that the couple does not obtain a divorce at that time.

The term separation agreement is also used to refer to agreements made by couples living apart which are later incorporated into divorce agreements.

TYPES OF DIVORCE

Default Divorce

If a spouse who is served with a summons and complaint for divorce fails to file a formal response with the court, the court will automatically grant the divorce, called a default or uncontested divorce. Many divorces proceed this way because the spouses have worked everything out and there's no reason for both to go to court (and pay the court costs). Without such cooperation, however, you should never ignore a summons and complaint unless you truly do not wish to contest the matter.

Divisible Divorce

A divisible divorce is one where the divorce itself is granted, terminating the marriage. Issues incident to the divorce, such as alimony, child support, custody, visitation and division of property, however, are decided at a later hearing or trial. Divisible divorces usually occur when a couple cannot agree on some incidental issues, but one spouse wishes to remarry or be divorced for income tax reasons. Divisible divorces may also occur when a court has subject-matter jurisdiction over the divorce (because the plaintiff lives in the state), but doesn't have personal jurisdiction over the defendant. (See the *Court Procedures* chapter for definitions of these terms.) In this situation, the court is authorized to grant the divorce itself, but can't rule on the other issues without personal jurisdiction over the defendant.

Bifurcated Divorce

A bifurcated divorce is another term for a divisible divorce.

Convertible Divorce

A convertible divorce is one which is obtained by converting a legal separation to a divorce.

Example: Kate and Robert have been married for 15 years. Kate has severe back problems and is unable to work. She has received extensive medical care, which has been paid for through Robert's medical insurance; she is unable to

obtain her own insurance. Kate and Robert agree that their m~~
working. If they divorce, however, Kate will have no health insuranc~
they legally separate so that Kate remains on Robert's health plan.

After a few years, Kate undergoes extensive surgery and her back problems are gone. She also obtains a job in which her employer's health insurer is willing to provide her with coverage. Because Kate no longer needs Robert's insurance, Kate and Robert now convert their legal separation into a divorce.

Foreign Divorce

A divorce obtained in a different state or country from where one spouse resides at the time of the divorce is called a foreign divorce. As a general rule, foreign divorces are recognized as valid in all states if the other spouse has become a resident of the state or country granting the divorce and if both parties consented to the jurisdiction of the foreign court to grant the divorce. A foreign divorce obtained by one person without the consent of the other is normally not valid, unless the non-consenting spouse later acts as if the foreign divorce was valid, for example, by remarrying.

UNIFORM DIVORCE RECOGNITION ACT

The Uniform Divorce Recognition Act was promulgated by the Uniform Law Commissions and then withdrawn in 1978, but not before it was passed by a few states. This law provides that if both members of a married couple are residing within one state and the couple obtains a divorce from another state, the state in which the couple resides will not recognize or enforce the foreign divorce. This means that if a married couple lives in Ohio and gets divorced in South Dakota, Ohio will not consider the divorce valid. Having an invalid divorce can have many effects, including changing the filing status on state and federal income tax returns, altering the disposition of property on death and, in rare cases, leading to prosecution for bigamy where a spouse, knowing she has an invalid divorce, remarries.

DOMINICAN REPUBLIC DIVORCE

Divorces granted by the Dominican Republic are called Dominican divorces. Married couples can obtain Dominican divorces without actually going to the Dominican Republic. Most states, however, do not recognize these divorces as valid unless at least one spouse was present in the Dominican Republic at the time the Dominican divorce was obtained.

The Dominican Republic is the current nation offering fast, mail-order divorces, but is by no means the only nation to do so. In past years, Mexico and Haiti were popular "quickie" divorce spots.

GROUNDS FOR DIVORCE

All states require a spouse to identify a legal reason for requesting a divorce when he initiates the proceedings by filing the complaint (or petition). Some states also allow the other spouse to identify reasons in her answer in the event she, too, wants the divorce. What constitutes a sufficient legal reason varies among the states; the reasons are laid out in state laws and referred to as the grounds for divorce. See Table 6.1 in the Appendix.

No-Fault Divorce

No-fault divorce describes any divorce where the spouse suing for divorce does not have to accuse the other of wrongdoing. Rather, the spouse can simply state that the couple no longer gets along, or that the couple has been living apart for a specified period.

Until the 1970s, the only way a person could get a divorce was to prove that the other spouse was guilty of marital misconduct and was at fault for the marriage not working. Today, all states allow divorces regardless of who is at "fault."

No-fault divorces are usually granted for reasons such as incompatibility, irreconcilable differences, or irretrievable or irremediable breakdown of the marriage. Also, some states allow incurable insanity as a basis for a no-fault divorce.

Incompatibility. Incompatibility refers to a conflict in personalities that makes married life together impossible.

Irreconcilable differences. Irreconcilable differences are those differences between spouses that are considered sufficiently severe to make married life together more or less impossible. As a practical matter, courts seldom, if ever, inquire into what the differences actually are, and routinely grant a divorce as long as the party seeking the divorce says the couple has irreconcilable differences.

Irremediable or irretrievable breakdown. An irremediable breakdown in a marriage occurs when one spouse refuses to live with the other and will not work toward reconciliation. As a practical matter, courts seldom, if ever, inquire into whether the marriage has actually broken down, and routinely grant a divorce as long as the party seeking the divorce says the marriage has broken down.

Fault Divorce

Traditionally, in order for a married couple to obtain a divorce, one spouse had to prove that the other spouse was legally at fault. The "innocent" spouse was then granted the divorce from the "guilty" spouse. If a husband was the guilty spouse, he would usually have to pay a substantial amount of alimony or give up marital property to which he was entitled; if a wife was at fault, her alimony might be reduced or eliminated or she may lose marital property she otherwise would have been awarded.

Today, about two-thirds of the states still allow a spouse to allege fault in obtaining a divorce. But alimony, property division and fault are linked less and less. For example, although a fault divorce is still available in Illinois, alimony is awarded and property divided regardless of fault. (§ 40-404.) Conversely, although fault divorces have been eliminated in Florida, adultery is a factor in determining the award of alimony. (§ 61.08.)

The various traditional fault grounds for divorce, such as adultery, cruelty and desertion, are also generally referred to as marital misconduct. Below are the standard fault grounds for divorce.

Adultery. Sexual relations by a married person with somebody other than his or her spouse is called adultery. In many states, adultery is technically a crime, but rarely is anyone prosecuted for it. In the states that have retained fault grounds for divorce, adultery is always a grounds. In addition, in some states, a parent accused by her spouse of adultery may find judges hostile to granting her custody of children of the marriage.

ELEMENTS OF ADULTERY

Co-respondent. The "other man" or "other woman" named in the court papers alleging adultery is called the co-respondent.

Inclination. Inclination is an element of adultery that a spouse must prove if there is no eyewitness to the adulterous act. Inclination means demonstrated signs of affection between the defendant and the co-respondent.

Opportunity. An actual chance a person has to perform an act is called an opportunity. A plaintiff seeking a divorce on the grounds of adultery must prove that his spouse had the opportunity to commit adultery. This opportunity may have been, for example, when the defendant and the co-respondent attended a convention together or stayed at the same motel on the same night.

Cruelty. Cruelty is often defined as any act of inflicting unnecessary emotional or physical pain. Cruelty or mental cruelty is the most frequently used fault grounds for divorce because as a practical matter, courts will accept minor wrongs or disagreements as sufficient evidence of cruelty to justify the divorce.

Desertion. Desertion (also called abandonment) is the voluntary abandonment of someone by his spouse without the abandoned spouse's consent. Commonly, desertion occurs when a spouse leaves the marital home for a specified length of time (which varies among the states).

Confinement in prison. In most states with fault divorce, the spouse not in prison can obtain a divorce from her spouse if he has been imprisoned for a set number of years. In New York, for example, the imprisonment must be at least three years. (Domestic Relations Law § 170.)

Physical incapacity. In some states with fault divorce, lack of the physical capacity to engage in sexual intercourse is grounds for annulment or divorce, assuming the incapacity was not disclosed to the other spouse before the marriage.

Incurable insanity. Incurable insanity of a spouse often is grounds for either a fault or a no-fault divorce. It is rarely used, however, because of the difficulty of proving both the insanity and its incurability.

WHEN BOTH ARE AT FAULT

Under the doctrine of comparative rectitude, a court will grant the spouse least at fault a divorce when both parties have shown grounds for divorce. Under common law, when both parties were at fault, neither was entitled to a divorce. The absurdity of this result gave rise to this concept.

DEFENSES TO DIVORCE

Under the traditional fault divorce scheme, a spouse who did not want a divorce usually defended against the divorce action by simply denying whatever the other spouse alleged. Sometimes, however, the evidence of the defendant's fault (also called marital misconduct) was overwhelming, and the defendant needed something other than just a denial. Under the laws of many states, the defendant was permitted to defeat a divorce action by proving that the plaintiff was also at fault and therefore shouldn't be granted the divorce. If both parties were deemed at fault, neither could be granted the divorce, and they were forced to remain married. (Courts sometimes got around this, however.)

Under this system, women who were financially dependent on their husbands could threaten to block a divorce by proving that a husband was at fault, unless he agreed to provide a greater share of marital property or alimony than he might otherwise be required to pay. Although it is still possible to obtain a fault divorce in most states, the fact that no-fault divorce is now also available in every state has made this type of bargaining much less common.

Other defenses to a divorce based on marital misconduct include the following:

Collusion

Collusion is the secret cooperation of two people in order to mislead or deceive a third person. Before no-fault divorces, many couples wanted to divorce, but neither spouse had a legal basis (ground) for the divorce. They would therefore pretend that one of them was committing adultery or was otherwise at fault in order to manufacture grounds for divorce. This was collusion because they were cooperating in order to mislead the judge. If, before the divorce, the defendant decided he no longer wanted a divorce, he could raise the collusion as a defense to the divorce.

Condonation

Condonation is someone's approval of another's activities. For example, a wife who does not object to her husband's adultery may be said to condone it. In a fault divorce, condonation may constitute a defense to divorce. If the wife sues her husband for divorce, claiming he has committed adultery, the husband may argue as a defense that she condoned his behavior.

Connivance

Connivance is the setting up of a situation so that the other person commits a wrongdoing. For example, a wife who invites her husband's co-respondent to the house and then leaves for the weekend may be said to have connived his adultery. In a fault divorce, connivance may constitute a defense to divorce. If the wife sues her husband for divorce, claiming he has committed adultery, the husband may argue as a defense that she connived—that is, set up—his actions.

Provocation

Provocation is the inciting of another to do a certain act. In a fault divorce, provocation may constitute a defense. For example, if the spouse suing for divorce claims that the other spouse abandoned her, her spouse might defend the suit on the ground that she provoked the abandonment.

DIVORCE REQUIREMENTS

To obtain a divorce, a plaintiff must meet several requirements—grounds for a divorce, legal adulthood and residency in the state.

Residency

Residency means living in a particular place with the intention of remaining there. States require a spouse to be a resident of a state before filing for a divorce there. States do not require someone who wants to file for a divorce to prove that he is a resident; instead, the state just looks to the fact that he is residing there as indication that he plans to stay indefinitely.

TRAVEL: EFFECT ON RESIDENCY

Travel for any length of time does not affect residency for the purpose of obtaining a divorce. Thus, if Henry moved to New Hampshire from Florida, lived there for several years, and then took a leisurely trip around the world, he could still return to New Hampshire and file for divorce based on his prior established residency.

Virtually all states require that someone live in the state for a certain period of time—often six months—before filing for divorce. This is called a durational residency requirement. (See Table 6.2 in the Appendix.) No state has a residency requirement for getting married.

DIVORCE AGREEMENTS

When a couple divorces, they may agree on some or all of the issues relating to the division of property, custody and visitation of the children, alimony and child support. If the agreement is put in writing, signed by the parties and accepted by the court, it is called a divorce agreement, marital settlement agreement, marital termination agreement or settlement agreement. The agreement becomes part of the divorce decree and does away with the necessity of having a trial on the issues covered by the agreement.

INTEGRATED PROPERTY SETTLEMENT AGREEMENT

Upon divorce, couples commonly enter into a divorce agreement which divides marital property and may set alimony. The agreement is called integrated if the property settlement and alimony payments are combined into either one lump sum payment or periodic payments. Integrated agreements are often used when the marital property consists of substantial intangible assets (for example, future royalties, stock options, future pension plans) or when one party is buying the other's interest in a valuable tangible asset (for example, a home or business). In addition, if a spouse is entitled to little or no alimony, but is not financially independent, periodic payments may help that spouse gain financial independence.

Most integrated property settlement agreements cannot later be changed at the request of one of the parties unless he can show the agreement was entered into under fraud or duress. This is because the alimony and property division are so intertwined that a later modification would create a substantial risk of unfairness to one of the parties.

RECONCILIATION AND MEDIATION

Reconciliation

Reconciliation is the getting back together of a couple who have continuously lived apart for a period of time. Reconciliation requires more than occasional sex or living together; it requires that the couple actually intend to resume their marriage. If a judge determines that parties to a divorce have reconciled, a pending divorce complaint may be denied. If, however, an interlocutory judgment of divorce has been issued prior to the reconciliation, the judgment's terms concerning the division of property will remain in effect unless the spouses seek to have it set aside.

Many states require a waiting period between the interlocutory and final judgments to give the parties an opportunity to reconcile. This is called a cooling-off period and can be three months to a year, depending on state law. Once the divorce becomes final, however, the marriage cannot be reconciled (that is, the couple must remarry).

Conciliation Service

In a few states, persons contemplating divorce can get help from court-provided services that attempt to bring the parties back together (conciliation) or help them work out some disputed issues (mediation). Some states also offer conciliation services and mediation to divorcing spouses to help resolve disputes over child support, alimony, custody, visitation and division of property through negotiation rather than adversarial court proceedings.

Mediation

Mediation is a non-adversarial process where a neutral person (a mediator) meets with disputing persons (often parties to a lawsuit or a threatened lawsuit) to help them settle the dispute. The mediator, however, does not have the power to impose a solution on the parties.

Mediation is often used to help a divorcing or divorced couple work out their differences concerning alimony, child support, custody, visitation and division of property. Some lawyers and mental health professionals employ mediation as part of their practice.

CONSEQUENCES OF DIVORCE

Former Name

A woman's surname given to her at birth is her maiden name. She may have another former name from a previous marriage or other name change. A divorcing woman who took her husband's name (or who created a new or hyphenated name) at marriage has the option of returning to her maiden name, a former married name (if she has been married more than once), keeping her married name or choosing something completely new. A woman's surname is not automatically changed by marriage; the change becomes effective only if the woman starts using her husband's surname. A divorcing husband who took a new name at marriage can also return to his old name at divorce.

Head of Household

Head of household is the federal income tax status of a single person who contributes more than one half toward the support of a non-spouse relative. The relative must be a parent (including a stepparent or grandparent), child (including stepchild or grandchild) or sibling (including half-sibling). The head of household tax rate is higher than that for married persons filing jointly, but lower than that for single persons.

Head of household tax status is important for single parents, and divorcing parents often argue over which one is entitled to the head of household filing status. Because the one who claims head of household must contribute more than half of the support, both parents cannot claim it.

Insurance

Divorce can affect a couple's life and health insurance. If a spouse is named as a beneficiary in a life insurance policy, some states' laws change the beneficiary automatically if the couple divorces and the holder of the policy remarries. Thus, even if the policyholder forgets to change the beneficiary, the new spouse, not the ex-spouse, will get the proceeds. In a few states, if there is no remarriage, the ex-spouse may still be automatically taken off the policy and the proceeds given to the insured's children. Some judges require an ex-spouse who pays alimony (or child support) to make the recipients of the support beneficiaries of a life insurance policy.

Divorce can also affect health insurance coverage. Some states have automatic conversion laws requiring the financially independent spouse to continue to cover the financially dependent spouse after divorce until the dependent spouse becomes financially independent. See, for example, Connecticut General Statutes Annotated 38-262(d); Florida Statutes Annotated 627.6675; Iowa Code Annotated 509(B)(3); Massachusetts General Laws Annotated 32A-11(A) and 175-110(I); Minnesota Statutes Annotated 62A and 21(A)(2A), 2(B); Annotated Missouri Statutes 376-428; New Jersey Statutes Annotated 17:48-6 and 48A;

DIVORCE

New Mexico Statutes Annotated 59A-47-34; Tennessee Code Annotated 56-7-1501.

Also, the federal Consolidated Omnibus Budget Reconciliation Act—COBRA—makes an ex-spouse eligible to receive for the three years following the divorce, any group rate health insurance provided by her ex-husband's employer. (26 U.S.C. § 4980B(f).) This law also applies to children of the parties and they may take these continuation and conversion options until they are no longer dependents.

In addition, all states require one or the other parent to provide health insurance for the minor children after divorce. Some states also require that the parent paying child support maintain a life insurance policy naming the children as beneficiaries in the event the parent dies before the children reach the age of majority.

Pets

Pets are a part of many families. In some divorces, spouses argue over who should keep the dogs, cats, rabbits and other pets. Some disagreements are so heated that the parties to the divorce cannot make the decision themselves. A growing number of judges (although still very few) are asked to make custody and visitation orders concerning the pets.

Divorce can also affect pets when a family breaks up and is forced to move to smaller living quarters. In this situation, there is often insufficient space for the pets, and they must be sold or given away.

UNIFORM DIVORCE LAWS

The Uniform Marriage and Divorce Act (UMDA) is an extensive uniform law which provides standards governing marriage, divorce, property distribution, alimony, child support and custody. It has been adopted by eight states—Arizona, Colorado, Illinois, Kentucky, Minnesota, Missouri, Montana and Washington.

The major provisions do the following:
- Eliminate fault divorces. The only grounds permitted is irretrievable breakdown, defined as either living apart for 180 days, or a serious marital discord adversely affecting the attitude of one or both spouses toward the marriage.
- Eliminate traditional defenses to divorce.
- Provide for equitable distribution of property in non-community property states; factors to include in making an equitable distribution are:
  — length of marriage and any prior marriages
  — agreement before marriage
  — age, health, station, occupation, income, vocational skills, employability, property and debts of each spouse
  — needs of the parties, including any future opportunities to acquire assets
  — who has custody
  — any economic misconduct, and
  — whether the property distribution is in lieu of, or in addition to, alimony.
- Provide for distributing community property; factors include:
  — non-monetary contributions to the marriage
  — value of property distributed to each spouse
  — length of marriage, and
  — any other economic circumstances including the need to award the family home to the custodial parent.
- Award alimony only if the supported spouse lacks property to provide for

reasonable needs, and is unable to support herself through employment or is a custodial parent unable to seek employment outside the home.

- Base child support on:
  - resources of the child and the custodial parent
  - standard of living the child enjoyed before the divorce
  - physical, emotional and educational needs of the child, and
  - resources and needs of the noncustodial parent.
- Base custody on:
  - parents' and child's preference
  - relationship of child with parents, siblings, and others affecting child, and
  - mental and physical health of all involved.

DOMESTIC VIOLENCE

TOPICS

**BATTERED WOMEN
PROTECTION FROM DOMESTIC VIOLENCE
REPORTING DOMESTIC VIOLENCE**

When a spouse or lover physically assaults his partner or a child, it is called domestic violence or abuse. When a child is the victim, it is called child abuse. Many states offer simplified civil court procedures through which the victim of domestic violence (or a parent, in the case of a child victim) may get a temporary restraining order (TRO) from the court, barring the abuser from entering the family home and prohibiting further acts of violence. In many localities, a TRO is registered with the local police so that immediate action may be taken if the abuser violates it and the victim phones the police for assistance. Violation of a TRO can result in criminal prosecution in most states. Many police officers, however, are reluctant to get involved in domestic violence situations; prosecutions are therefore infrequent.

In all states, domestic violence is also a crime. See California Civil Code 546, Illinois Annotated Statutes 750 ¶ 5/112A-14; 750 ¶ 60-214, New Jersey Statutes Annotated 2C:25-28, New York Family Court Act 828, Texas Family Code 71.15. Victims may make formal complaints to their police departments, regardless of whether they have obtained or registered TROs. Unfortunately, however, because of police reluctance and victim fear of retaliation by the abuser, arrests and prosecutions are often difficult to bring.

Civil Liability

A tort is an act that injures someone in some way, and for which the injured person may sue the wrongdoer for damages. Legally, torts are called civil wrongs, as opposed to criminal ones, although some acts, like battery, may be both torts and crimes. The wrongdoer may face both civil and criminal penalties.

Torts fall into two categories—negligent and intentional. Negligent torts are generally acts of carelessness. Intentional torts are deliberate acts which cause harm to others. Battery—domestic violence—is always an intentional tort.

Many states prohibit one family member from suing another for tortious acts, even battery. Other states allow intrafamilial tort suits only for intentional torts. States that still prohibit one family member from suing another except for intentional torts include Arizona, Delaware, Hawaii, Illinois, Iowa, Louisiana, Missouri, Ohio, Texas, Utah, Wyoming and Washington, DC. See, for example, *Bounds v. Candle*, 611 S.W.2d 685 (Texas 1980); *Townsend v. Townsend*, 708 S.W.2d 646 (Missouri, 1986) and *Green v. Green*, 446 N.E.2d 837 (Ohio 1982).

In Alabama, Georgia, Nevada, New York and Tennessee, a spouse is encouraged by the courts to combine a tort case for domestic violence with any pending divorce case; New Jersey requires it.

Criminal Liability

A crime is a wrongdoing classified by the state or Congress as a felony or misdemeanor.

Felony. A felony is a serious crime punishable by at least one year in prison. People convicted of felonies lose certain rights, such as the right to vote or hold public office. During the term of sentence, the convicted person may also be prohibited from making contracts, marrying, suing or keeping certain professional licenses. Upon release from prison, the convict may also be required to register with the police.

Misdemeanor. A misdemeanor is a crime for which the punishment is usually a fine and/or up to one year in a county jail. Often a crime which is a misdemeanor for the first offense becomes a felony for repeated offenses. All crimes that are not felonies are misdemeanors.

Battery is the crime of physically injuring someone intentionally. Assault is the crime of threatening to use unlawful force against another. Assault is a part of battery, thus the phrase "assault and battery." Battery is usually a misdemeanor, although it is a felony in some states.

BATTERED WOMEN

Women who are the victims of domestic violence are often called battered women.

Battered Women's Syndrome

Battered women's syndrome describes a cycle of violence and reconciliation that exists in a battering relationship. In the cycle, the abuser grows tense and angry in the first stage, explodes into violence in the second and then becomes tender and apologetic in the third stage. Both the abuser and the victim often convince themselves that the abuse will not happen again. Fear, guilt, lack of confidence, love, shame and ignorance of alternatives are common factors preventing the victim from leaving or stopping the relationship.

Battered women's syndrome exists in all races and economic classes, and may be exacerbated (but not usually caused) by drug or alcohol abuse. Counseling and removing the victim from the relationship can help to break the cycle. Battered women's shelters can provide a temporary respite, and often refer women to lawyers who will seek temporary restraining orders for police protection.

Battered Women's Shelters

Many areas have temporary homes called battered women's shelters where women (and their children) who are victims of domestic violence may stay until the crisis passes or until they are able to find a permanent place to relocate. The best way to find these shelters is to consult the local police, phone book, welfare department, neighborhood resource center or women's center. In California, the police must provide an apparent battering victim a list of referrals for emergency housing, legal services and counseling services.

Spousal Rape

Under traditional common law, still followed in many states, a husband cannot be criminally prosecuted for rape of his wife, although he can be prosecuted for assault and battery if he beats her. Some states, however, have changed their laws to define rape as any sexual act carried out without the consent of the other person, regardless of marital status. On the other hand, a few states have extended the spousal rape exemption (that is, no prosecution for the rape) to cohabiting partners.

PROTECTION FROM DOMESTIC VIOLENCE

When a spouse threatens to harm the other spouse, or to wrongfully take children or property, a court has the power to temporarily order the wrongdoer not to take any further action until the court has had more time to fully consider the situation. In some states, these laws also apply to a lover or even a roommate who threatens to harm his lover or roommate.

Temporary Restraining Order (TRO)

An order that tells a wrongdoer to stop acting is called a temporary restraining order (TRO). A TRO is usually issued after one party makes a request for an ex parte hearing (ex parte means that only the party asking for the TRO appears before the judge). Once the TRO is issued, the court holds a second hearing, where the other side can tell his story and the court can decide whether the TRO should be made permanent in the form of an injunction.

Although a piece of paper will often not stop an enraged spouse from acting violent, the police are more willing to intervene if the victim has a TRO.

Emergency Protective Order

A protective order is any order issued by a court which is meant to protect a person from harm or harassment. A temporary restraining order issued to prohibit domestic violence is referred to as a protective order. An emergency protective order is similar to a temporary restraining order, but is issued directly by the police when court is out of session. An emergency protective order usually lasts only for a brief period of time, such as a weekend or a holiday.

The trend in many states makes it relatively easy for the victim to obtain a TRO. In New York, California and some other states, for example, the court clerk will hand the victim a package of forms and will even assist the victim in filling them out. In other areas, non-lawyers may be available to help the victim complete the forms.

REPORTING DOMESTIC VIOLENCE

Police Report

After responding to a call of suspected criminal activity, police officers often make an official report of the incident. Because of police officers' reluctance to get involved in domestic violence cases, they often never make a police report and, as a result, there is no documentation of the incident. Documentation is crucial if the victim wants to press criminal charges or requests a restraining order from the court. Victims of domestic violence should insist that the officer responding to the call make an official report and get its prospective number or a receipt before the officer leaves the premises.

If you do press charges, keep in mind that only the district attorney decides whether or not to prosecute the abuser. But if you *don't* press charges, the chance is extremely low that the district attorney will prosecute.

Child Abuse

Physical, emotional or sexual mistreatment of a child is child abuse. Physical abuse generally consists of causing physical harm to a child, even if the injury is temporary. Thus, corporal punishment that causes bruising or burning, and deprivations of food, water or needed medical treatment are all examples of physical abuse. While some parents who rely on force to discipline their children may be unable to tell the difference between child abuse and proper parental treatment, most parents know where the line is, even if it can't be defined.

Emotional abuse includes speech and conduct calculated to deprive the child of dignity and self-esteem, such as humiliating the child in front of family or friends, isolating the child from other persons for long periods of time and habitually directing language or gestures at the child that are designed to punish rather than instruct.

Sexual mistreatment includes virtually all behavior toward the child that is designed to lead to sexual gratification of either the adult or the child. While the most common forms of sexual mistreatment are outright sexual acts such as fondling or sexual intercourse, sexual mistreatment may also consist of placing the child in compromising situations such as nudity, inappropriate clothing, and methods of discipline that are commonly associated with sexual gratification.

FAMILY RELATIONS

TOPICS

**SPOUSES
PARENTS
CHILDREN
SIBLINGS
OTHER TERMS TO DESCRIBE YOUR FAMILY
FAMILIES AND CRIMES**

SPOUSES

Spouses are people legally married to each other.

Putative Spouse

A person who reasonably but erroneously thinks he is married is called a putative (meaning reputed or supposed) spouse. If one spouse believes the marriage is valid while the other knows it is not, the innocent or putative spouse is entitled to the legal rights and privileges normally enjoyed by a regularly married spouse (for example, the right to alimony or property division upon divorce). The guilty spouse—the one who knew the marriage was not valid—may not have these same rights.

PARENTS

Legal Mother

The legal mother of a child is the woman recognized under the law as the female parent of the child. This is usually the woman who conceives and gives birth to the child. Technological advances, however, now permit one woman to conceive an embryo through in vitro fertilization and another to bring it to term. In such a case, the legal mother and the biological mother are the same, but the birth mother is different.

Some infertile couples may hire a surrogate mother to conceive and bear a child from the husband's sperm, intending that the wife, not the birth mother, be the legal mother.

Birth Mother

A birth mother is a woman who gives birth to a child but who may or may not raise the child. The term is usually used when a birth mother does not intend to keep the child, such as with surrogate mothers or adoptions. In adoptions and most surrogacy arrangements, the birth mother and the natural mother are the same person. But if an embryo conceived with another woman's egg is implanted into the surrogate mother's uterus, the birth mother is the one who gives birth and the natural mother is the one who conceives.

Surrogate Mother

A surrogate mother is a woman who is paid to bear a child for someone else. Most surrogate mothers are impregnated with the semen of a man. A few others have already-fertilized eggs of other women implanted in their wombs. In either case, upon the birth of the child, the surrogate mother relinquishes all rights in and responsibilities for the child and turns the child over to either the man (in the former case), or the man and/or the woman (in the latter situation).

Natural Mother

The term natural parent has different meanings in different contexts. With adoptions, it means the biological mother who conceived and gave birth to a child, as opposed to the adoptive parents who raise the child.

In the context of artificial insemination, surrogacy and in vitro fertilization, the natural mother is the one who provides the egg for conception, but not necessarily the one who carries the child to term or gives birth.

Legal Father

A legal father is the man recognized under law as the male parent of a child. Legal recognition is automatic if he was married to the child's mother when the child was born or has been declared the father in a paternity action. A male stepparent is not the legal father of his stepchildren unless he adopts them.

Single Father or Mother

A divorced, separated, widowed or unwed father or mother is often referred to as a single parent, or a single father or mother.

Presumed Father

If any of the following are true, a man is presumed to be the father of a child, unless he or the mother proves otherwise to a court:

- he was married to the mother when the child was conceived or born
- he attempted to marry the mother (even if the marriage was not valid) and the child was conceived or born during the "marriage"
- he married the mother after the birth and agreed either to have his name on the birth certificate or to support the child, or
- he welcomed the child into his home and openly held the child out as his own.

In some states, the presumption of paternity is considered conclusive, which means it cannot be disproven, even with contradictory blood tests. In *Michael H. v. Gerald D.*, 491 U.S. 110 (1989), the U.S. Supreme Court upheld California's presumed father statute as a rational method of protecting the integrity of the family against challenges based on the due process rights of the father and the child. Nevertheless, in some states, the putative father might be able to get visitation rights based on the best interests of the child, if he has an existing relationship with the child, and his involvement would not threaten the integrity of the marriage.

Putative Father

A putative father is the man named the father of a child born to unwed parents, but for whom paternity has not yet been established. Many states apply a conclusive presumption that the husband is the father of any child conceived by or born to his wife during marriage. This may prevent a putative father from proving that he is the father, even where blood tests show a 99.85% likelihood of his paternity.

Stepparent

A stepparent is a person married to a man or woman who has a child. In general, the stepparent and stepchild have no legal relationship. This means, in most states, that there is no right of inheritance between a stepparent and a stepchild (absent a will) and no obligation to support nor any rights of visitation if the legal parent and the stepparent divorce.

Co-Parent

An adult who is not legally responsible for the care, support and custody of a child, but who has assumed the care, support and custody of a child together with the child's legally responsible parent, is sometimes called a co-parent.

Stepparents who have not adopted their stepchildren are co-parents; however, the term is rarely used for stepparents. It is more commonly used by unmarried couples jointly raising a child for whom only one of them is legally responsible. Because same-sex couples cannot biologically parent a child, cannot marry (and become stepparents) and because few can jointly adopt (instead, one person usually adopts and together the couple raises the child), co-parenting has become an important concept in the lesbian and gay community.

Equitable Parent

In Michigan (*Atkinson v. Atkinson*, 408 N.W.2d 516 (1987)) and Wisconsin (*In re Paternity of D.L.H.*, 419 N.W.2d 283 (1987)), a spouse who is not a legal parent may be granted custody or visitation under the notion of equitable parent. Courts apply it when a spouse and child have a close relationship and consider themselves parent and child, or where the biological parent encouraged this relationship. If the court grants an equitable parent custody or visitation, then the parent will also be required to pay child support.

Equitable parenthood arose to protect husbands who discover, in the course of a divorce, that they are not the biological fathers. It could also protect a stepparent who is divorcing a biological parent when the other biological parent is either deceased or absent. The theory of equitable parent has not been extended to cohabitants and foster parents.

Foster Parent

Adults who take children into their homes when those children have been removed from their legal parents' home by a court are called foster parents. Foster parents usually become the guardians of the children placed in their homes. If the legal parents are unable to make the necessary changes to have the children return to them, their parental rights may be terminated and the children made available for adoption. When this occurs, foster parents usually have priority in adopting. In fact, many states have Fost-Adopt programs, where the foster placement is intended to lead to the adoption of the children by the foster parents.

Foster parents are often entitled to receive payments from the state welfare department to assist them in supporting the children. Foster parents who parent disabled children may receive even higher payments. The payments usually terminate, however, if the foster parents adopt the children.

CHILDREN

Issue

Issue is the legal term used to denote a person's children, grandchildren and great-grandchildren down the line, especially in laws governing wills and inheritance.

PRIMOGENITURE LAWS

Primogeniture laws gave first born sons the exclusive right to inherit their father's property (their mothers did not own property). These laws no longer exist in the U.S.

Generation

Generation is a single step in line of descent from or to an ancestor.

Illegitimate Children

Children born to parents not legally married to each other are sometimes termed illegitimate unless and until the parents marry. This term is used infrequently today, and has little legal effect except where the law expressly gives rights only to legitimate children. For instance, illegitimate children are denied the right to inherit from their fathers in some states. Also, some states do not allow unwed fathers to sue for the wrongful deaths of their children, although married fathers and all mothers—married and unmarried—can.

In most states, once paternity of the child is established by acknowledgment of the father or by court order, there is no difference in the legal treatment between children born in and children born out of wedlock.

After-Born Child

An after-born child is one born after his parent signs a will. Even if the will is not changed to mention or provide for the child before the parent dies, the laws of most states allow the child to inherit a portion of the parent's property. The law assumes the parent would have wanted the child to inherit. If, however, the evidence shows that the parent did intend that the child receive nothing, the after-born child will probably get nothing. The legal term for any child omitted from a parent's will (either after-born or living at the time the will was executed) is pretermitted heir.

Stepchildren

A stepchild is the child of a person married to a man or woman who is not the child's other parent. In general, the stepparent and stepchild have no legal relationship. This means, in most states, that there is no right of inheritance between a stepparent and a stepchild (absent a will). In addition, the stepparent generally has no obligation to support the child and no right to seek custody of or visitation with the child if the stepparent and the legal parent divorce.

SIBLINGS

Siblings is the term used to refer to brothers and sisters—that is, people who, through biology or adoption, have the same parent or parents. For legal purposes (such as inheriting property which a deceased person did not dispose of through a will), siblings generally include half-brothers and half-sisters (people who have only one parent in common), but do not include stepbrothers and stepsisters (people who are not related biologically or through adoption, but whose parents are married to each other).

OTHER TERMS TO DESCRIBE YOUR FAMILY

The word family may be used to define immediate relatives (parents and children), people related by blood, marriage or adoption, or any extended group of people living together.

Extended Family

An extended family is one which includes persons in addition to or other than parents and children. Some extended families include grandparents, stepparents and stepchildren, nieces and nephews, etc.

Extended family can also mean a circle of people in a close relationship. For example, for many lesbians, gay men and other non-married people, the term extended family refers to a small, close group of friends who provide support for one another in much the same way a traditional family supports its members.

Intact Family

A family that has not gone through a divorce or separation is sometimes called an intact family.

Kin or Next of Kin

Kin refers to persons related by blood. Kin can be close, as in brother and sister, or distant, as in third cousin twice removed. When used to determine the right of inheritance in the absence of a will, the term is commonly limited to specifically designated relationships.

See Table 8.1 in the Appendix.

Consanguinity

Consanguinity describes any blood relationship, such as between parent and child, brother and sister, grandparent and grandchild, and uncle and nephew.

Affinity

Affinity is the term used to describe any relationship created by marriage. A husband, for example, is related to his wife's sister by affinity. Direct affinity is the relationship of a spouse to his mate's blood relatives, such as the example of the husband and his wife's sister. Secondary affinity describes the relationship of a spouse to his mate's marital relatives, such as a husband and his wife's sister's husband. Collateral affinity is the relationship between a spouse's relatives and his mate's relatives, such as a husband's brother and a wife's sister.

FAMILY RELATIONS

Head of Family

The head of the family is the person who supports and maintains one or more people who are related by blood, marriage or adoption. In some states, the head of the family has the legal right to choose and establish where the family resides.

Head of Household

Head of household is the federal income tax status of a single person who contributes more than one half toward the support of a non-spouse relative. The relative must be a parent (including a stepparent and grandparent), child (including a stepchild and grandchild) or sibling (including half-sibling). The head of household tax rate is higher than that for married persons filing jointly, but lower than that for single persons.

Head of household tax status is important for single parents, and divorcing parents often argue over which one is entitled to the head of household filing status. Because the one who claims head of household must contribute more than half of the support, both parents cannot claim it.

FAMILIES AND CRIMES

Incest

Sexual relations (or marriage) between close relatives is called incest and is a crime. Incest between an older relative and a minor is also punishable as child abuse under the laws of all states. See Table 8.2 in the Appendix.

Domestic Violence

When a spouse or lover physically assaults his partner or a child, it is called domestic violence or abuse. Many states offer simplified civil court procedures through which the victim of domestic violence (or a parent, in the case of a child victim) may get a temporary restraining order (TRO) from the court barring the abuser from entering the family home and prohibiting further acts of violence. Violation of a TRO can result in criminal prosecution in most states. (See also the *Domestic Violence* chapter.)

Spousal Rape

Under traditional common law, still followed in many states, a husband cannot be criminally prosecuted for rape of his wife, although he can be prosecuted for assault and battery if he beats her. Some states, however, have changed their laws to define rape as any sexual act carried out without the consent of the other person, regardless of marital status. On the other side, a few states have extended the spousal rape exemption (that is, no prosecution for the rape) to cohabiting partners.

Child Abuse

Physical, emotional or sexual mistreatment of a child is child abuse. In some situations, an abused child is removed from the home by a court and placed in the care of the state. Many are placed in foster homes. In addition, the abuser may be criminally prosecuted.

MARRIAGE

TOPICS

GETTING MARRIED
EFFECTS OF MARRIAGE
AGREEMENTS AFFECTING MARRIAGE
LAWSUITS AFFECTING MARRIAGE
MARITAL CRIMES
FAMILY BUSINESSES

Marriage is the legal union of two people. Once they become married to each other, their responsibilities and rights toward one another concerning property and support are defined by the laws of the state in which they live. A couple may be able to modify the rules set up by their state. A marriage can only be terminated by a court granting a divorce or an annulment.

Marriage entails many legal rights and benefits, including the right to:

- file joint income tax returns with the IRS and state taxing authorities
- claim family partnership tax income
- create a marital life estate trust
- receive marital and dependency Social Security, disability, unemployment, veterans', pension and public assistance benefits
- receive a share of the deceased spouse's estate under intestate succession laws
- claim an estate tax marital deduction
- sue for wrongful death, loss of consortium, alienation of affection and criminal conversation
- receive family rates for insurance
- avoid the deportation of a non-citizen spouse
- enter hospital intensive care units, jails and other places where visitors are restricted to immediate family
- live in neighborhoods zoned "families only"
- make medical decisions about one's spouse in the event of disability, and
- claim the marital communication privilege.

There are several types of marriages.

Common Law Marriage

In Alabama, Colorado, Georgia, Idaho, Iowa, Kansas, Montana, Oklahoma, Pennsylvania, Rhode Island, South Carolina, Texas, Utah and Washington, D.C., couples can become legally married by living together for a long period of time and either holding themselves out to others as husband and wife or intending to be married. These are called common law marriages. Contrary to popular belief, however, even if two people cohabit for a certain number of years, if they don't intend to be married or don't hold themselves out as married, there is no common law marriage—even in those states which recognize such marriages.

When a common law marriage does exist, the spouses receive the same legal treatment given to other married couples, including the requirement that they go through a formal divorce to end the marriage.

New Hampshire and Oregon recognize common law marriages only when one partner dies without a will or other estate plan.

Confidential Marriage

In California, couples may undergo a marriage in which only the two parties and the official performing the marriage are present. This is called a confidential marriage. Confidential marriages are not witnessed, nor are they entered into public county records. (They are entered into "non-public" records.) Although they are rarely performed, they are legally binding. In order to obtain a confidential marriage, the parties must:
- each be at least 18
- be a man and a woman (that is, no same-sex marriages), and
- have lived together "for a long period of time."

Second (or Third, Etc.) Marriage

Remarriage is a subsequent marriage by a divorced person. In many states, a divorced person must wait a certain length of time (20 days to 18 months, depending on the state) after her divorce becomes final before marrying again.

Proxy Marriage

A proxy marriage is a marriage where someone is permitted to stand in for and represent an absent bride or groom at a wedding. Proxy marriages are usually resorted to only in extreme circumstances—for example, when one person is detained for an indefinite period in prison or in a foreign country.

Proxy marriages were not uncommon during World War II and the Korean War. States allowed women who discovered they were pregnant after their fiancés had been sent overseas to have a friend or relative stand in for the groom. Today, only a few states allow proxy marriages.

Shot-Gun Marriage

A marriage which results from an unmarried couple getting pregnant is sometimes referred to as a shot-gun marriage.

Out-of-State Marriage

When a couple hoping to divorce was married in a state or country different from where they are seeking their divorce, the marriage is referred to as an out-of-state marriage.

Mixed-Race Marriage

Miscegenation means the mixing of races. Miscegenation statutes prohibited people of one race from marrying people of other races. Typical was a statute that prohibited a white person from marrying a black person or Asian, but not prohibiting a black person from marrying an Asian. Miscegenation statutes were declared unconstitutional in 1967 by the U.S. Supreme Court in *Loving v. Virginia*, 388 U.S. 1, and are not enforced in any state.

Marriage of Convenience

A marriage of convenience is one where the couple is legally married, but only for appearances, rather than because of a romantic or sexual relationship. A marriage of convenience often occurs where one or both partners wants to appear married for professional or social reasons, such as a gay man or lesbian who has succeeded in a very traditional profession and for whom the only obstacle to full acceptance is the failure to conform socially.

A marriage of convenience is a perfectly legal marriage.

Voidable Marriage

A voidable marriage is one that is invalid at the outset, but can be made valid by some act of the couple. Parties to a voidable marriage must obtain an annulment or a divorce in order to have it declared invalid.

Example: In some states, a marriage by a person under the age of consent is voidable—that is, if she or her parents object before she reaches the age of consent, the marriage may be legally terminated. If, however, neither she nor her parents object before she reaches the age of consent, her marriage becomes valid.

Putative Marriage

When two people reasonably and honestly think that they are married, but for some technical reason are not (for example, the person who married them was not authorized to do so), the couple is said to have a putative (meaning reputed or supposed) marriage. In virtually all situations, the law treats putative marriages the same as any valid marriage. A putative marriage need not be formalized, though the couple may do so by repeating the marriage ceremony.

To terminate a putative marriage, the couple must get a divorce, where the court will determine alimony, child support, custody, visitation and the division of property as if the couple had been actually married.

QUASI-MARITAL PROPERTY

Quasi means like. Quasi-marital property is the term used to describe any assets, property or debts accumulated during a putative marriage. In most states, quasi-marital property is treated the same as marital property for purposes of property division upon divorce or separation, and for property distribution upon the death without a will of one of the spouses.

Void Marriage

A void marriage is one that is invalid at the outset and cannot be made valid. The parties to a void marriage may go their separate ways without obtaining a divorce or an annulment. In virtually all states, incestuous marriages (for example, between a brother and a sister) are void marriages.

Fraudulent Marriage

If a person marries relying on a false statement made by her spouse before the marriage, the marriage is considered fraudulent, and the defrauded spouse may obtain an annulment or divorce. The false statement must concern something of fundamental importance, such as the ability to have sex, the ability or desire to have children, or religious beliefs or practices. For example, if Ben represented himself to be Roman Catholic, but then confessed to being Shaker and having taken vows of celibacy, his wife could probably get an annulment.

Sham Marriage

When a U.S. citizen (or permanent resident) marries a citizen of another country solely to make the foreign citizen a permanent resident of the U.S., the marriage is called a sham marriage. (It is also called a green-card marriage because the U.S. Immigration and Naturalization Service (INS) used to issue green cards—they are now pink—to permanent residents.)

These marriages are illegal because they are meant to defraud the INS. If the INS becomes aware of a sham marriage and takes action, either spouse may be fined up to $250,000, imprisoned for up to five years or both. In addition, the foreign citizen can be deported and is forever barred from obtaining permanent residency. If the couple lives together, appears to the outside world to be married, and remains married for the period of time necessary for the foreign citizen to become a permanent resident, fraud will be difficult to prove and the couple usually can avoid INS involvement.

GETTING MARRIED

Blood Test

All states but Maryland, Minnesota, Nevada, South Carolina and Washington require a couple planning to marry to take blood tests to find out whether either is afflicted with venereal disease or with rubella (measles). These tests may also disclose the presence of genetic disorders such as sickle-cell anemia or Tay-Sachs disease. In addition, Illinois and Louisiana briefly required pre-marital testing for the AIDS virus. These states repealed those laws because few couples tested positive and many went to other states to marry to avoid taking the test. Instead, like California, Hawaii and Indiana, Illinois and Louisiana now simply provide AIDS information to marrying couples. Couples who marry under California's confidential marriage statute do not have to have blood tests.

Marriage License

A marriage license is a piece of paper issued by local officials authorizing a couple to get married in a wedding and obtain a marriage certificate. The normal procedure for getting married is to obtain a marriage license, have the ceremony, and then file a marriage certificate with the county recorder within a few days after the ceremony.

Marriage Certificate

In order for people to be legally married, most states require that a couple undergo a wedding and then file a marriage certificate with the proper authorities, usually the county clerk. (Usually, whoever performs the wedding may file the marriage certificate for the couple.) The filing usually must be done within a few days (often five) after the ceremony.

Wedding

Most states require a ceremony of some type for persons to be legally married. This ceremony, called a wedding, must be performed by a clergy member (priest, minister or rabbi) or other person (justice of the peace, judge or court clerk) given authority by law to perform weddings. Usually, no special words are required as long as the bride and groom acknowledge their intention to marry each other; in fact, many people write their own ceremonies. Although it is customary to have witnesses, they are required only in some states.

REQUIREMENTS TO MARRY

Most states have certain requirements in order for people to marry. These include:
- being at least the age of consent (usually 18)
- being not too closely related (see Table 8.2 in the Appendix)
- having the mental capacity—that is, understand what she is doing and what consequences her actions may have
- being sober at the time of the marriage, and
- not being married to anyone else

Dower and Curtesy

Under the traditional common law, dower was the portion of a husband's property (almost always real property) which he brought into the marriage or acquired during the marriage to which his wife was automatically entitled if he died leaving children. Dower laws barred a husband from selling, giving away or disposing of in his will the portion his wife was entitled to, unless she consented. Some dower laws provided the wife and children use of the husband's property until the wife died, and then passed the property as laid out in the husband's will or under the state's intestate succession laws if he died without a will. Other dower laws provided the wife with one-third of the husband's property on his death, even if his will left her less.

Curtesy was the portion of a wife's property that the husband was entitled to when the wife died. Commonly, a husband received 100% of his wife's property if she died leaving children, who could later inherit the property from their father. If the woman died without children, her property returned to her parents, siblings or other relatives. Some states, however, did not require the woman to leave children in order for her husband to receive her property.

Dower and curtesy laws don't exist in community property states. All common law states, however, still retain some version of dower and curtesy (although many have dropped the old terminology). No such legal protections are needed in community property states because each spouse owns one-half of all property acquired from the earnings of the other during the marriage.

In most common law property states, a spouse is entitled to one-third of the property left by the other. In a few, it's one-half. The exact amount of the spouse's minimum share often depends on whether the couple has minor children. In some states, the surviving spouse must be left only a certain percentage of the estate transferred by will. In other states, property transferred by means other than a will, such as a living trust, is included when calculating whether a spouse has received his or her minimum legal share of property.

What happens if a person leaves nothing to a spouse or leaves less than the spouse is entitled to under state law? In most states, the surviving spouse has a choice of either taking what the will or other transfer document provides or rejecting the gift and instead taking the minimum share allowed by state law. Taking the share permitted by law is called taking against the will.

Example: Leonard's will gives $50,000 to his second wife, June, and leaves the rest of his property, totaling $400,000, to his two children from his first marriage. June can take the $50,000 or elect to take against the will and receive her statutory share of Leonard's estate. Depending on the state, this will normally be from one-third to one-half of Leonard's total estate.

When a spouse decides to take against the will, the property which is taken must come out of one or more of the gifts given to others by the will (or in many states, other transfer documents, such as a living trust, as well). In other words, somebody else is going to get less. In the above example, the children will receive much less than Leonard intended. So, if you don't provide your spouse with at least the statutory share under your state's laws, your gifts to others may be seriously reduced.

EFFECTS OF MARRIAGE

Marital Status

Marriage changes your marital status from single, divorced, separated or widowed to married.

Former Name

A woman's surname given to her at birth is her maiden name. She may have another former name from a previous marriage or other name change. A woman's surname is not automatically changed by marriage; the change becomes effective only if the woman starts using her husband's surname. A man who wishes to legally change his name at marriage must often obtain a court order authorizing the change.

HOW THEY DESCRIBED MARRIAGE IN THE "OLD" DAYS

Spousals. Spousals is an old English term meaning the mutual promises of a man and a woman to marry.

Conjugal. Conjugal means relating to marriage. Conjugal rights are a husband and wife's rights to mutual love, affection, comfort, companionship and sex.

Nuptials. Nuptials is a Latin word meaning marriage or wedding. Nuptial means relating to marriage.

Et ux. Et ux is Latin for "and wife." It was used in referring to married men when married women had few legal rights. The phrase is rarely used today.

AGREEMENTS AFFECTING MARRIAGE

Agreement Before Marriage

Before a couple marries, they may make an agreement concerning certain aspects of their relationship, including how they will characterize their property during marriage, whether alimony will be paid in the event they later divorce and other issues. A spouse, however, cannot agree to give up child support in the event of divorce. These agreements are called ante-nuptial, pre-nuptial or pre-marital agreements. They are usually upheld by courts unless one person shows that the agreement is likely to promote divorce (for example, by including a large alimony amount in the event of divorce), was written and signed with the intention of divorcing or was unfairly entered into (for example, a spouse giving up all of his rights in his spouse's future earnings without the advice of an attorney). Eleven states limit these agreements to issues of property ownership only, and refuse to enforce any provisions which force or encourage one spouse to give up alimony.

Agreement During Marriage

Contracts made between a husband and wife during their marriage are interchangeably called post-nuptial, marital and post-marital agreements. Usually these agreements involve how property ownership is to be handled during the marriage and upon divorce, but occasionally they also cover matters such as chore division or child responsibility. A spouse, however, cannot agree to give up child support in the event of divorce. In most states, it is legal for a couple to transfer property from one to the other, from one to both or from both to one, or to agree that earnings will be solely or jointly owned, even though the state's law would treat the earnings or property differently in the agreement's absence. Courts usually enforce legally executed property agreements which are fair to both spouses, but will not enforce agreements where a spouse has been deceived. In addition, courts do not want to get involved with personal matters (such as the division of chores), and it is wise to keep personal agreements separate from property agreements.

LAWSUITS AFFECTING MARRIAGE

Heart-Balm Lawsuits

Heart-balm lawsuits were those brought to soothe broken hearts and include the following:

Breach of promise to marry. Under traditional common law, a broken engagement could be treated as a breach of promise to marry which would support a lawsuit for money damages against the person who broke the engagement. Today, most states have done away with this type of lawsuit. It may be possible, however, for the giver of an engagement ring or other gift made in contemplation of marriage to get the gift back if the other person broke off the engagement and the couple understood that the ring or other gift was a precursor to marriage.

Alienation of affection. When a person intentionally came between a husband and wife, he was technically guilty of alienation of affection. At one time, courts in all states but Louisiana allowed the injured spouse to sue the interloper for the harm done to the marriage. Most states have eliminated alienation of affection lawsuits. They still exist in a few states, however, including Hawaii, Kansas, Rhode Island and Tennessee.

Seduction. A seduction lawsuit is brought by a father against a man who has induced the father's unmarried daughter into having sexual intercourse by means of promises or bribes (but not force), regardless of whether the woman is a minor or an adult. Seduction suits are based on the notion that once an unmarried woman has had sexual intercourse, it is more difficult for her father to "marry her off." Seduction suits have been done away with in most states.

Criminal conversation. Criminal conversation is grounds for a lawsuit brought by a husband for damages against a man who seduced the husband's wife. This action is no longer available in most states.

Loss of Consortium

Consortium is the relationship between a husband and wife, which includes love, affection, fellowship and sexual companionship. If a third party interferes with that relationship (for example, a neck injury disables the husband from having sexual intercourse), the spouse who loses elements of consortium can sue the third party on that grounds.

Wrongful Death Action

A wrongful death action is a lawsuit brought by a survivor (someone who outlives another) of a deceased person. In such a lawsuit, the survivor claims that the deceased was killed due to the wrongful act of a third person (the defendant). Only a person who had a certain relationship with the deceased person (a parent, child or spouse, usually) may sue for wrongful death.

MARITAL CRIMES

Bigamy

A person who knows he is already legally married and marries another person is guilty of the crime of bigamy in every state. Prosecution for this crime may occur when the already married person enters into the second marriage and harms his new spouse (for example, by spending money earned by his second wife on his first wife). There is no crime if one person makes a legitimate mistake (such as remarrying when one mistakenly believes that his divorce has been finalized).

Polygamy

Polygamy is intentionally having more than two spouses at a time. Polygamy is a crime in every state. Bigamists and polygamists are usually prosecuted only when they have defrauded their spouses and when prosecutors find out about the multiple marriages, which they frequently don't.

Prohibited Marriage

A prohibited marriage is a marriage that is a crime because our culture considers it harmful to society. Prohibited marriages include incestuous marriages and bigamous marriages. These marriages are void (not valid) and legally do not exist. No divorce is required to end them.

Uniform Desertion and Non-Support Act

This uniform statute has been adopted in a few states. It requires all husbands to support their wives and their children under the age of 16, and makes failure to provide such support a crime.

FAMILY BUSINESSES

Federal Partnership Income Tax

Under federal tax law (26 U.S.C. § 704), a married couple may create a family partnership to divide business income among family members, assuming the family members qualify as partners in the business. Dividing income this way will frequently lower the total tax on the income more than if all the income were received by one person.

MINORS AND PARENTS

TOPICS

MINORS
MINORS IN TROUBLE
PARENTS AND GUARDIANS
PARENTS IN TROUBLE
**INSTITUTIONS THAT DEAL WITH MINORS OR
PARENTS IN TROUBLE**

MINORS

A minor is a person under the age of majority. The age of majority is the age at which a minor, in the eyes of the law, becomes an adult. This age is 18 in most states. In a few other states, the age of majority is 19 or 21. (See Table 11.1 in the Appendix.) A minor is considered to be a resident of the same state as her custodial parent or guardian.

Once a person reaches the age of majority, she may vote, sign a will, enter into a binding contract, buy property, and generally act without parental consent. An unwed mother who is under the age of majority, however, may be required to notify, or obtain the consent of, her parents or a court before having an abortion. In addition, a person must be 21 before he or she can buy alcoholic beverages. A state may not have one age of majority for men and a different one for women.

Dependent Child

A dependent child is one who still depends on his parents for financial support, a child who can be claimed by an adult on an income tax return because he receives at least one-half of his support from that adult or a child who is eligible to receive Aid to Families with Dependent Children (AFDC).

Changing a Child's Name

When a custodial parent seeks to change either a child's given name (first name) or surname (last name), the change is permitted in most states as long as the court determines it to be in the best interest of the child. A child's name cannot legally be changed without a court order, however. In some states, courts refuse to grant a name change if one parent objects.

Age of Consent to Marry

Every state sets an age under which people must obtain the consent of a parent or guardian in order to marry. The age at which no parental consent is needed is called the age of consent and is 18 in most states (a few states allow younger persons to marry without a parent's consent). Some states require professional counseling and the approval of a judge instead of parental consent if a person under 18 wants to get married.

AGE OF CONSENT TO HAVE SEX

In all states, sexual intercourse with a woman (except by a husband with his wife) under the age of consent is irrebuttably presumed to be the rape of that woman. Her consent is irrelevant; she is presumed to be unable to consent to sexual intercourse until she reaches the age of consent. For this purpose, the age of consent varies among the states and is usually 14 to 18. Depending on the state, the age of the man may determine the severity of the punishment. If he, too, is very young, a court may view the situation as an experiment, rather than rape; young men, however, may very well be prosecuted for rape.

In addition to statutory rape laws, most states have unlawful sex statutes that prohibit adults from engaging in sexual intercourse with minors, even if they are over the age of consent. Unlawful sex statutes are usually misdemeanors (punishable by a fine, or a jail sentence not to exceed one year), whereas statutory rape is a felony (punishable by a sentence of a year or longer in jail).

Emancipated Minor

A minor demonstrating freedom from parental control or support is considered emancipated, or may be declared emancipated by a court. An emancipated minor is considered an adult for purposes such as entering into contracts (for employment or buying a car, for instance) and signing a will. Emancipated minors are treated like adults and establish their residency by where they live and intend to remain. An unwed mother or father who is a minor, moves out of her or his parents' home and raises the child, is usually considered emancipated.

A minor who goes on active military duty is considered emancipated without a court order. A minor who gets a job and moves out of the family home is usually considered emancipated, but some states require a court order of emancipation before a parent's duty to support ends. In most states, minors who wish to get married before reaching the age of consent to marry need to obtain a court order of emancipation or, in some states, their parent's consent.

Child support obligations to the parents of emancipated minors may be canceled by the court. For obvious reasons, most states do not allow parents to unilaterally declare their children emancipated; rather, a special proceeding must be brought to have the child declared emancipated by a court.

MINORS IN TROUBLE

Incorrigible Children

Children who refuse to obey their parents are classified by the juvenile laws of many states as incorrigible. The same label applies to children who engage in behavior which is noncriminal, but prohibited for persons of their age (for example, running away from home, chronic truancy or endangering their own or another's health or morals).

Incorrigible children are often referred to as status offenders because they would not be in court but for their status as minors. Incorrigible children may be brought into the court system by police, welfare or school officials or by parents seeking help.

Delinquent Children

When a person under the age of majority engages in an act which would be a crime if committed by an adult, she is said to have committed a delinquent act and is referred to as a juvenile delinquent, delinquent or delinquent child.

PARENTS AND GUARDIANS

Parental Control

Parental control is the right and responsibility a parent has to rear and nurture her child. If parental control is not being exercised, the child may be considered the victim of child neglect; if a parent is unable to control her child, the child may be considered incorrigible. If a minor becomes emancipated, he is no longer legally under parental control.

Guardian

A guardian is an adult given the legal right to control and care for a minor child or a disabled adult, called the ward. A guardian may be awarded custody of a minor. Courts order guardianships over children when their parents are unavailable to care for them and another adult has assumed that responsibility. Guardianships are necessary so that schools, hospitals and other authority figures have an adult to turn to in the event a decision needs to be made about the child. Guardians are accountable to courts for the well being and financial best interests of their wards.

> ### NEXT FRIEND
>
> When a child or an adult unable to legally care for himself wants to bring an action in court, a competent adult (often a parent, child or spouse) must usually bring the case for him as his next friend, as in "John Doe, a minor, through his next friend, Sally Doe, his mother."

GUARDIAN AD LITEM

If a party in a lawsuit is a minor or an adult unable to legally care for herself, the court must appoint a person to protect and manage the person's interests in any legal proceedings that directly affect her. That person is called a guardian ad litem and is often, although not always, a parent or close relative, or an attorney. Twenty-five states also authorize the appointment of a guardian ad litem to represent the child's interests, without the child actually becoming a party to the case, when custody is an issue.

If a guardian ad litem is not an attorney, the minor or disabled adult is frequently represented by an attorney as well. Both the guardian ad litem and the attorney are to act in and articulate the best interests of the minor or disabled adult. When the attorney and the guardian ad litem differ, the attorney often disregards the guardian ad litem's advice.

Parental Liability

Parental liability is the term used to refer to a parent's obligation to pay for damage done by negligent, intentional or criminal acts of his child. In 47 states, parents are responsible for all malicious or willful property damage done by their children; in 30 states, parents are liable for all malicious or willful personal injuries inflicted by their children. Eight states obligate parents only when their children have acted illegally. Hawaii, Louisiana and Oregon hold parents responsible for all torts committed by their children. Only Washington, D.C. does not hold parents liable at all. All parental liability laws limit the amount of liability to between $300 and $15,000, depending on the state. See Table 11.2 in the Appendix.

Parental liability usually ends when the child reaches the age of majority and does not begin until the child reaches somewhere between eight and ten. (No one is liable for damage done by a child younger than eight or so unless the parent was grossly negligent—for example, giving the child a loaded gun.)

Family Car Doctrine

The family car doctrine holds the owner of a family car legally responsible for any damage caused by a family member when driving if the owner knew of and consented to the family member's use of the car. This doctrine is followed by the courts of approximately 20 states.

PARENTS IN TROUBLE

Unfit Parent

If a parent's lifestyle is found to be detrimental to a child, a court may declare that parent unfit to have any contact—including supervised visitation—with her child. What constitutes unfitness depends on many issues, including the social, psychological and sexual behavior of the parent. Unfitness is an extreme determination. It often leads to a termination of parental rights, and usually involves abuse or severe neglect.

Abandoned Child

When a parent fails to provide any financial assistance to, and/or communicate with, his child over a period of time, a court may deem the child legally abandoned by that parent. Two important consequences of a court finding of abandonment are that the parent's rights are terminated and the child may be adopted through court proceedings without the parent's permission. This determination is made at a court hearing. Abandonment actions are often initiated by stepparents or foster parents who want to adopt but cannot get permission from one or both of the legal parents.

Abandonment also describes situations where a child is physically abandoned—left on a doorstep, delivered to a hospital or placed in a trash can, for example. These children are usually placed in orphanages or foster homes and made available for adoption. Parents who abandon their children in this way may be criminally prosecuted.

Neglected Child

When a parent or guardian fails to provide a child with adequate necessaries, education, supervision or general guidance, the adult may be guilty of child neglect. If child neglect is suspected, the local welfare department will conduct an investigation. In severe cases, the child will be removed from the home after a court hearing and placed in a foster home. If the parents do not improve their situation within a reasonable time (usually between six months and two years, depending on the state), the child may be taken away permanently and placed for adoption. In especially severe cases, the parents or guardian may be criminally prosecuted.

In some situations, parents may be unable to properly care for their children by themselves, but may have the ability to perform their responsibilities with appropriate outside help. In these instances, courts often allow the children to stay with the parents as long as the parents accept help, usually from a social service agency.

Child Abuse

Physical, emotional or sexual mistreatment of a child is child abuse. Physical abuse generally consists of causing physical harm to a child, even if the injury is temporary. Thus, corporal punishment that causes bruising or burning, and deprivation of food, water or needed medical treatment are all examples of physical abuse. While some parents who rely on force to discipline their children may be unable to tell the difference between child abuse and proper parental treatment, most parents know where the line is, even if it can't be defined.

Emotional abuse includes speech and conduct calculated to deprive the child of dignity and self-esteem, such as humiliating the child in front of family or friends, isolating the child from other persons for long periods of time and habitually directing language or gestures at the child that are designed to punish rather than instruct.

Sexual mistreatment includes virtually all behavior towards the child that is designed to lead to sexual gratification of either the adult or the child. While the most common forms of sexual mistreatment are outright sexual acts such as fondling or sexual intercourse, sexual mistreatment may also consist of placing the child in compromising situations such as nudity, inappropriate clothing, and methods of discipline that are commonly associated with sexual gratification.

In some situations, an abused child is removed from the home by a court and placed in the care of the state. Many are placed in foster homes. In addition, the abuser may be criminally prosecuted.

MINORS AND PARENTS

Dependent Child

A dependent child is also one found by a court to have been neglected or abused by his parents or guardians. He is placed under the protection of the court or appropriate social welfare agency. He may be placed in a foster home and eventually released for adoption.

Termination of Parental Rights

Parental rights are rights to exercise parental control and custody of a child. When a child is placed up for adoption, the birth parents' rights are terminated. (If a child is adopted by her stepparent, only the noncustodial parent's rights are terminated.)

If a court finds a parent unfit, or places a child in a foster home, parental rights may be temporarily suspended while the parent tries to rehabilitate herself. If the rehabilitation succeeds, parental rights may be restored.

INSTITUTIONS THAT DEAL WITH MINORS OR PARENTS IN TROUBLE

Juvenile Court

Most states have established a special juvenile court to consider cases involving minor children who:
- are neglected, abandoned or abused by their parents
- are considered incorrigible (also called status offenders), or
- commit crimes.

The original purpose of these courts was to provide a judicial procedure for troubled children that would be less harsh than the regular criminal court process. To this end, judges are given broad discretion in an effort to counsel and rehabilitate minors. In addition, many juvenile court systems have introduced new vocabulary: crimes are called delinquent acts; the court adjudges a minor to be a ward of the court, rather than find him guilty; and the court disposes of a case rather than pronounces sentence. Despite these new terms, many observers have noted that the system works more or less the same as the regular criminal system, with similar results. On occasion, juveniles are sent to reform institutions for acts that would not constitute crimes if they were adults.

Probation Department Investigation

When a child is suspected of being abused, neglected or incorrigible, the court handling the matter will normally want the family environment investigated. The investigation usually consists of one or more visits to the home by a social worker, who physically views the surroundings and talks to whomever is present. Most visits are scheduled; often, however, the social worker makes at least one unannounced visit. Depending on the state and kind of case, the investigation will be conducted by the juvenile probation department, the adult probation department or the welfare department.

Foster Home

When a child is temporarily placed by a court or welfare department in a home other than her parents', it is termed a foster home.

FOSTER PARENT

Adults who take children into their homes when those children have been removed from their biological parents' home by a court are called foster parents. Foster parents usually become the guardians of the children placed in their homes. If the biological parents are unable to make the necessary changes to have the children return to them, their parental rights may be terminated and the children made available for adoption. When this occurs, foster parents usually have priority in adopting. In fact, many states have Fost-Adopt programs, where the foster placement is intended to lead to the adoption of the children by the foster parents.

Foster parents are often entitled to receive payments from the state welfare department to assist them in supporting the children. Foster parents who parent disabled children may receive even higher payments. The payments usually terminate, however, if the foster parents adopt the children.

Group Home

When delinquent children or incorrigible children are taken away from their parents by juvenile courts, they are supposed to be placed in the least restrictive environment. In most states, private individuals have obtained licenses to operate special group homes in which juvenile courts place children who don't need to be confined to state or county institutions or reform schools. These group homes function much like regular homes, except that the operators specialize in providing supervision to troubled children.

Orphanage

An orphanage is a group home maintained for the care, custody and control of children who have no parents or guardians.

PROPERTY AND DEBTS

TOPICS

PROPERTY DEFINED
PROPERTY OWNED DURING MARRIAGE
STATE MARITAL PROPERTY SCHEMES
DUTIES OF CO-OWNERS TOWARD EACH OTHER
PROPERTY DIVISION AT DIVORCE—GENERAL CONCEPTS
FIGURING OUT HOW MUCH THE PROPERTY IS WORTH
OTHER FACTORS TO CONSIDER WHEN DIVIDING PROPERTY
SPECIAL CONCEPTS WHEN DIVIDING REAL PROPERTY
SPECIAL CONCEPTS WHEN DIVIDING RETIREMENT PLANS
AND SURVIVORS' BENEFITS
SPECIAL CONCEPTS WHEN DIVIDING A BUSINESS
WHEN ONE SPOUSE PUTS THE OTHER THROUGH SCHOOL
DEBTS
FEDERAL AND UNIFORM LAWS AFFECTING PROPERTY

PROPERTY DEFINED

Virtually anything one can own is considered property. Generally, we think of items with monetary value as property, but valueless items can also constitute property.

Asset

Asset is another term for property of all kinds—usually referring to property with some value. Property includes tangible things—things you can see and touch, like furniture, houses, cars, cats, clothing, jewelry, record albums, photographs, bank accounts, boats, art collections and motorcycles, and intangible items such as business good will, the right to receive future pensions, patents, stocks and money owed to a person by others.

Debts

Debts are also considered property—actually negative property or a negative asset.

PROPERTY AND DEBTS

Real Property

Land and structures permanently attached to the land (houses, sheds, pools, etc.) are referred to as real property or real estate. All other kinds of property are called personal property. Mobile homes are usually considered personal property unless they have been rendered immobile by being placed on a foundation. Crops are real property while they are growing and personal property after they have been harvested.

Personal Property

All property that is not classified as real property is called personal property, sometimes referred to as chattel. It includes such widely diverse items as money, stocks, furniture, cars, bank accounts, pensions, jewelry, oil paintings and patents.

PROPERTY OWNED DURING MARRIAGE

In a divorce where the parties cannot agree on how to divide their property, the court must classify the disputed items as either marital property or separate property in order to decide who gets what. (For a discussion on property rights of people who are not married, see the *Rights of Unmarried People* chapter.)

A couple may sign an agreement during marriage to change the nature of any property from marital to separate or from separate to marital if they follow the rules of their state for doing this. If they divorce, the property will be divided according to the agreement if a judge finds the agreement valid. While these agreements may sometimes be legal if made orally, they are easier to refer to and to prove if they are in writing.

Separate Property

In all states, a married person is permitted to treat certain types of earnings and assets as his separate property. This means that the property can be disposed of (sold, given away or left in a will) without the consent of the other spouse. Also, at divorce, the property is not divided under the state's property distribution laws, but rather is kept by the spouse who owns it.

Marital Property

Most property accumulated by a married couple is called marital property. In community property states, marital property is called community property. The rules as to what constitutes marital property in non-community property states differ. Some states include all property and earnings during marriage. Others exclude gifts and inheritances from this general rule. Some states exclude certain types of property even if acquired during marriage, while others exclude improvements to property that existed before marriage.

Upon divorce, marital property in community property states is divided equally. In virtually all other states, marital property is divided equitably (fairly). In practice, equitable means equal, or nearly so, unless the court believes it is fairer to award one spouse more.

STATE MARITAL PROPERTY SCHEMES

Equitable Distribution

Equitable distribution is a principle under which assets and earnings accumulated during marriage are divided equitably (fairly) at divorce. In theory, equitable means equal, or nearly so. In practice, however, equitable is often two-thirds to the higher wage earner and one-third to the lower (or non-) wage earner, unless the court believes it is fairer to award one or the other spouse more. In some equitable distribution states, if a spouse obtains a fault divorce, the "guilty" spouse may receive less than her equitable share of the marital property upon divorce.

Equitable distribution principles are followed in Washington, D.C. and 41 states—all states *except* Arizona, California, Idaho, Louisiana, Nevada, New Mexico, Texas, Washington and Wisconsin.

Example: Maureen and Frank, who live in New York, are divorcing after ten years of marriage. During their marriage, they bought a house, some furniture and a car with their earnings and they made investments. Maureen earns substantially more than Frank; they shared the work around the house. Upon divorce, a court is likely to divide the property in a way which takes into account the money and work put into the marriage and property as well as the economic realities of the parties. Maureen, because of her higher earnings, will probably keep the house (and its mortgage), the furniture will be divided, the party who needs the car more will get it, and Maureen will pay Frank a sum of money equal to his portion of the house—probably near half.

Community Property

Community property is a method of defining the ownership of property acquired (including earnings) during a marriage and the responsibility for debts incurred during marriage. Community property principles are followed in Arizona, California, Idaho, Louisiana, Nevada, New Mexico, Texas, Washington and Wisconsin.

Generally, all earnings during marriage and all property acquired with those earnings are considered community property. This includes wages, stock options, pensions and other employment compensation, family business profits, business good will, household goods, motor vehicles, bank accounts, life insurance policies, tax refunds, real property, art collections, copyrights and inventions. Additionally, all debts incurred during marriage, unless the creditor was specifically looking for payment from the separate property of one spouse, are community property debts.

The major exceptions to these rules are that gifts and inheritances specifically made to one spouse during marriage, personal injury awards received by one spouse during marriage and the proceeds of a pension which had already vested (that is, the pensioner is legally entitled to receive it) before marriage are separate property.

Property purchased with the separate funds of a spouse remains that spouse's separate property. A business owned by one spouse before the marriage remains his separate property during the marriage, although a portion of the value of the business may be attributed to the community if it increased in value during the marriage or both spouses worked at it. Property purchased partially with separate funds and partially with community property funds is part community and part separate property.

Upon divorce, community property is generally divided equally between the spouses. (In many community property states, for purpose of divorce, property held in joint tenancy is presumed to be community property.) A spouse who contributed separate property to a community asset may be entitled to reimbursement for that contribution. Conversely, the community estate may be reimbursed for community property contributions to a spouse's separate property.

On death, one-half of each item of community property automatically goes to the remaining spouse. (This discussion does not apply to property held in joint tenancy.) The other half goes to the remaining spouse if the deceased person died without a will or living trust and there are no minor children of the marriage. If there are children, they commonly will get a share. Otherwise, the half goes to whomever the deceased person left it to in her will or living trust. (This could result in the surviving spouse owning half of an item and the deceased's brother, aunt, friend or lover owning the other half.)

In most community property states, upon divorce a court has the discretion to divide the property equitably, if dividing the property equally would result in unfairness to one party. Additionally, in some community property states which still have fault divorce, a spouse deemed at fault in ending the marriage may be awarded less than 50% of the community property. (These exceptions do not apply in California, the most populated community property state.)

Example: Aaron and Rachel own Rachel's boat, purchased before their marriage; oil paintings Rachel inherited; Aaron's photo equipment from before their marriage; Aaron's stamp collection, part of which was acquired before they married and part acquired during the marriage; a stereo system Aaron purchased during the marriage with money he had earned before the marriage; a jointly purchased house and household furniture; a Mercedes they won in a raffle; and various record albums and compact discs, some acquired by each before the marriage and some acquired during the marriage.

Their property is characterized as:

Rachel's	Aaron's	Community
boat	photo equipment	house
oil paintings	stamp collection (part)	stamp collection (part)
music collection (part)	music collection (part)	music collection (part)
	stereo system	Mercedes
		furniture

If a court divides their property, Rachel and Aaron each would keep what they owned before they married. The house, furniture, Mercedes and stamp collection would be appraised and, along with the remaining portion of the music collection, divided equally. One way to divide the community property would be to sell it all and split the proceeds. Another way would be to sell the house, split the rest of the property and divide the house proceeds, evening up the balance. If Rachel and Aaron divide their property without court intervention, they can agree on whatever division they want.

QUASI-COMMUNITY PROPERTY

Quasi means like. Quasi-community property is a term used only in California and Arizona. It refers to the property accumulated by a married couple living in a non-community property state when the couple later moves to California or Arizona. (Property accumulated in another community property state during a marriage already is and remains community property when the couple moves to California or Arizona.)

At divorce, quasi-community property is treated exactly like community property.

Example: Harold and Darlene married in Atlanta and bought a house, two boats, furniture for the house and a car there. Later, they moved to Tucson and got divorced. The Arizona courts will categorize the house, boats, furniture and car bought in Atlanta—which would have been community property had the couple been living in Arizona—as quasi-community property. It will be treated, for purposes of division, just like community property.

Quasi-community property rules operate a little differently when someone dies. Personal property (wherever situated) is treated like community property. Real property, however, is treated according to the laws of the state in which it is located.

Example: Harold and Darlene married in Atlanta, bought and furnished a condo there and another in Tucson. After a few years in the southeast, they moved to Tucson and Harold died. In this situation, Arizona courts will treat the furnishings in the Atlanta condo, and the Tucson condo and its furnishings, as quasi-community property. The Atlanta condo itself, however, will be distributed according to Georgia property laws.

Common Law Property

Under the traditional common law as developed in England and later adopted by the U.S., property acquired during marriage was divided upon divorce according to who had legal title to the property—that is, who owned it. This property division system was also sometimes referred to as title division. Only property jointly owned by the couple could be divided by the court. Virtually all states that originally followed this common law rule have since adopted equitable distribution rules, which provide that property acquired during marriage is equitably divided at divorce, regardless of who has legal title. No state strictly follows the common law property scheme of dividing marital property.

WAYS TO HOLD MARITAL OR COMMUNITY PROPERTY

When any two or more people (including spouses) are the legal owners of a piece of property, they are generally said to be joint owners. Where the property is the type to which the owners have title (real property, cars or boats, for instance), the joint ownership is called joint title. There are several different ways in which jointly owned property may be held, including in only one spouse's name, as community property or as husband and wife. Here are the others.

Joint tenancy. Joint tenancy is a method by which people jointly hold title to property. All joint tenants own equal interests in the jointly owned property. When two or more persons expressly own property as joint tenants, and one owner dies, the remaining owner(s) automatically take over the share of the deceased person. This is termed the right of survivorship. For example, if two people own their house as joint tenants and one of them dies, the other person ends up owning the entire house, even if the deceased person attempted to give away her half of the house in her will.

In most states, one joint tenant may, on her own, end a joint tenancy by signing a new deed changing the way title is held; then, she is free to leave her portion of the property through her will. Because joint tenancy property isn't passed through a will and thus doesn't go through probate, joint tenancy is a popular probate-avoidance technique.

In most community property states, property held in joint tenancy is presumed to be community property upon divorce unless there is proof to the contrary. This makes sense because a married couple's joint tenancy property is divided in half when they divorce, and a married couple's community property is divided equally at the end of their marriage.

In community property states, when purchasing real estate or valuable personal property that comes with a written title (for example, a recreational vehicle), a married couple must choose whether to take title to the property as community property or as joint tenants. If the property is taken as community property, there may be significant federal income tax advantages if one spouse dies. On the other hand, if the property is held in joint tenancy and one spouse dies, that spouse's creditors (if she has any) will not be able take the property.

Tenancy by the entirety. Tenancy by the entirety is a way married couples can hold title to property in some states. Tenancy by the entirety is very similar to joint tenancy; upon the death of one of the spouses, the property automatically passes to the surviving spouse, regardless of will provisions to the contrary. Unlike joint tenancy, however, one person cannot unilaterally sever the tenancy by the entirety.

Tenancy in common. Tenancy in common is a way for any two or more people to hold title to property together. Each co-owner has an undivided interest in the property, which means that no owner holds a particular part of the property and all co-owners have the right to use all the property. Each owner is free to sell or give away his interest. On his death, his interest passes through his will or by intestate succession if he had no will.

Tenancy in common differs from joint tenancy and tenancy by the entirety, where the property passes automatically to the surviving co-owners on one's own death, regardless of any will provision. Tenancy in common is a more appropriate form of title than joint tenancy when co-owners do not have a close personal relationship, such as when individuals are all willed a home and find themselves joint owners.

DUTIES OF CO-OWNERS TOWARD EACH OTHER

Most states provide that both spouses have equal management and control over all jointly owned property. This includes the power to buy it, sell it, give it away or invest it. Until the mid-1970s, most states placed the management and control of jointly owned property exclusively with the husband. (For a discussion on duties of people who are not married, see the *Rights of Unmarried People* chapter.)

In most states today, certain property—usually necessaries of life, such as clothing, furniture and similar items—cannot be sold or disposed of without the consent of both spouses.

Each spouse has management and control over all his separate property, even necessaries of life.

Confidential Relationship

A confidential relationship is one between two people who have gained the confidence of the other, purport to act or advise with the other's interest in mind, and therefore have a duty to act toward the other with good faith and honesty (sometimes termed a fiduciary duty). The most common confidential relationship is between spouses. People in confidential relationships have a duty not to conceal or misappropriate property from one another, not to incur debts holding the other liable without authorization, and to be open and honest with each other even during divorce. If a spouse breaches any of these duties, in virtually all states she will be awarded less than her share of the marital property on divorce. Other confidential relationships commonly recognized are between parents and children, and sometimes between non-marital partners.

Fraud

Fraud is intentional perversion of the truth in order to gain an advantage (usually economic) over another person. Common types of fraud are deceit, misrepresentation and concealment. To prove deceit or misrepresentation, a person must show that another person made a material false statement with the intention of deceiving the first person, who justifiably relied on the statement and was hurt by it. To prove concealment, a person must show that the other person withheld something that she had a duty to disclose, and that the first person was hurt by the withholding. A spouse who conceals jointly owned property may be awarded less than her full share on divorce. See Table 12.1 in the Appendix.

PROPERTY DIVISION AT DIVORCE—GENERAL CONCEPTS

In the course of a divorce, a couple must divide the property and debts accumulated during their marriage. It is common for the couple to do their own dividing rather than leave it to the judge. There is no requirement that the couple follow their state's laws in making the division. But if a couple cannot agree on a division, they may submit their property dispute to the court, which will use state laws to characterize and divide their marital property keeping to the schemes described above.

Division of property does not mean a physical division. Rather, each party is awarded by a court a percentage of the value of the property. Each item of property is assigned a monetary value and the values are totaled. The items are distributed, with each party getting items totaling his or her percentage.

In some states, regardless of whether fault divorces are still available, fault is a factor in dividing property and a guilty spouse might not receive her full share of the marital property.

FIGURING OUT HOW MUCH THE PROPERTY IS WORTH

Fair Market Value

The fair market value of an item of property is the amount a willing buyer would pay a willing seller. Fair market value can be determined by comparing the price for which similar items recently have been sold. Factors that commonly influence an item's fair market value are:

- Supply—If an item is relatively rare, its fair market value will tend to be higher than if the item is commonly available.
- Demand—If demand for the item is high, the fair market value will be higher than if the item is not wanted.

Divorcing couples (or the court, if the spouses cannot agree on the property division) often want or need to know the fair market value of their assets. This is because marital property is usually divided by totaling up the value of the items to be divided, and then giving each spouse a more or less equal share.

Appraisal or Valuation

An appraisal or valuation is the process of determining the fair market value of an asset. Appraisals of real property and automobiles are common when the item is to be sold or divided. One common method of appraising real property is to compare the property in question to similar property recently sold. Another common method, especially with vehicles, is to start with the purchase price and then to adjust the value based on inflation, appreciation and depreciation. To obtain an appraisal, it is usually necessary to consult an expert in the field (for example, a real estate broker, art dealer or actuary). Evaluating a professional degree or license may also require an appraisal.

Equity

Equity in property is the portion of the property's value that is claimed by the property owner. For example, a real property owner's equity in her property is the fair market value of the property less the mortgage and taxes due. In evaluating real property as part of a division of property during a divorce, other debts which must be subtracted from the fair market value are any real estate commission, closing costs or lawyer's fees necessary to sell the property.

Example: Terri and her husband own a house with a fair market value of $125,000, and owe $50,000 on the mortgage and $2,500 in taxes. The equity in the house is $72,500—that is, $125,000 − ($50,000 + $2,500).

If Terri and her husband are dividing it as part of their divorce settlement, the equity must take into consideration the costs of selling the house; the closing costs, commissions and lawyer's fee would be approximately $5,000. The equity in the house is now $67,500—that is, $125,000 − ($50,000 + $2,500 + $5,000).

OTHER FACTORS TO CONSIDER WHEN DIVIDING PROPERTY

Non-Monetary Contributions to Marriage

Spouses make monetary and non-monetary contributions to the marriage. Monetary contributions tend to be in the form of earnings and benefits (and result in the acquisition of assets, such as furniture, a car and a house). Non-monetary contributions include homemaking, child care, entertaining the employed spouse's business associates and working without a salary in a spouse's business.

Normally, when couples get divorced, only the monetary contribution is treated as having value and divided accordingly. Now, however, in over 35 states, when a couple divorces and their property is divided, the non-monetary contributions of a spouse are recognized to have monetary value. In some cases, the spouse who contributed the non-monetary services is compensated from the couple's property for the full value of the services. If that spouse's future earning capacity has been impaired by her absence from the income-earning world, she may be compensated by a large alimony award.

Some statutes specify that a spouse's contribution to acquiring marital property can be fulfilling the duties of a homemaker. See, for example, Illinois Annotated Statutes § 503(d)(1), Massachusetts General Laws Annotated § 34 and New York Domestic Relations Law § 236B(5)(d)(6). Other statutes are not as specific, but recognize the importance of non-monetary contributions by factoring in the spouse's contribution to the marriage or to the well being of the family. See, for example, Florida Statutes Annotated § 61.075(1)(a), Maryland Family Code Annotated § 8-205(b)(1) and Virginia Code § 20-107.3(e)(1). Still other states, through their case law, permit consideration of non-monetary contributions as a factor in dividing marital property.

Reimbursement

Reimbursement is the right to be repaid for money paid out. This becomes a core concept when a couple divorces. This is because when a marriage is working, the spouses don't pay too much attention to property ownership laws. Money comes in and money goes out, and whether the money is marital property or separate property isn't important. If the marriage fails, however, whose money or property was spent by which spouse, and for what purpose, suddenly becomes important. One or both of the spouses will want the full benefit of the state's property ownership laws. Thus, an accounting of money earned and money spent during the marriage will be necessary.

If, during the marriage, one spouse contributed her separate property to marital property or to the other spouse's separate property, she may be entitled to reimbursement for the amount. Or, if one spouse paid a separate debt of the other, he may be reimbursed for the amount paid.

Improvements to Property

In community property states, improvements to separate property (such as additions, renovations and substantial upkeep) are usually considered community property upon divorce if they were paid for out of community funds, unless there is a written agreement to the contrary. Also in community property states, improvements to community property paid for by separate funds usually remain separate property unless a written agreement states otherwise. The spouse making the separate contribution is entitled to reimbursement upon divorce. Community property improvements to community property remain community property, and separate property improvements to (one's own or one's spouse's) separate property remain the separate property of the contributor.

In equitable distribution states, separate property improvements by one spouse to the other's separate property or to jointly owned property may result in the first spouse acquiring a monetary interest (equal to the value contributed, or equal to any increase in the value of the property) in the improved property. In Mississippi, the contributing party will obtain a monetary interest in the other's property generally only if title to the property was changed to reflect the contribution.

Example: Bill owned a house before he married Tricia. During the marriage, Tricia used her inheritance from her Uncle Roy (Tricia's separate property) to build a $3,000 deck on the house. Bill and Tricia are now divorcing.

If Bill and Tricia live in Idaho (a community property state), Tricia is entitled to either a $3,000 reimbursement from Bill's separate property or $3,000 more than Bill from the community property.

If Bill and Tricia live in New Hampshire (an equitable distribution state), Tricia may argue that she has a monetary interest in Bill's house for $3,000 or an amount equal to the house's increase in value caused by the addition of the deck. More than likely, Tricia will receive $3,000 (plus any increased value) more than Bill in their marital property when they divide their assets. Or Tricia may file a lien against the house, giving her a right to be paid when the house is sold.

Transmutation

In community property states, when property is changed from separate property to community property, or vice versa, the change is called a transmutation. Property can be automatically transmuted, as when it is commingled, or changed by an agreement during marriage.

Commingling

Commingling is the mixing together by spouses of their marital property with the separate property of one spouse, or one spouse's separate property with the other spouse's separate property. For instance, if cash belonging separately to one spouse is put in a bank account containing marital property, the separate property is commingled with the marital property. Upon divorce, commingled funds are often treated as marital property, and property purchased from commingled funds is treated as marital unless very careful records have been kept tracking the separate property funds from the time they were deposited until the time they were spent on the property in question.

Tracing of Funds

In community property states, when one spouse's separate property is commingled with community property, the mixed assets are presumed to be community property. Upon divorce, community property is divided equally, while each spouse keeps his own separate property. The owner of the separate property, however, may be able to overcome the presumption of community property created by the commingling by establishing the separate source of the funds. This is called tracing the funds. Tracing usually involves careful analysis of financial institution deposits and withdrawals.

Example: Jim and Leslie live in Texas, a community property state. They deposited their paychecks (community property) into a bank account which usually had a balance of about $2,000 to pay the household bills. Leslie also deposited into the account $5,000 in proceeds from the sale of a boat she owned before marrying Jim (her separate property). Four thousand dollars from the account was then used to buy exercise equipment for the house. Jim and Leslie divorce, and Jim claims that half of the equipment is his. Leslie says it's all hers.

There are two ways Leslie can prove her position. First, she can show that at the time the exercise equipment was bought, there was an excess of her separate property deposits over her separate property expenses—for example, a student loan she incurred before marrying Jim—in the account. This must be done by reconstructing each separate property deposit and expenditure from the account. She then must show that the excess was used to buy the equipment. Second, she can show that other than the equipment, they only used the commingled funds to pay for household expenses; the law presumes that household expenses are paid for from the community portion, leaving the separate property portion to pay for the exercise equipment.

Agreement Before Marriage

Before a couple marries, they may make an agreement concerning certain aspects of their relationship, including how they will characterize their property during marriage. These agreements are called ante-nuptial, pre-nuptial or pre-marital agreements. They are usually upheld by courts unless one person shows that the agreement is likely to promote divorce, was written and signed with the intention of divorcing or was unfairly entered into (for example, a spouse giving up all of his rights in his spouse's future earnings without the advice of an attorney). Eleven states limit these agreements to issues of property ownership only.

Agreement During Marriage

Contracts made between a husband and wife during their marriage are interchangeably called post-nuptial, marital and post-marital agreements. Usually these agreements involve how property ownership is to be handled during the marriage and upon divorce.

In most states, it is legal for a couple to transfer property from one to the other, from one to both or from both to one, or to agree that earnings will be solely or jointly owned, even though the state's law would treat the earnings or property differently in the agreement's absence. Courts usually enforce legally executed property agreements which are fair to both spouses, but will not enforce agreements where a spouse has been deceived.

PROPERTY AND DEBTS

Necessaries

Necessaries (also called necessities, necessities of life or necessaries of life) are the articles needed to sustain life, such as food, clothing, medical care and shelter. In all states, the law requires men to pay for necessaries for their wives and children; in many states, women must provide them for their spouses and offspring. When it comes to enforcing this obligation, however, courts have been notoriously reluctant to intervene as long as the couple is living together. The barest provision of food and shelter has been found sufficient under the law.

In some states, debts incurred by a spouse for necessaries are considered to be joint debts of the spouses even if the couple is living apart but not yet divorced. This means that in most states, creditors may sue either spouse for debts incurred for necessaries by either spouse.

SPECIAL CONCEPTS WHEN DIVIDING REAL PROPERTY

Partition

Partition means selling real property and dividing the proceeds among the joint owners. A partition action is a lawsuit brought by one owner of jointly owned real property to force its sale and split the proceeds in accordance with the state's property laws.

Partition actions are commonly brought by a divorcing spouse who wants to sell the family home when the other spouse doesn't want to. A request for partition may be refused if custody, visitation and child support have not yet been determined or if selling the home would not be in the best interest of the child who has been living there.

Deed

A deed is a written document, signed by the owner of real property, that transfers title to the property to another person. There are several types of deeds:

- bargain and sale deed—document includes getting something of value in exchange for the transference of the property.
- grant deed—document guarantees that the title hasn't already been passed to someone else or isn't encumbered (burdened with a mortgage, lien or past-due tax bill) except to the extent disclosed by public records or the person signing the deed.
- quitclaim deed—one person transfers what ownership interest in the property he has, but makes no promises about the title. When divorcing spouses jointly own real property, often one spouse is required to sign a quitclaim deed in favor of the other spouse as part of the overall property division.
- sheriff's deed—document is given to the purchaser and signed by the sheriff after property is sold at a sheriff's sale (that is, sold to pay a court judgment on a foreclosure).
- tax deed—document is given to the purchaser and signed by the government after property taken by the government from a previous owner is sold to pay due taxes.
- warranty deed—the person signing the deed guarantees that he has good title to the property. These deeds are rarely used today, as their function has been replaced by title insurance.

Sweat Equity

Sweat equity is a non-monetary improvement or contribution to jointly owned or the other spouse's property.

Example: When Bob and Carol got married, Carol moved into Bob's one-bedroom cottage. Since they wanted to have a family, Carol decided to make some improvements to the house. She built an additional bedroom for the nursery and a laundry room. Upon divorce, Carol would not only be entitled to reimbursement of any of her separate property money that she put into improving Bob's house, but also for her labor (the sweat).

SPECIAL CONCEPTS WHEN DIVIDING RETIREMENT PLANS AND SURVIVORS' BENEFITS

A fund into which payments are made to provide an employee an income after retirement is termed a pension or retirement fund. The benefits the employee eventually receives are called pension or retirement payments. Because pensions are deferred employment benefits for work already done, in many community property and equitable distribution states, the portion of the pension earned during marriage is considered marital property and subject to division on divorce—especially if the pension has already vested.

When a pension has vested, the employee has the right to receive payments (that is, it can't be taken away), even if he gets fired the next morning or quits the next month. Pensions vest after the employee works for a certain number of years. Many pensions don't vest until after the employee works 15 or 20 years. Other pensions vest gradually, that is, after five years the employee is entitled to a percentage of the pension (for example, 25%); after ten years, he's entitled to more (for example, 50%), and then after 15 or 20 years he's entitled to it all.

Many federal retirement benefits, including Social Security, disability military pay and railroad pensions are always the separate property of the spouse who earned them, no matter what state property distribution laws say. State courts, however, may divide disposable military retirement pay, however. This means that the amount of the monthly military pension is first reduced by income taxes and other necessary withholdings. The net amount is then subject to division. *Mansell v. Mansell*, 490 U.S. 581 (1989).

Once a pension vests, the employee may still have to wait before actually receiving the benefits. Usually, vested pensions do not pay out (mature) until the worker reaches a certain age, such as 62 or 65. Some employees choose to continue to work even after the pension matures because the pension payments increase the longer the employee works past the maturity date.

In addition, a spouse who divorces after ten or more years of marriage is entitled to receive a share of the working spouse's Social Security benefits.

Profit-Sharing Plan

Many employers provide their employees with a benefit of sharing in the profits of the company as an incentive for years of productive service. Since the profit-share is essentially a bonus for work already done, in many community property and equitable distribution states, it is considered marital property and subject to division on divorce.

Survivor's Benefits

Survivor's benefits are support payments for the spouse and children of a worker who dies. They come from pension, Social Security or veteran's benefits deducted from the deceased's wages or owed him for his military service. Generally, survivor's benefits are payable only if the worker has enough years of work credits at the time of death. Survivor's benefits differ from pension or retirement benefits. Private retirement benefits can be divided at divorce, but survivor's benefits cannot.

A divorced spouse may or may not be the beneficiary of survivor's benefits. Veteran's survivor's benefits generally go only to current spouses, while Social Security survivor's benefits go to a former spouse if the marriage lasted ten years or a child under 16 is at home. Children's benefits usually end when the child turns 18 unless she is disabled.

SPECIAL CONCEPTS WHEN DIVIDING A BUSINESS

In a divorce, the value of a business owned by one or both spouses is often divided by the court to reflect the portion that belongs to each spouse. How much of a business will be considered marital or community property subject to division by a court depends on whose money went into the business, the amount of time spent by each spouse in making the business grow and the law of the state where the divorce occurs. When the business has been run or managed by one spouse only, that spouse will most likely be awarded the business, and the other spouse will be given his share in other marital or community property. If both spouses have run or managed the business, one spouse often will purchase the other's share.

Example: Judy and Roy owned and operated a gasoline station during their marriage. Roy put down an initial $30,000 of his own property while Judy contributed $15,000 of hers. Judy, however, ran the business alone for its first three years; Roy worked there only during the last two. All improvements to the business were paid for out of marital property. At divorce, the court divides the business evenly (for example, Judy buying Roy's share from him, or Roy is given the gas station and Judy is given different marital property equal in value to her share of the business), because although Roy contributed twice as much money, Judy has contributed significantly more time.

Business Good Will

Any established business has a name and reputation which by themselves can be expected to generate a certain amount of income in the future. A shorthand name for the value of a business's name and reputation is good will. The good will of a business depends on a number of factors including its name recognition, length of existence and revenues. IBM, for example, has a significant good will based on name recognition alone.

In virtually all states, a business owned by one or both spouses is treated like any other item of marital property in a divorce—that is, it is appraised to determine its value and then divided between the spouses. Most states require that the business good will be included as part of the overall appraisal of the business. A few states, including Hawaii (*Antolik v. Harvey*, 761 P.2d 305 (1988)) and Maryland (*Prahinski v. Prahinski*, 582 A.2d 784 (1990)), have expressly rejected the argument that business good will is a part of the business appraised during divorce. For example, a Maryland court in *Prahinski v. Prahinski* held that the good will of a husband's law practice could not be divided between the husband and wife upon divorce despite the fact that the wife worked in the practice during the 18 years of their marriage.

Special Equity

Special equity is a concept in equitable distribution states used in the division of property at divorce. A special equity award grants a non-owning spouse a share of her husband's separate property business when she has worked in his business but has not been paid or otherwise compensated for her work.

WHEN ONE SPOUSE PUTS THE OTHER THROUGH SCHOOL

Professional Degree or License

Some spouses support their mates financially as well as emotionally through professional, graduate or trade school. When they divorce, alimony is rarely awarded to the spouse who supported the couple. Yet, she often made sacrifices (such as delaying her own education) in order to support the other.

Where the spouse who supported the couple earns less than the other at divorce, courts have tried a number of solutions to even up the income imbalance. Michigan views a professional degree as marital property to be valued and divided. (*Thomas v. Thomas*, 417 N.W.2d 563 (1987).) New York values and divides the licenses and degrees. (*McSparron v. McSparron*, 597 N.Y.S.2d 743 (1993).) Arkansas and Missouri will value and divide degrees when no other way exists to equally divide the property. (*Wilson v. Wilson*, 741 S.W.2d 640 (Arkansas 1987); *Marriage of Dusing*, 654 S.W.2d 938 (Missouri 1983).) Georgia, however, views the degree and license as being too personal to the holder to be transferred into marital property. (*Lowry v. Lowry*, 413 S.E.2d 731 (1992).)

Many other states, such as California, Indiana and Pennsylvania, reimburse the supporting spouse for the costs contributed to the education or support while the student was in school. (California Family Code § 2641; Indiana Statutes Annotated § 31-1-11.5-11(d); Pennsylvania Consolidated Statutes Annotated § 23-3502.) Other states which allow such reimbursement are Arizona, Florida, Iowa, Kentucky, Maryland, Michigan, Mississippi, New Jersey, Ohio and Vermont. Some states use the degreed spouse's ability to earn in setting alimony. Others states, when setting alimony, look at the post-graduation living standard, not the standard of living during the student days. A few states combine these methods.

DEBTS

A debt is money owed. Common debts are home mortgages, alimony and child support obligations, credit card bills, phone bills, gas bills, car payments and student loans.

For a married couple, responsibility for paying a debt depends on when the debt was incurred, the state in which the couple lives, who incurred the debt and for what the debt was incurred. As a general rule, both spouses are responsible for debts incurred by either or both during marriage if the debt is for property or a service which benefits both spouses.

COMMUNITY DEBTS

Community debts are debts incurred during marriage by a couple living in a community property state. Both partners are responsible for community debts. If a creditor was specifically looking for payment from the separate property of one spouse, however, the debt is not a community debt, and only the spouse to whom the creditor looked is responsible for the debt. In addition, most community property states require that the debt benefit the community (the couple)—that is, not promote the breakdown of the marriage. If the debt does not benefit the community, the spouse who does benefit by the debt will be solely responsible for it.

Example: Lee buys herself a motorcycle; that is a community debt because the community benefits by Lee's enjoying the motorcycle, even if her husband never uses the motorcycle. If Lee takes a trip to the Caribbean with her lover, however, that debt will be her separate debt because the community of Lee and her husband does not benefit by Lee and her lover's trip.

Debts Incurred Before Marriage

In community property and equitable distribution states, debts incurred by a spouse before marriage are the responsibility of the spouse incurring them. During the marriage, the debtor-spouse's separate property must first be looked to by creditors to pay the pre-marital debt. After that, marital property may be used. In no case, however, is the separate property of one spouse liable for debts incurred by the other spouse before marriage. In some community property states, community property earnings of the non-debtor spouse are not liable for the other's pre-marital debts if the earnings are kept in a separate bank account and not mixed with other marital property.

Example: When Marie and Pierre married, Marie had student loan debts of $10,000. She had defaulted on four payments of $150 each, and continued not to pay during the marriage. Pierre had a vested pension from before the marriage and kept the proceeds in a separate bank account. When the bank which loaned Marie the money sued her for repayment, it could go after Marie's separate property, and Marie and Pierre's community property. None of Pierre's separate property, however, can be used.

Debts Incurred During Marriage

Debts incurred during a marriage are usually considered joint debts—that is, during the marriage, both spouses are legally responsible for them. Creditors first look to jointly owned property to satisfy debts; if there is no jointly owned property, they look to each spouse's separate property.

If a couple divorces, responsibility for marital debts is allocated in accordance with the property division laws of the state. This usually means that the debts are divided equally or equitably, especially when they were incurred for food, shelter, clothing and medical care (called necessaries). The court also considers who is better able to pay the debts (the spouse with the higher income and/or lower living expenses). If a couple has many debts but also has much property, a common result is for the spouse better able to pay the debts to assume their payment and also to receive a larger share of the property to even up the division.

Regardless of the court's assignment of responsibility of a joint debt, a creditor may sue either or both spouses and will do so on the basis of who is more likely to pay. Any agreement which the husband and wife may make regarding these debts is not binding on creditors, but entitles a spouse to reimbursement if the agreement is not honored by the other.

Example: Aaron and Alice purchased a table for cash, bought a car on credit and charged a vacation to Hawaii on their credit card while they were married. After they divorced, Alice agreed to pay off the vacation (in exchange for keeping the table), and Aaron took the car and assumed the car payments. If Alice doesn't pay off the vacation, or if Aaron doesn't make the car payments, the creditor can seek payment from the other and leave the two of them to fight out who must pay and who is entitled to reimbursement.

One member of a couple may also incur a separate debt during the marriage, but only that partner is responsible for repayment. In most states, a separate debt is when the creditor requested credit information about only one spouse when making the debt and intends for only that spouse to repay the debt.

Debts Incurred Between Separation and Divorce

State law varies on who is responsible for debts incurred after a married couple permanently separates but before the divorce is final. In some states, each spouse is responsible for his own debts. In many states, however, creditors may sue both the husband and the wife for a debt incurred by either one of them before a separation agreement is signed or divorce papers are filed. If a creditor obtains payment from the wife, but the husband incurred the debt, the wife must request the court to order her husband to reimburse her.

In a few states, debts incurred between separation and divorce for necessaries (food, housing, clothing and health care) for the spouse or children (unless there is a child support order stating who must pay) are considered joint debts. A creditor may obtain payment from either spouse. If the wife pays, but the husband incurred the debt, the wife will not be entitled to reimbursement.

Bankruptcy

Bankruptcy is a federal court proceeding in which a person unable to pay her debts asks the court to either cancel them (Chapter 7 bankruptcy) or allow their payment—often in less than the full amount—in an orderly manner over a three- to five- year period (Chapter 13 bankruptcy). For married couples, either or both spouses may file for bankruptcy; if both wish to file, the couple may use one set of forms. In equitable distribution states, it is usually a good idea for both spouses to file for bankruptcy when a couple is having debt problems. Otherwise, if only one declares bankruptcy, a creditor may still go after the other for payment of any debts attributable to the marriage. In community property states, it is not necessary that both spouses file. All community debts eligible for elimination are wiped out for both spouses, even if only one files for bankruptcy.

Alimony and child support obligations are usually not erasable (called dischargeable) in bankruptcy, but three kinds of alimony or child support debts can be discharged.

- Support owed under a state's general support law, not a court order. If your support debt arose under a general law of your state that requires parents to support their children, or spouses to support each other, and no court actually ordered the support, the debt is dischargeable. This is true even if the creditor is the welfare department and is seeking reimbursement for benefits paid to the family before a child support order was obtained.

- Support paid under an agreement between unmarried persons. If an unmarried couple enters into an agreement about their obligations to each other, as many do, the agreement often covers support (who pays whom) in the event the couple separates. In most states, these agreements are enforceable—the recipient can sue if the other person doesn't pay. But unlike alimony or child support ordered by a court, if the person who must pay files for bankruptcy, the obligation can be discharged unless the recipient sues and wins a court judgment against the other person.

- Support owed someone other than a spouse, ex-spouse or child. If a former or current spouse or a child has given (assigned, in legal terms) the right to receive the support to someone else, or a creditor has garnished the payments, the debt is dischargeable unless it's owed to the welfare department.

Alimony and child support debts aren't dischargeable if they're owed under a separation agreement, divorce decree, court order or property settlement.

A court order setting the amount of child support payments is clear enough. Some other debts, however, may also be considered non-dischargeable child support or alimony. The most common are marital debts—the debts a spouse was ordered to pay when the couple divorced.

Often, the spouse who's paying alimony or child support agreed at the time of the divorce to pay more than half of the marital debts, in exchange for a lower support obligation. If that spouse later files for bankruptcy, a portion of the debt is really support. Consequently, it's considered a non-dischargeable debt owed to the other spouse. Similarly, one spouse may have agreed to pay some of the other spouse's or children's future living expenses (shelter, clothing, health insurance, transportation) in exchange for a lower support obligation. The obligations for the future expenses are treated as support owed to the other spouse and aren't dischargeable.

Example: When Erica and Tom divorced, they had two young children. Tom offered to pay most of the marital debts in exchange for low child support payments; Erica agreed because she had a good income of her own and felt able to support the children without too much help from Tom. If Tom files for bankruptcy before paying off the marital debts, the bankruptcy judge won't grant a discharge for all the marital debts.

Obligations that are generally considered support and aren't dischargeable include debts that:

- are paid to a spouse who is maintaining the primary residence of the children while there is a serious imbalance of incomes
- terminate on the death or remarriage of the recipient spouse
- depend on the future income of either spouse, or
- are paid in installments over a substantial period of time.

Until October 1994, the only marital debts that could not be discharged in bankruptcy were child support and alimony. Now, any debt arising from a separation or divorce, or in connection with a marital settlement agreement, divorce decree or other court order, can be considered nondischargeable, provided that the non-debtor former spouse or child of the debtor challenges the debt in the bankruptcy court and proves that either:

- the debtor has the ability to pay the debt from income or property not reasonably necessary for the debtor's support and not reasonably necessary for the debtor to continue, preserve and operate a business, or
- discharging the debt would not result in a benefit to the debtor that would outweigh the detrimental consequences to a spouse, former spouse or child of the debtor.

FEDERAL AND UNIFORM LAWS AFFECTING PROPERTY

Employee Retirement Income Security Act

The Employee Retirement Income Security Act (ERISA) is a federal law governing retirement pay and pension benefits. It was set up to protect employees in the event their employers went out of business. All employers who choose to adhere to ERISA's rules get special tax breaks. ERISA's rules, however, may affect a state's ability to divide pension and retirement benefits upon divorce.

Retirement Equity Act

The Retirement Equity Act of 1984 (REA) amended ERISA. REA is intended to equalize pension/retirement benefit rules that penalize women because of their unique work patterns. REA liberalizes the amount of leave (paid or unpaid) a worker can take before losing pension benefits and shortens the number of years needed for accrual of pension benefits. It also governs the ways states can divide pensions during a divorce.

Qualified Domestic Relations Order (QDRO)

A QDRO (pronounced "quadro") is an order which complies with REA and uses pension or retirement benefits to provide alimony or child support, or to divide marital property, at divorce. The REA dictates when and how retirement benefits may be divided or paid to a child or former spouse. Although state laws govern divorce and property rights, the REA supersedes state law on the issue because retirement pay is covered by the federal law ERISA.

If the QDRO does not meet the REA requirements, the pension plan administrator need not pay out the benefits. Thus, divorcing spouses with pension plans must understand and comply with QDRO requirements whenever dividing pension benefits.

Federal Partnership Income Tax

Under federal tax law (26 U.S.C. § 704), a married couple may create a family partnership to divide business income among family members, assuming the family members qualify as partners in the business. Dividing income this way will frequently lower the total tax on the income more than if all the income were received by one person.

Uniform Marital Property Act

The Uniform Marital Property Act provides for division of property at divorce, in a manner identical to the method used in community property states. This uniform statute has been enacted only in Wisconsin. (Statutes Annotated §§ 766.001 through 766.97.)

Uniformed Services Former Spouses' Protection Act (10 U.S.C. § 1408)

This law provides various benefits for former spouses of military service members, including:

- treating disposable military retirement pay as marital or community property
- enabling the former spouse's share of military retirement pay to be disbursed directly from military finance centers
- having military benefits, including health care, continue after the divorce, and
- enabling the former spouse to be designated as a Survivor Benefit Plan beneficiary.

REPRODUCTIVE RIGHTS AND REPRODUCTIVE TECHNOLOGY

TOPICS

**CONTRACEPTION
REPRODUCTION
WHO IS THE MOTHER?
ABORTION**

CONTRACEPTION

Contraception, or birth control, is any procedure used by persons engaging in sexual intercourse to minimize the chances of the woman getting pregnant.

In 1965, the U.S. Supreme Court ruled that married couples have a constitutional right of privacy, which includes the right to use birth control. The case is significant because it was one of the first Supreme Court decisions recognizing a right to privacy under the U.S. Constitution. (The case is *Griswold v. Connecticut,* 381 U.S. 479.)

> ## RIGHT OF PRIVACY
>
> The right of privacy, although not expressly provided for in the U.S. Constitution, stems from the Bill of Rights (the first ten amendments to the Constitution) as a whole. In the family law context, the right of privacy currently includes:
> - the right to have an abortion
> - the right to procreate, and
> - the right to use birth control.
>
> Because there is no express right of privacy, its scope can change depending on the make up of the U.S. Supreme Court.
>
> Some state constitutions, such as the constitutions of Alaska (Article 1, § 22), California (Article 1, § 1), Florida (Article 1, § 23) and Montana (Article 1, § 10), contain a right of privacy, and thus add independent safeguards against intrusion by state governments.

REPRODUCTION

Zygote

A zygote is a two-cell organism formed by a sperm and an egg, which begins a series of cell divisions and will eventually become an embryo. Between fertilization (the division of the first cell) and the development of the embryo, a zygote divides 16 times. This process takes about two weeks.

Embryo

An embryo is a group of cells developing from a fertilized egg into a fetus. Embryo generally describes the stage of development from the second to ninth weeks after conception. Whether an embryo constitutes human life is significant for legal purposes in the debates over abortion and how courts should treat developing human cells or frozen embryos.

For example, in the case of *Davis v. Davis*, 842 S.W.2D 588 (1992), a divorcing couple in Tennessee battled over control of their frozen embryos. The issue in the case was whether a frozen embryo, fertilized with two to eight cells, but unable to resume its growth unless thawed and implanted in a uterus, is human life or property. The Tennessee Supreme Court held that they were neither human life nor property and that the relative interests of the mother and father in using or not using the embryos must be balanced. The judges ruled that the father's interest in avoiding procreation in this instance outweighed the mother's interest in donating the frozen embryos to a couple unable to conceive.

In Vitro Fertilization

In vitro fertilization is fertilization that takes place outside a woman's body. An egg is removed from a woman, fertilized with a man's semen and then placed back in the woman's womb where the embryo develops. Children conceived this way are often referred to as test-tube babies.

Artificial Insemination

Artificial insemination is a procedure by which a woman is inseminated by a means other than sexual intercourse. If the semen came from her husband, (homologous artificial insemination), the law considers this father-child relationship the same as any father-child relationship where the child is born during marriage. If the semen is from a man other than her husband, the procedure is termed artificial insemination by donor (AID) or heterologous artificial insemination.

If the woman is married when the insemination and birth occur, and her husband consented to the insemination, the husband, and not the donor, is considered the father. If the woman is unmarried when the insemination occurs, whether the donor is considered the father depends on a number of factors, including the details of the procedure and the state. In Oregon (*McIntyre v. Crouch*, 780 P.2d 239) and New Jersey (Statutes Annotated § 9:17-43), for example, the woman and the donor may enter into an agreement outlining their intentions, including declaring the donor not to be the father. In California (Family Code § 7613), if the insemination procedure for an unmarried woman is performed by a doctor, the donor is not considered the father. If no doctor is used, the donor may be considered the father. See *Jhordan C. v. Mary K. and Victoria T.*, 179 Cal. App. 3d 386 (1986).

Sperm Banks

Sperm banks are private businesses to which men donate (or sell) their semen. The semen is bought by women, or doctors on their behalf, who want to become pregnant by artificial insemination. Sperm banks have advantages over inseminations arranged through friends or acquaintances in that the banks obtain complete medical histories of the donors, often know where the donors are located should there be a need to contact them in the future, and allow women to proceed without knowing the identity of the donors. Most sperm banks will not reveal the identity of the donor to the woman unless the donor has consented in advance and the woman requests the information.

INABILITY TO CONCEIVE

Infertile. An infertile person is unable to conceive or bear a child. Either a man or a woman can be infertile. Infertility is treatable in a variety of ways, from surgery to hormone therapy. Recent technological advances also make it possible for infertile couples who can produce eggs or sperm (though not a viable fetus) to conceive in vitro and have the resulting embryo frozen or implanted in the uterus of the woman of the couple or another woman.

Sterilized. Sterilization is the process of rendering someone, through surgery, incapable of producing children. The most common methods for women are tying the fallopian tubes or removing the uterus; the most common method for men is a vasectomy. Although most forms of sterilization are permanent, recent advances in medical science permit reversal under some circumstances.

Involuntary court-ordered sterilization of mentally retarded people, people with severe emotional disturbances, epileptics and some prisoners is authorized today in a number of states and quite controversial.

WHO IS THE MOTHER?

Birth Mother

A birth mother is a woman who gives birth to a child but who may or may not raise the child. The term is usually used when a mother does not intend to keep the child, such as with surrogate mothers (see below) or adoptions. In adoptions and most surrogacy arrangements, the birth mother and the natural mother are the same person. But if an embryo conceived with another woman's egg is implanted in the surrogate mother's uterus, the birth mother is the one who gives birth and the natural mother is the one who conceives.

Natural Mother

The term natural mother has different meanings in different contexts. With adoptions, it means the biological mother who conceived and gave birth to a child, as opposed to the adoptive parents who raise the child.

In the context of artificial insemination, surrogacy and in vitro fertilization, the natural mother is the one who provides the egg for conception, but not necessarily the one who carries the child to term or gives birth.

Legal Mother

The legal mother of a child is the woman recognized under the law as the female parent of the child. This is usually the woman who conceives and gives birth to the child. If one woman conceives an embryo through in vitro fertilization and another brings it to term, however, the legal mother and the biological mother are the same, but the birth mother is different.

Surrogate Mother

A surrogate mother is a woman who is paid to bear a child for someone else. Most surrogate mothers are impregnated with the semen of a man. A few others have already-fertilized eggs of other women implanted in their wombs. In either case, upon the birth of the child, the surrogate mother relinquishes all rights in and responsibilities for the child and turns the child over to either the man (in the former case), or the man and/or the woman (in the latter situation).

The most common scenario with surrogate motherhood is where a woman is unable to bear children; her husband's semen is used to impregnate another woman who acts as the surrogate mother. After the child is born, the man's wife formally adopts the child.

The best-known surrogate motherhood case is the New Jersey case, *Matter of Baby M.* (537 A.2d 1227), where the surrogate mother changed her mind after the baby was born and decided that she wanted to keep the baby. The baby's father and his wife sued the surrogate mother to enforce the contract. The trial court declared the contract valid, terminated the surrogate mother's parental rights, and allowed the father's wife to adopt the baby. The New Jersey Supreme Court reversed that decision, ruled that surrogate motherhood contracts are unenforceable, and then treated the case like any other disputed custody case, awarding custody to the father and visitation rights to the surrogate mother.

In response to the *Baby M.* case, about a dozen states now regulate or prohibit surrogate motherhood arrangements, and many other states are considering legislation which would do the same. See Table 13.1 in the Appendix.

Surrogate motherhood raises a number of social issues. Some people object to surrogacy arrangements because they believe that women who serve as surrogate mothers are turning their bodies into baby-making machines. Others feel that a woman's right to do with her body what she pleases means that it is her choice whether or not to serve as a surrogate mother.

ABORTION

Abortion is the medical termination of pregnancy, either elective (by choice) or therapeutic (to save the mother's life). Since the 1973 landmark U.S. Supreme Court case, *Roe v. Wade* (410 U.S. 113), every woman has had the legal right to an elective abortion during the first three months of pregnancy (called the first trimester). But the 1989 U.S. Supreme Court decision of *Webster v. Reproductive Services* (492 U.S. 490) has permitted the states to erode that right in many ways.

States may now pass laws prohibiting public facilities or employees from performing elective abortion, even if paid for by private funds. States may also ban the use of public funds for family planning programs that include abortion counseling and referral. Since the early 1980s, neither the federal government nor the states have had to fund non-therapeutic abortions for indigent women, though some states, such as California, have chosen to do so.

States may also ban or limit abortion at any time after viability (when the fetus may survive outside the mother's womb), and may require testing as early as 20 weeks into pregnancy to determine viability. Viability is the point at which the law begins to protect a fetus as a potential human life. As medical technology advances, the moment of viability is occurring earlier and earlier.

In response to *Webster v. Reproductive Services,* many state legislatures are now battling over abortion. Some states impose obstacles to obtaining elective abortions, such as delays in scheduling the procedure and requiring anti-abortion counseling.

In 1990, the U.S. Supreme Court in *Ohio v. Akron Center for Reproductive Health* (110 S.Ct. 2972) declared that women under the age of majority can be required to notify one of their parents before obtaining an abortion. The Court held that these laws do not infringe on the U.S. Constitution's right to privacy, as long as the state has set up an alternative procedure where a court can waive parental notification. If a state has adopted a privacy right greater than the federal one, the parental notification law still may be declared invalid. In the states with parental notification laws, many are not enforced while the state constitutional challenges make their way through the courts.

In 1992, the U.S. Supreme Court reaffirmed its decision allowing a woman the right to choose to have an abortion before her fetus is viable without undue interference from the state in *Planned Parenthood of Southeastern Pennsylvania v. Casey* (112 S.Ct. 2791). The court did hold, however, that a state's requirements of a 24-hour waiting period and parental consent to a minor's decision to have an abortion were constitutional.

RIGHTS OF FATHERS

An unmarried man who impregnates a woman is referred to as an unwed father. Unwed fathers have few rights concerning their children. For example, an unwed father does not have the right to require the mother of the child to obtain his consent, or even notify him, before she undergoes an abortion. If the mother decides to bear and keep the child, however, the unwed father will be required to pay child support if a court determines or he acknowledges that he's the father; in addition, he may seek custody or visitation.

Married fathers don't have any more rights in the abortion area. In the case of *Planned Parenthood of Southeastern Pennsylvania v. Casey*, the court held that a husband had no enforceable right under state law to require his wife to notify him regarding her choice to have an abortion.

WRONGFUL LIFE ACTION

A wrongful life action is a lawsuit seeking damages for the harm that occurs when a child is accidentally conceived or born injured in a way that should have been diagnosed. Usually the plaintiffs argue that the act of giving life to the child was wrong and the defendants were negligent in not preventing the birth. The lawsuit often alleges misdiagnosis of a hereditary birth defect, misrepresentation of the risks of conception and birth, misinterpretation of diagnostic tests or negligent sterilization.

The plaintiff may be the child or his parents. Most courts refuse to allow these cases unless a statute expressly authorizes them. California, Illinois, Indiana, New Jersey and Washington authorize cases for special damages only, like the extraordinary expenses of the child's illness.

Wrongful birth action refers to a medical malpractice action by parents for the birth of a severely disabled child, alleging negligent advice or treatment, or the failure to abort.

RIGHTS OF UNMARRIED PEOPLE

TOPICS

LIVING TOGETHER
PARENTING
UNMARRIED COUPLES' PROPERTY RIGHTS
WAYS TO OWN PROPERTY
INHERITANCE
SEX BETWEEN UNMARRIED PARTNERS
INTERFERENCE WITH THE COUPLE'S RELATIONSHIP
UNWED PARENTS

LIVING TOGETHER

Cohabitation generally refers to a man and a woman living together in an intimate sexual relationship without marrying. Occasionally, the term is used to describe gay or lesbian couples who live together.

In a few states, cohabitation (in this context, living intimately with a person of the *opposite* sex) brings about a termination of alimony, if the paying spouse can show that the recipient spouse and new lover live together, share expenses and are generally recognized as a couple. In other states, an alimony recipient who begins cohabiting is automatically presumed to need less alimony than originally awarded. If the recipient objects, it is her burden to show that her needs have not decreased.

Also, in some states, a parent who cohabits may have difficulty obtaining custody of her children. Cohabitation is still a crime in some places, though rarely is anyone prosecuted for it. Some people describe a cohabiting couple's relationship as a meretricious relationship.

Only two states, Illinois (*Hewitt v. Hewitt*, 394 N.E.2d 1204 (1979)) and Georgia (*Rehak v. Mathis*, 238 S.E.2d 81 (1977)), have expressly failed to recognize cohabitation agreements.

RIGHTS OF UNMARRIED PEOPLE

Extended Family

An extended family is one which includes persons in addition to or other than parents and children. Extended family can also mean a circle of people in a close relationship. For example, for many lesbians, gay men and other non-married people, the term extended family refers to a small, close group of friends who provide support for one another in much the same way a traditional family supports its members.

POSSLQ (Persons of the Opposite Sex Sharing Living Quarters)

POSSLQ is a U.S. Census Bureau phrase coined to describe members of the opposite sex who live together without getting married.

Domestic Partner

This phrase is used to describe two people (either of the opposite sex or of the same sex) who cohabit, have a sexual relationship and experience economic and social integration—that is, two people who have created their own family.

Same-Sex Marriage

Currently, all states restrict marriages to the union of one man and one woman. Same-sex couples, therefore, cannot marry. (This may change, however—an important case is working its way through the Hawaii court system.) Denying lesbian and gay couples the right to marry means they cannot obtain the legal and economic benefits of marriage, such as:

- filing joint income tax returns
- claiming dependency benefits, such as leave to care for a sick or disabled spouse, as well as Social Security and death benefits
- inheriting from each other under state automatic inheritance laws (although they may leave each other property in their wills), and
- obtaining family rates for insurance, mortgage, loans and credit.

Same-sex couples are also denied the emotional and psychological benefits of marriage. To compensate, many lesbian and gay couples enter into cohabitation agreements, purchase property together, name each other as beneficiaries in wills and insurance policies, and participate in "union" ceremonies.

Only Scandinavian countries let lesbians and gay men have legally sanctioned relationships. Denmark and Norway permit same-sex couples to form a registered partnership, with full inheritance rights and the same duty to support each other that married heterosexual couples have. They must also divorce to end the relationship. Sweden gives gay and lesbian couples the same common law rights as unmarried heterosexual couples. France has a nationwide domestic partners law.

PARENTING

Co-Parent

An adult who is not legally responsible for the care, support and custody of a child, but who has assumed the care, support and custody of a child together with the child's legally responsible parent, is sometimes called a co-parent.

Stepparents who have not adopted their stepchildren are co-parents; however, the term is rarely used for stepparents. It is more commonly used by unmarried couples jointly raising a child for whom only one of them is legally responsible. Because same-sex couples cannot biologically parent one child, cannot marry (and become stepparents) and virtually all have been denied the right to jointly adopt (usually one person adopts and together they raise the child), co-parenting has become an important concept in the lesbian and gay community.

Second-Parent Adoption

A second-parent adoption (also called a co-parent adoption) is an adoption of a child by the unmarried partner of the child's legal parent. Second-parent adoptions have been granted to lesbians and gay men who are the partners of the biological parents.

Two-Parent Adoption

A two-parent adoption is an adoption of a child by an unmarried couple. Like second-parent adoptions, a number of two-parent adoptions have been granted to lesbian and gay couples.

States that have granted second-parent or two-parent adoptions to lesbian or gay couples include Alaska, California, Illinois, Indiana, Massachusetts, Michigan, Minnesota, New Jersey, New York, Oregon, Pennsylvania, Texas, Vermont and Washington. They've also been granted in Washington, DC.

Gay or Lesbian Parents: Rights to Custody

If a divorced or separated parent is gay or lesbian, many courts deny or strictly limit the parent's custody of or visitation with her children. In addition, some courts, when the parent's sexual orientation becomes known, modify existing custody and visitation orders. In a few states, however, a parent's sexual orientation cannot in and of itself prevent a parent from being given custody of her child. As a practical matter, however, lesbian and gay parents in those states may still be denied custody. This is because judges, when considering the best interests of the child, may be motivated by their own prejudices as well as by the prejudices of the community and may find reasons other than the parent's sexual orientation to deny the lesbian or gay parent custody.

UNMARRIED COUPLES' PROPERTY RIGHTS

Property Agreements

A property or cohabitation agreement is a contract entered into by an unmarried couple (heterosexual, lesbian or gay) living together to arrange property rights. Sometimes, the agreements also spell out custody, child support and alimony-like support arrangements in the event the couple breaks up or one partner dies.

Until 1976, courts generally did not enforce cohabitation agreements because they reasoned that the underlying sexual relationship formed the basis of the contractual relationship and that the agreement therefore improperly arranged an exchange of sex for money (that is, prostitution). In 1976, however, the California Supreme Court ruled in *Marvin v. Marvin* (18 Cal.3d 660) that cohabiting couples in California could contract.

MARVIN V. MARVIN

The decision said that unmarried couples may make enforceable contracts with each other regarding property and alimony-like support, and that where there is no explicit contract but the actions of the parties make it appear as though there is an understanding, the court may imply a contract to exist and enforce it. The decision does not give cohabiting couples the property rights of married people, but rather allows them to have their contracts and understandings enforced in court. There is no minimum number of years that a cohabiting couple must live together in order to obtain these rights. The *Marvin* case has been extended to same-sex couples. (*Whorton v. Dillingham*, 202 Cal. App. 3d 447 (1988).) The result is that adults who live together and engage in sexual relations are legally able to form contracts regarding their earnings and property rights.

Example: Let's look at the *Marvin* case itself. Michelle Triola (who called herself Michelle Marvin) lived with actor Lee Marvin for a number of years. She claimed that she gave up her own career in exchange for becoming Lee Marvin's homemaker and an agreement that she would be entitled to half his income. When the couple separated, Michelle sued Lee for a lot of money. No written contract was produced, but Michelle insisted that an oral agreement had been made. The California Supreme Court allowed her to proceed on the basis of the oral contract and on the implied contract theory. In the end, a jury awarded Michelle nothing because she was unable to prove the contract or that her worth as a homemaker was worth the money she claimed.

Marvin in toto is followed by only a few states. Most states follow the express written and oral contract theories, but many have rejected the implied contract theory. Also, no court will apply the *Marvin* principle when the sole "services" provided by a person are sexual in nature. In fact, even in states which follow *Marvin*, courts do not recognize a contract which contains any mention of sex. Other states that have enforced cohabitation agreements include:

- Alaska—*Levar v. Elkins*, 604 P.2d 602 (1980)
- Arizona—*Carroll v. Lee*, 148 Ariz. 10, 712 P.2d 923 (1986), *Cook v. Cook*, 142 Ariz. 573, 691 P.2d 664 (1984)
- Connecticut—*Boland v. Catalano*, 202 Conn. 333, 521 A.2d 142 (1987)
- Florida—*Poe v. Estate of Levy*, 411 So. 2d 253 (1982)
- Hawaii—*Maria v. Frietas*, 832 P.2d 259 (1992)
- Indiana—*Glasgo v. Glasgo*, 410 N.E.2d 1325 (1980)
- Iowa—*Slorum v. Hammond*, 346 N.W.2d 485 (1984)
- Maryland—*Donovan v. Seuderi*, 51 Md.App. 217, 443 A.2d 121 (1982)
- Massachusetts—*Green v. Richmond*, 369 Mass. 47, 337 N.E.2d 691 (1975)

- Michigan—*Carnes v. Sheldon*, 109 Mich. App. 204, 311 N.W.2d 747 (1981), *Tyranski v. Piggins*, 44 Mich. App. 570, 205 N.W.2d 595 (1973)
- Mississippi—*Pickens v. Pickens*, 490 So. 2d 872 (1986)
- Nebraska—*Kinkenon v. Hue*, 207 Neb. 698, 301 N.W.2d 77 (1981)
- Nevada—*Hay v. Hay*, 100 Nev. 196, 678 P.2d 672 (1984), *Warren v. Warren*, 94 Nev. 309, 579 P.2d 772 (1978)
- New Hampshire—*Joan S. v. John S.*, 121 N.H. 96, 427 A.2d 498 (1981), *Tapley v. Tapley*, 122 N.H. 727, 449 A.2d 1218 (1982)
- New Jersey—*Crowe v. DeGioia*, 90 N.J. 126, 447 A.2d 173, *appeal after remand*, 303 N.J. Super. 22, 495 A.D.2d 889, *aff'd*, 102 N.J. 50, 505 A.D.2d 591 (1986)
- New Mexico—*Dominguez v. Cruz*, 95 N.M. 1, 617 P.2d 1322 (1980)
- New York—*Morone v. Morone*, 50 N.Y.2d 481, 429 N.Y.S.2d 592, 407 N.E.2d 438 (1980)
- North Carolina—*Suggs v. Norris*, 88 N.C. App. 539, 364 S.E.2d 159, *cert. denied*, 322 N.C. 486, 370 S.E.2d 236 (1988)
- Oregon—*Beal v. Beal*, 282 Or. 115, 577 P.2d 507 (1978), *Ireland v. Flanagan*, 51 Or. App. 837, 627 P.2d 496 (1981)
- Pennsylvania—*Mullen v. Suchko*, 279 Pa. Super. 499, 421 A.2d 310 (1980)
- Texas—*Small v. Harper*, 638 S.W.2d 24 (1982)
- Washington—*In re Estate of Thornton*, 81 Wash.2d 72, 499 P.2d 864 (1972)
- Wisconsin—*Watts v. Watts*, 137 Wis.2d 506, 405 N.W.2d 303 (1987), *Matter of Estate of Steffes*, 95 Wis.2d 490, 290 N.W.2d 697 (1980)
- Wyoming—*Kinnison v. Kinnison*, 627 P.2d 594 (1981)

Example 1: Rose and Ted have lived together for four years. They've never had any written agreement, but their behavior has been consistent: they've purchased a car, an oak table and a china set, with each one paying half. If they split up, a court is likely to imply an agreement and equally divide the items purchased together.

Example 2: Jon and Steve plan to buy a fixer-upper house and move in together. Jon is a carpenter; Steve is a university professor who makes nearly twice as much as Jon. Jon and Steve plan to own their home equally, so they agree in writing as follows: Steve will pay two-thirds of the mortgage, and Jon will pay one-third. Steve and Jon will equally pay for the materials to fix up the house, and Jon will contribute all the labor. Steve and Jon also agree to equally own all the property, furniture and fixtures they buy once they move in together.

Palimony

Palimony isn't a legal term; it was coined by journalists to describe the division of property or alimony-like support given by one member of an unmarried couple to the other after they break up.

Trusts: Resulting and Constructive

A trust is a right in property held by one party for the benefit of another. When there is no official trust instrument, a trust may still be found under certain circumstances in order to enforce agreements as to property and income of domestic partners:

- Resulting Trust: If the transaction indicates a trust was intended by the parties, it is called a resulting trust.
- Constructive Trust: When no such intent can be found, but the one holding the property would benefit unjustly, especially where there is a close relationship

between the parties or there is a difference in financial sophistication, then a constructive trust is said to occur.

Uniform Pre-Marital Agreement Act

This act has been adopted in 20 states (Arizona, Arkansas, California, Hawaii, Illinois, Iowa, Kansas, Maine, Montana, Nebraska, Nevada, New Jersey, North Carolina, North Dakota, Oregon, Rhode Island, South Dakota, Texas, Utah and Virginia). It provides legal guidelines for unmarried couples who wish to make agreements in anticipation of marriage regarding ownership, management and control of property; property disposition on separation, divorce and death; alimony; wills and life insurance beneficiaries. The statute expressly prohibits couples from including provisions concerning child support. Pre-marital agreements are permitted in states that haven't adopted this uniform statute, but are subject to different guidelines in those states.

WAYS TO OWN PROPERTY

Joint Tenancy

Joint tenancy is a method by which people jointly hold title to property. All joint tenants own equal interests in the jointly owned property. When two or more persons expressly own property as joint tenants, and one owner dies, the remaining owner(s) automatically take over the share of the deceased person. This is termed the right of survivorship. For example, if two people own their house as joint tenants and one of them dies, the other person ends up owning the entire house, even if the deceased person attempted to give away her half of the house in her will.

In most states, one joint tenant may, on her own, end a joint tenancy by signing a new deed changing the way title is held; then, she is free to leave her portion of the property through her will. Because joint tenancy property isn't passed through a will and thus doesn't go through probate, joint tenancy is a popular technique to avoid the costs and delay often associated with the probate process.

Tenancy in Common

Tenancy in common is a way for any two or more people to hold title to property together. Each co-owner has an undivided interest in the property, which means that no owner holds a particular part of the property and all co-owners have the right to use all the property. Each owner is free to sell or give away his interest. On his death, his interest passes through his will or living trust, or by intestate succession if he had no will or living trust.

Tenancy in common differs from joint tenancy, where property passes automatically to the surviving co-owners at any one owner's death, regardless of any will provision. Tenancy in common is a more appropriate form of title than joint tenancy when co-owners do not have a close personal relationship, such as when individuals are all willed a home and find themselves joint owners.

INHERITANCE

Intestate succession is the method prescribed by a state to distribute a person's property when he has not provided for its distribution in a will. Although the details of these laws vary from state to state, the normal scheme is to distribute the deceased person's property to his spouse and children. When an unmarried partner dies, this means that unless she created a will or other estate planning document, her property will be divided among her parents, siblings, aunts and uncles, nieces and nephews and then more distant relatives. Her partner will receive nothing.

Wills

A will is a legal document in which a person (called the testator) states various intentions about what he wants done with his debts, property and minor children after his death. Will provisions must be carried out unless they are illegal or impossible. A will allows a person to:

- name beneficiaries (people or organizations) to receive the testator's real property and personal property
- forgive debts owed to the testator
- name a guardian of the testator's children in the event there is no other biological or adoptive parent to care for the children
- create trusts in which property can be put and managed by a trustee until the person who is left the property reaches a certain age or dies
- name an executor of the will—that is, the person who will manage the testator's property, deal with the probate court, collect the testator's assets and distribute them as identified in the will after the testator dies; and
- disinherit relatives by specifically excluding them, not naming them in the will or leaving them very little, such as $1.

Trusts

A trust is a right in property held by one party for the benefit of another. Trusts are entered into for many reasons, including maintaining control over assets, avoiding probate and avoiding inheritance taxes.

There are two basic types of trusts:

- *Testamentary.* This trust is created by a will or living trust and takes effect only at death. It does not have tax advantages, but allows the beneficiary to use the property during her lifetime; the remaining principal goes to a second person after the beneficiary's death.
- *Living (also called inter-vivos trusts).* The trust creator establishes this trust during his lifetime; the trust continues after his death. It is used to avoid probate. There are two kinds of living trusts:
  - Revocable. The terms, conditions or even beneficiaries of a revocable trust can be altered or revoked. It is managed by a trustee and income is paid to the creator of the trust during his lifetime. At death, the principal is paid to the beneficiaries. The advantage of creating this type of trust is avoiding probate. The property is still considered part of the trust creator's estate, however, so the estate will have to pay inheritance tax.
  - Irrevocable. Once this type of trust is set up, it cannot be revoked or altered. The advantage of forming this type of trust is that the trust creator pays no taxes on the trust income he receives during his life. At his death, the trust property passes to the beneficiaries, but because the property is not considered part of the trust creator's estate, the estate pays no inheritance tax.

SEX BETWEEN UNMARRIED PARTNERS

Fornication

Fornication means sexual intercourse between unmarried persons. In some states, if one person is married, it is still fornication; other states call sexual intercourse between an unmarried person and a married person adultery. Other states, when referring to sexual intercourse between an unmarried person and a married person, call the unmarried person a fornicator and the married person an adulterer. Fornication is illegal in many states. If a state prohibits fornication, a court may refuse to uphold a cohabitation agreement on the grounds that because the relationship covered by the agreement is illegal, the agreement is unenforceable.

Meretricious Relationship

Some courts, especially those in states where fornication is illegal, describe a cohabitation relationship as meretricious, meaning "of an unlawful sexual nature."

Sodomy

Sodomy generally refers to any "unnatural" sexual intercourse. It usually means anal and oral sex. Consensual sodomy is a crime in just less than half the states; most of these laws are interpreted as prohibiting homosexual sex. The U.S. Supreme Court upheld the constitutionality of state laws prohibiting homosexual sodomy in *Bowers v. Hardwick*, 478 U.S. 186 (1986).

Sodomy laws are often used to justify various forms of discrimination against lesbians and gay men, including the denial of child custody and the refusal to recognize cohabitation agreements. The rationales used by the courts include:

- people who are criminals (that is, engage in the crime of sodomy) should not be allowed custody, and
- if a state prohibits sodomy, the relationship covered by the agreement is illegal and therefore the agreement is unenforceable.

INTERFERENCE WITH THE COUPLE'S RELATIONSHIP

Loss of Consortium

Consortium is the relationship between a husband and wife, which includes love, affection, fellowship and sexual companionship. If a third party interferes with that relationship (for example, a neck injury disables the husband from having sexual intercourse), the spouse who loses elements of consortium can sue the third party on that ground. Although cohabiting and same-sex couples have argued that loss of consortium statutes should apply to their relationships as well, no states have applied the law to them.

Wrongful Death

A wrongful death action is a lawsuit brought by a survivor (someone who outlives another) of a deceased person. In such a lawsuit, the survivor claims that the deceased was killed due to the wrongful act of a third person (the defendant). Only a person who had a certain relationship with the deceased person (a parent, child or spouse usually) may sue for wrongful death. In nearly all states, cohabiting and same-sex couples are not allowed to sue for wrongful death.

UNWED PARENTS

Unwed Father

An unmarried man who impregnates a woman is referred to as an unwed father. Unwed fathers have few rights concerning their children. For example, an unwed father does not have the right to require the mother of the child to obtain his consent, or even notify him, before she undergoes an abortion. If the mother decides to bear and keep the child, however, the unwed father will be required to pay child support if a court determines or he acknowledges that he's the father; in addition, he may seek custody or visitation.

If the mother of the child decides to place the child up for adoption, or if she has married and her husband (that is, the child's stepparent) wants to adopt, the court must terminate the parental rights of the unwed father before granting the adoption. The unwed father may oppose the termination of his rights and the adoption. Whether his opposition will succeed depends on his relationship with the child. If he lived with the mother and helped raise the child, he has a greater chance of succeeding than if he neither visited nor supported the child. If the child to be adopted is a newborn (and thus the unwed father has had no opportunity to create a relationship with the child), 20 states allow the father to prevent the adoption and obtain custody. In some of the remaining states, the father has no right to prevent the adoption; other states decide the question case-by-case.

Unwed Mother

An unmarried woman who becomes pregnant is often referred to as an unwed mother. Unwed mothers have virtually all the same rights as do married women who become pregnant—they cannot be denied the right to have an abortion; they cannot be required to obtain the father's consent before having an abortion and they may raise the child or place the child up for adoption. An unwed mother who is under the age of consent, however, may be required to notify, or obtain the consent of, her parents or a court before having an abortion.

APPENDIX

Table 2.1

FACTORS IN SETTING AND TERMINATING ALIMONY

In 28 states and the District of Columbia, a spouse guilty of fault (such as adultery, mental cruelty or desertion) may either be barred from receiving or receive less than her full share of alimony. Ironically, some of these states are states that have done away with fault as a basis for the divorce! In addition, some states reduce or terminate alimony if the recipient cohabits. Iowa, Kansas, Maine, Nebraska and Vermont are silent on the issue of fault considerations and alimony. (For a discussion on fault as a basis of divorce, see "Grounds for Divorce" in the Divorce chapter.)

Fault has no bearing on alimony		Fault may bar or limit alimony		Cohabitation may end or reduce alimony	
STATE	CODE SECTION	STATE	CODE SECTION	STATE	CODE SECTION
Alaska	25.24.160(3)	Alabama	30-20-52	Alabama	30-2-55
California	Fam. 2600	Arizona[1]	25-319	California	Fam. 4323
Colorado	14-10-114	Arkansas	9-12-312	Georgia	30-220
Delaware	T. 13, 1512(c[a]	Connecticut	466-82	Illinois	Ch. 40, 504
Illinois	Ch. 40, 504	Florida	61.08(1)	Louisiana	Art. 112
Indiana	31-1-11.5-11	Georgia	30-217	New York	DRL 248
Kentucky	403.200	Hawaii	580-47	Oklahoma	43-134
Massachusetts[2]	Ch. 208-1A	Idaho	32-705	Pennsylvania	23-3706
Minnesota	518.552	Louisiana	Art. 112	Tennessee	36-5-19
Montana	40-4-203	Maryland	FL 11-106	Utah	30-3-5
New Jersey[2]	2A:34-23	Michigan	25.103		
Ohio	3105.18	Mississippi	93-5-23		
Oklahoma	43-121	Missouri	452.335		
Oregon	107.036	Nevada	125.150		
Washington	26.09.090	New Hampshire	458:19		

(continued on next page)

Table 2.1 (continued)

FACTORS IN SETTING AND TERMINATING ALIMONY

Fault has no bearing on alimony		Fault may bar or limit alimony		Cohabitation may end or reduce alimony	
STATE	CODE SECTION	STATE	CODE SECTION	STATE	CODE SECTION
Washington, DC[1]	16-913	New Mexico	40-4-7		
Wisconsin	767.26	New York	DRL 236(B)(6)		
		North Carolina	50-16.6		
		North Dakota	14-05-24		
		Pennsylvania	23-3701		
		Rhode Island	15-5-16		
		South Carolina	20-3-130		
		South Dakota	25-4-41		
		Tennessee	36-5-101		
		Utah	30-3-5		
		Virginia	20-107.1		
		West Virginia	48.2-15.1		
		Wyoming	20-2-114		

[1] Economic misconduct—such as concealing assets from your spouse—may affect alimony award.

[2] If divorce is based on no-fault grounds.

Table 5.1

Permitted

Alabama	*Yates v. Yates*, 607 S.E.2d 207 (1991)
Alaska	25.20.060
Arizona	25-332
Colorado	14-10-123.5
Delaware	13-727
Georgia	19-9-3
Hawaii	571-46.1
Illinois	750 ¶ 5/602.1
Indiana	31-1-11.5-21
Kentucky	403.270
Maine	19-752
Maryland	Family Law 5-203
Massachusetts	208:31
Michigan	25.3126(a)
Nebraska	42-364
New York	*Guarnier v. Guarnier*, 547 N.Y.S.2d 455 (1989)
North Carolina	50-13.2
Ohio	3109.041
Oklahoma	43-109
Pennsylvania	23-5304
Rhode Island	*Cok v. Cok*, 479 A.2d 1184 (1984)
South Carolina	20-3-160
South Dakota	25-5-7.1
Tennessee	36-6-101
Texas	Family Code 14.01
Utah	30-3-10.2
Vermont	15-665
Virginia	20-124.2
Washington	26.09.184
West Virginia	*Lewis v. Lewis*, 433 S.E.2d 536 (1993)
Wisconsin	767.24
Wyoming	20-2-113

Preferred

California	if parents agree; otherwise permitted—Family Code 3080, 3081
Connecticut	46b-56a
Florida	61-13
Idaho	32-717B
Iowa	598.41
Kansas	60-1610
Louisiana	9:335
Minnesota	when a parent requests; otherwise permitted—518.17
Mississippi	if parents agree; otherwise permitted—93-5-24
Missouri	452.375
Montana	40-4-222
Nevada	125.480
New Hampshire	458:17
New Jersey	9:2-4
New Mexico	40-4-9.1
Oregon	107.105

Law Silent

Arkansas	9-13-101
North Dakota	14-05-22
Washington, DC	16-911

Table 5.2

MEDIATION OF CUSTODY AND VISITATION DISPUTES

Required

California	Family Code 3170
Delaware	Family Court Rule 16(b)(1)
Florida	(in circuits with family mediation programs) 44.102(2)(b)
Idaho	Rules of Civil Procedure 16(j)
Maine	19-752
Maryland	Rule S73A
Nevada	(if county has mediation program) 3.500
New Jersey	1:40-5, Court Rule 1
New Mexico	40-4-9.1
North Carolina	50-13.1
Oregon	107.755 through 107.795
South Dakota	25-4-56
Utah	(in districts with pilot mediation programs) 30-3-21
Virginia	20-124.4
West Virginia	(in counties with pilot mediation programs) 48A-5-7a
Wisconsin	767.11

Permitted

Alabama	Rule of Civil Procedure 16(6), Civil Court Mediation Rule 1-15
Alaska	25.20.080, Rule of Civil Procedure 100
Arizona	25-332, 12-134
Colorado	14-10-123.5(4) (custody), 14-10-129.5(1)(c) (visitation)
Connecticut	46b-53a
Florida	(in circuits without family mediation programs) 61.183
Georgia	ADR Rule I
Illinois	750 ¶ 5/602.1
Indiana	31-1-11.5-19
Iowa	598.41, 679.1 through 679.14
Kansas	23-601 through 23-607
Kentucky	403.170
Louisiana	9:332
Maine	19-665
Massachusetts	Probate Court Order 1-88
Michigan	552.505, 552.513, Special Proceedings & Actions Rule 3.210(C)
Minnesota	518.167, 518.003
Missouri	487.100, Supreme Court Rule 88.01
Montana	40-4-301
Nebraska	25-2911, 43-2904
New Hampshire	(parties may volunteer; court cannot order) 458:15-a
North Dakota	14-09.1-01
Ohio	3109.052
Oklahoma	12-1801, ADR Rule 12-7(D)(4)
Pennsylvania	Rule of Court 1915.15
Rhode Island	15-5-29
South Carolina	20-7-420
Tennessee	36-4-130
Texas	Civil Practice & Remedies 152-11-001
Vermont	15-666(b)
Washington	5.60.070, 7.75.020, 26.09.015, 26.09.184
Wyoming	1-43-101 through 1-43-104

Table 5.3

DEFENSES TO CUSTODIAL INTERFERENCE

State	Code Section	Taker has or seeks legal custody	Guardian (or child over certain age consented)	Protecting child or self from bodily harm	Reported to police or parent; returned promptly	Type of Crime
Alabama	13A-45	•				Felony
Alaska[1]	11-31-330	•				Both[2]
Arizona	13-1302	•			•[3]	Felony
Arkansas	5-26-502	•[3]				Both[2]
California	Penal 278		• (child over 14)	•	•	Felony
Colorado	18-3-304			•		Felony
Connecticut[1]	53a-97					
	53a-98	•				Both[2]
Delaware	11-785	•				Both[2]
Florida	787.03	•	• (child over 12)	•		Felony
Georgia[4]	16-5-45	•				Both[2]
Hawaii[5]	707-726	•				Both[2]
Idaho	18-4506	•	• (child over 12)	•		Both[2]
Illinois	720 ¶5/10-5	•		•		Felony
Indiana[5]	35-42-3-4				•	Both[2]
Iowa[1,6]	710.6				•	Both
Kansas[6]	21-3422	•			•[3]	Both[2]

(continued on next page)

Table 5.3 (continued)

DEFENSES TO CUSTODIAL INTERFERENCE

State	Code Section	Taker has or seeks legal custody	Guardian (or child over certain age consented)	Protecting child or self from bodily harm	Reported to police or parent; returned promptly	Type of Crime
Kentucky	509.070	•				Felony
Louisiana[1]	14:45-1	•				Misdemeanor
Maine[1]						Not a crime
Maryland[1]	FL 9-301	•		•		Both[2]
Massachusetts[1]	265:26A			•		Both[2]
Michigan[1]	28.582			•		Felony
Minnesota	609.26	•[7]	• (child over 12)	•	•	Felony
Mississippi[1, 8]	97-3-51	•				Felony
Missouri	565.149-565.169			•	•	Both[2]
Montana	45-5-304				•	Both[2]
Nebraska	28-316	•[3]			•	Both
Nevada	200.359	•	• (child over 12)	•		Felony
New Hampshire	633:4	•		•		Felony
New Jersey	2C:13-4	•	• (child over 12)	•	•	Both[2]
New Mexico	30-4-4	•		•	•	Felony

(continued on next p

Table 5.3 (continued)

DEFENSES TO CUSTODIAL INTERFERENCE

State	Code Section	Taker has or seeks legal custody	Guardian (or child over certain age consented)	Protecting child or self from bodily harm	Reported to police or parent; returned promptly	Type of Crime
New York[1]	Penal 135.45	•				Both
	135.50					Both
North Carolina[1]	14-41			•		Felony
North Dakota[1]	14-14-22.1		• (child over 12)		•	
Ohio	2919.23			•	•	Misdemeanor
Oklahoma					•	Not a crime
Oregon	163.245	•				Felony
	163.257	•			•[3]	Both
Pennsylvania[1]	18-2904	•	• (child over 12)	•	•	Felony
Rhode Island	11-26-1.1	•		•	•[3]	Both
	11-26-1.2	•	• (child over 12)			Felony
South Carolina[1]	16-17-495	•			•	Both
South Dakota[1]	22-19-7	•			•[3]	
Tennessee[1]	22-19-10	•	• (child over 12)[9]			Both
	39-13-306	•			•[3]	Both
Texas	Penal 25.03	•			•	Felony

(continued on next page)

Table 5.3 (continued)

DEFENSES TO CUSTODIAL INTERFERENCE

State	Code Section	Taker has or seeks legal custody	Guardian (or child over certain age consented)	Protecting child or self from bodily harm	Reported to police or parent; returned promptly	Type of Crime
Utah[1]	76-5-303			•		Both
Vermont[1]	13-2451	•		•[8]		Felony
Virginia[1]	18.2-49.1	•				Both
Washington[1]	9A.40.060		•(child over 15)	•		Both
	9A.40.070	•		•	•	Felony
West Virginia	61-2-14d	•		•	•	Felony
Wisconsin	948.31		•(child over 12)	•		Misdemeanor
Wyoming	6-2-204		•(child over 12)	•		Both
Washington, DC[1]	16-1023	•			•[3]	Both[2]

[1] Applies only to parents and relatives.
[2] Usually a misdemeanor; felony if the child is taken out of state or it's the second offense.
[3] Reduces the penalty, but is not an absolute defense.
[4] Includes harboring a runaway.
[5] Harsher penalties for younger children.
[6] Lighter penalties for a parent.
[7] Action dismissed if taker is involved in custody action and child is kept within state.
[8] A crime only if child is removed from the state.
[9] No crime if legal custodian does not report taking within 90 days.

Table 6.1

GROUNDS FOR DIVORCE

In twelve states, the only grounds for divorce are irreconcilable differences, incompatibility, irretrievable breakdown or irremediable breakdown (called pure no-fault grounds). In the District of Columbia, the only grounds is separation. Five states have a pure no-fault grounds and separation. Thirteen states have retained the traditional fault grounds (such as adultery) and added a pure no-fault grounds. Nine states have retained the traditional fault grounds and added separation. Eleven states have retained the traditional fault grounds and added a pure no-fault grounds and separation.

State	Fault grounds	No-fault grounds	Separation	Length of separation
Alabama	•	•	•	2 years
Alaska	•			
Arizona		•		
Arkansas	•		•	3 years
California		•		
Colorado		•		
Connecticut	•	•	•[1]	18 months
Delaware	•	•		
Florida		•		
Georgia	•	•		
Hawaii		•	•	2 years
Idaho	•	•	•	5 years
Illinois	•	•[2]	•[2]	2 years
Indiana	•	•		
Iowa		•		
Kansas	•	•		
Kentucky		•		
Louisiana	•		•	6 months
Maine	•	•		
Maryland	•		•	1–2 years
Massachusetts	•	•		
Michigan		•		
Minnesota		•	•	180 days
Mississippi	•	•		
Missouri	•	•		
Montana		•	•	180 days
Nebraska		•		
Nevada		•	•	1 year
New Hampshire	•	•		
New Jersey	•		•	18 months
New Mexico	•	•		
New York	•		•	1 year
North Carolina	•		•	1 year
North Dakota	•	•		
Ohio	•	•	•	1 year
Oklahoma		•		
Oregon		•		

(continued on next page)

Table 6.1 (continued)

GROUNDS FOR DIVORCE

State	Fault grounds	No-fault grounds	Separation	Length of separation
Pennsylvania	•	•	•	2 years
Rhode Island	•	•	•	3 years
South Carolina	•		•	1 year
South Dakota	•	•		
Tennessee	•	•	•[3]	3 years
Texas	•	•	•	3 years
Utah	•	•	•	3 years
Vermont	•		•	6 months
Virginia	•		•[4]	1 year
Washington		•		
West Virginia	•	•	•	1 year
Wisconsin		•		
Wyoming	•	•		
Washington, DC			•	6 months

[1] Separation-based divorce must also allege incompatibility.

[2] Must allege irretrievable breakdown and separation for no-fault; if both parties consent, two years may be reduced to six months.

[3] Separation-based divorce allowed only if there are no children.

[4] May be reduced to six months if there are no children.

167

Table 6.2

DURATIONAL RESIDENCY REQUIREMENTS FOR DIVORCE

The durational residency requirement is the length of time the plaintiff must live in a state before filing for divorce.

None	6 Weeks	60 Days	90 Days	6 Months or 180 Days	12 Months or 1 Year
Alaska	Idaho	Arkansas	Arizona	Alabama	Iowa
South Dakota	Nevada	Kansas	Colorado	California	Louisiana
Washington		Wyoming	Connecticut	Delaware	Maryland
			Illinois	Florida	Massachusetts
			Missouri	Georgia	Nebraska
			Montana	Hawaii	New Hampshire
			Utah	Indiana	New Jersey
				Kentucky	New York
				Maine	Rhode Island
				Michigan	South Carolina
				Minnesota	West Virginia
				Mississippi	
				New Mexico	
				North Carolina	
				North Dakota	
				Ohio	
				Oklahoma	
				Oregon	
				Pennsylvania	
				Tennessee	
				Texas	
				Vermont	
				Virginia	
				Wisconsin	
				Washington, DC	

Table 8.1

WHO IS YOUR KIN?

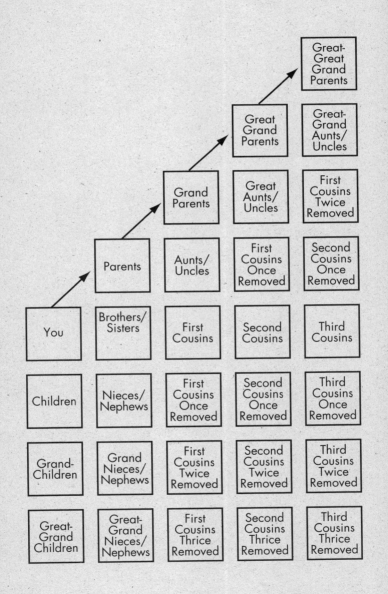

You	Brothers/Sisters	First Cousins	Second Cousins	Third Cousins
	Parents	Aunts/Uncles	First Cousins Once Removed	Second Cousins Once Removed
		Grand Parents	Great Aunts/Uncles	First Cousins Twice Removed
			Great Grand Parents	Great-Grand Aunts/Uncles
				Great-Great Grand Parents

Children	Nieces/Nephews	First Cousins Once Removed	Second Cousins Once Removed	Third Cousins Once Removed
Grand-Children	Grand Nieces/Nephews	First Cousins Twice Removed	Second Cousins Twice Removed	Third Cousins Twice Removed
Great-Grand Children	Great-Grand Nieces/Nephews	First Cousins Thrice Removed	Second Cousins Thrice Removed	Third Cousins Thrice Removed

Table 8.2

INCEST AND MARITAL PROHIBITIONS

All states prohibit a person from marrying her/his sibling, half-sibling, parent, grandparent, great-grandparent, child, grandchild, great-grandchild, aunt, uncle, niece and nephew. Additional prohibitions are listed below.

State	None	First cousin	Stepchild or stepparent	Parent-in-law or child-in-law	Spouse's grandchild or grandparent, or grandparent or grandchild's spouse
Alabama			•[1]	•	•
Alaska	•				
Arizona		•			
Arkansas		•			
California	•				
Colorado	•				
Connecticut			•	•	•
Delaware		•			
Florida	•				
Georgia	•				
Hawaii		•			
Idaho		•[2]	•	•	•
Illinois		•[3]			
Indiana		•			
Iowa		•			
Kansas		•			
Kentucky		•[4]			
Louisiana		•			

(continued on next page)

Table 8.2 (continued)

INCEST AND MARITAL PROHIBITIONS

State	None	First cousin	Stepchild or stepparent	Parent-in-law or child-in-law	Spouse's grandchild or grandparent, or grandparent's spouse or grandchild's spouse
Maine	•				
Maryland			•	•	•
Massachusetts			•⁵	•	•
Michigan		•	•	•	•
Minnesota		•	•	•	•
Mississippi		•			
Missouri		•			
Montana		•			
Nebraska		•			
Nevada		•		•	
New Hampshire		•	•		
New Jersey	•				
New Mexico	•				
New York	•				
North Carolina		•			
North Dakota		•			
Ohio		•			
Oklahoma		•	•		
Oregon		•	•		
Pennsylvania		•			•

(continued on next page)

171

Table 8.2 (continued)

INCEST AND MARITAL PROHIBITIONS

State	None	First cousin	Stepchild or stepparent	Parent-in-law or child-in-law	Spouse's grandchild or grandparent, or grandparent's spouse
Rhode Island			•	•	•
South Carolina			•	•	•
South Dakota		•	•		
Tennessee			•		•
Texas			•		•
Utah		•			
Vermont			•		
Virginia	•				
Washington		•[6]	•	•	•
West Virginia		•[7]			
Wisconsin		•			
Wyoming		•			
Washington, DC					•

[1] Only while the marriage creating the relationship exists.
[2] First cousins may marry if both are over 50 or either is sterile.
[3] First cousins may marry if both are over 65.
[4] Includes first cousin once removed.
[5] Includes step-grandparent and step-grandchild.
[6] Includes double first cousin.
[7] First cousins may marry if the woman is 55 or older, or either is sterile.

Table 11.1

AGE OF MAJORITY

State	Age	Code Section
Alabama	19	26-1-1
Alaska	18	25.20.010
Arizona	18	1-215
Arkansas	18	9-25-101
California	18	Family Code 6502
Colorado[1]	21	2-4-401[6]
Connecticut	18	1-1d
Delaware	18	1-701
Florida	18	743.07
Georgia	18	39-1-1
Hawaii	18	577
Idaho	18	32-101
Illinois	18	43-131
Indiana	18	34-1-2-5.5
Iowa	18	599.1
Kansas	18	38-101
Kentucky	18	2.015
Louisiana	18	Civil Code 29
Maine	18	tit. 22-2
Maryland	18	art. 1-24
Massachusetts	18	ch. 4-7
Michigan	18	722.51-.55
Minnesota	18	645.451
Mississippi	21	67-3-53
Missouri	18	431.055
Montana	18	41-1-101
Nebraska	19	43-2101
Nevada	18	129.010
New Hampshire	18	ch. 175-6
New Jersey	18	tit. 9, ch. 17B-3
New Mexico	18	28-6-1
New York	18	Dom. Rel. 2
North Carolina	18	48A-1
North Dakota	18	14-10-02
Ohio	18	3109.01
Oklahoma	18	15-13
Oregon	18	109.510
Pennsylvania	21	23-5101
Rhode Island	18	15-12-1
South Carolina	18	20-7-250
South Dakota	18	26-1-1
Tennessee	18	1-3-13
Texas	18	Civil Practice 129.001
Utah	18	15-2-1
Vermont	18	1-173
Virginia	18	1-13.42
Washington	18	26.28.010
West Virginia	21	ch. 36, art. 7-1
Wisconsin	18	990.01[3]
Wyoming	19	14-1-101
Washington, DC	18	30-401

[1] In certain situations, age may be different.

Table 11.2

PARENTAL LIABILITY LAWS

Parental liability laws impose an obligation on parents to pay for damage done by their children. Only Washington, D.C. imposes no obligation. Nearly all states impose liability on parents for property damage caused by their children's malicious or willful (deliberate) acts and many hold parents liable for personal injuries caused by their children's malicious or willful acts. Parental liability ceases in all states when the child reaches 18, except Nebraska (19) and Maine, South Carolina, Vermont and Wyoming (17). Parental liability usually doesn't apply with children under the age of eight, unless the parent was grossly negligent, such as giving the child a loaded gun. Most states limit the extent of damages to about $3,000, although Tennessee ($10,000) and Texas ($15,000) are substantially higher. Only the parent who had custody and control at the time is liable, unless otherwise noted.

State	Code Section	None	All torts	Malicious or willful property damage	Illegal property damage	Malicious or willful personal injury	Illegal personal injury
Alabama	6-5-380			•			
Alaska[1]	34.50.020			•			
Arizona[2]	12-661			•		•	
Arkansas	9-25-102			•			
California	Civil 1714.1			•		•	
Colorado	13-21-107						
	13-21-107.5						
Connecticut[3]	52-572			•		•	
Delaware	10-3922			•		•	
Florida	741.24			•	•	•	
Georgia	105-108			•			
	105-113			•			
Hawaii	577-3		•				

(continued on next page)

Table 11.2 (continued)

PARENTAL LIABILITY LAWS

State	Code Section	None	All torts	Malicious or willful property damage	Illegal property damage	Malicious or willful personal injury	Illegal personal injury
Idaho	6-210			•		•	
Illinois	70-53			•		•	
Indiana[4]	34-4-31-1			•	•	•	•
Iowa[4]	613.16			•			
Kansas	38-120			•		•	
Kentucky	405-025						
Louisiana[3,4]	Civil 237,2318 Civil Procedure 732		•				
Maine	217-19			•		•	
Maryland	27-640			•		•	
Massachusetts	Civil Justice 3-829 231-85G			•	•	•	•
Michigan	600.2913			•		•	•
Minnesota[4]	540.18 332.51		•	•			
Mississippi	93-13-2			•			
Missouri	537.045					•	
Montana	20-5-201 40-6-237 40-6-238			•			

(continued on next page)

175

Table 11.2 (continued)

PARENTAL LIABILITY LAWS

State	Code Section	None	All torts	Malicious or willful property damage	Illegal property damage	Malicious or willful personal injury	Illegal personal injury
Nebraska	43-801			•		•	
Nevada	41.470			•		•	
New Hampshire	169-B:45			•			
New Jersey	2A:53A-14						
	2A:53A-15						
New Mexico	40-1-97			•	•	•	
New York	General Obligations 3-112			•	•	•[5]	
North Carolina	1-538.1			•			
North Dakota	32-03-39			•		•	
Ohio	3101.01			•		•	
Oklahoma	10-20						
	10-15						
	10-25						
	10-26						
	23-10						
Oregon	30.765		•		•		•
Pennsylvania	11-2002			•			
Rhode Island[2]	9-1-3			•		•	
South Carolina[2]	20-7-360			•		•	

(continued on next page)

Table 11.2 (continued)

PARENTAL LIABILITY LAWS

State	Code Section	None	All torts	Malicious or willful property damage	Illegal property damage	Malicious or willful personal injury	Illegal personal injury
South Dakota	25-5-15			•	•		
	26-1-4						
Tennessee	37-10-101			•	•		
	37-10-103			•			
Texas	33.02			•			
Utah[4,5]	78-11-20,21			•		•	
Vermont[3,4]	15-901			•			
Virginia[3]	20-38.1			•			
Washington	26.04.020			•		•	
West Virginia	55-7A-1,2			•	•	•	•
Wisconsin	895.035			•		•	
Wyoming[4]	14-2-203						
Washington, DC		•					

1 Either or both parents liable.
2 Both parents liable.
3 Either parent liable.
4 Parent without legal custody not liable.
5 To a house of worship or the articles inside.

177

Table 12.1

FAULT CONSIDERATIONS IN DISTRIBUTING MARITAL PROPERTY

Although no-fault divorce is available in every state, some states reduce a spouse's share of marital property for marital fault (for example, adultery, mental cruelty or desertion). In addition, some states reduce a spouse's share of the marital property for economic misconduct (such as fraud or concealing assets). In many states, courts may consider all "relevant factors" or other factors "as may appear just and equitable." In these states, it's up to the judge to decide if marital fault or economic misconduct affects the property division.

Marital Fault Irrelevant		Marital Fault May Reduce Share		Economic Misconduct May Reduce Share	
Alaska	25.24.160(4)	Alabama	Case Law	Alaska	25.24.160(4)(E)
Arizona	25-318	Arkansas	9-12-315	Arizona	25-318
California	Family Code 2560	Connecticut	466-81	California	Family Code 2602
Colorado	14-10-113(1)	Florida	61.075	Colorado	Case Law
Delaware	13-1513	Georgia	30-118	Connecticut	46b-81
Idaho	32-712	Hawaii	580-47	Delaware	13-1513(a)(6)
Illinois	40-503	Maryland	FL 8-205(b)(4)	Florida	61.11
Indiana	31-1-11.5-11	Massachusetts	208-334	Georgia	30-118
Iowa	598.21	Michigan	25.103	Idaho	32-712(1)(a)
Kansas	60-16-1610	Mississippi	Case Law	Illinois	40-503(d)(1)
Kentucky	403-190.1	Missouri	452.330(1)	Indiana	31-1-11.5-11(c)
Louisiana	Civ. § 2336	New Hampshire	458.160II(1)	Iowa	598.21(1)(m)
Maine	19-722-A	North Dakota	3A-14-05-24	Kansas	60-1610(b)(1)
Minnesota	518-58(1)	Rhode Island	15-5-16.1(a)	Maine	19-722-A
Montana	40-4-202(1)	South Carolina	20-7-472(2)	Maryland	Family Law 8-205
Nebraska	42-365	Texas	Family 3.63	Minnesota	518.58(1)

(continued on next page)

178

Table 12.1 (continued)

FAULT CONSIDERATIONS IN DISTRIBUTING MARITAL PROPERTY

Marital Fault Irrelevant		Marital Fault May Reduce Share		Economic Misconduct May Reduce Share	
Nevada	125.150	Utah	30-3-3, -5	Montana	40-4-202[1]
New Jersey	2A:34-23.1	Vermont	15-751[b][12]	New Hampshire	458.16-all[f]
New Mexico	40-4-7	Virginia	20-107.3[E][5]	New Jersey	2A:34-23.1[i]
New York	Dom. Relations 2368	Wyoming	20-20-2-114	New York	Dom. Relations 236B(6)[d][11]
North Carolina	50-50-20			North Carolina	50-20(c)[11a]
Ohio	3105.17-18			Ohio	3105.171[E][3]
Oklahoma	43-121			Oklahoma	Case Law
Oregon	2-107.036			Pennsylvania	23-3501
	2-107.105			South Carolina	20-7-472(2)
Pennsylvania	23-401[d]			South Dakota	25-4-45.1
South Dakota	25-4-44			Tennessee	36-4-121[c][5]
	25-4-45.1			Texas	Family Code 3.63
Tennessee	36-4-12[a]			Vermont	15-751[b][11]
Washington	26.09.080			West Virginia	48-2-32(c)[4]
West Virginia	48-2-32(c)			Washington, DC	16-9-910[b]
Wisconsin	767.255				
Washington, DC	16-9-910				

179

Table 13.1

STATE SURROGACY CONTRACT LAWS

State	Code Section	All surrogacy contracts prohibited	Surrogacy contracts allowed if no money is exchanged	Surrogacy contracts allowed even if money is exchanged
Arizona	25-218	•		
Arkansas	10-201			•
Florida	63.212		•	
Indiana	31-8-2-1	•		
Kentucky	199.590		•	
Louisiana	9:2713	•		
Michigan	722.855	•		
Nebraska	25-21,2000	•		
Nevada	126.045		•	
New Hampshire	168-B:25	•		
New York	Dom. Rel. 122		•	
North Dakota	14-18-05	•		
Utah	76-7-204		•	
Virginia	20-159		•	
Washington	26.26.240		•	
West Virginia	48-4-16(e)(3)			•
Washington, DC	16-402	•		

INDEX

	EDITION	PRICE	CODE

BUSINESS

		EDITION	PRICE	CODE
	Business Plans to Game Plans	1st	$29.95	GAME
	Helping Employees Achieve Retirement Security	1st	$16.95	HEAR
	Hiring Indepedent Contractors: The Employer's Legal Guide	1st	$29.95	HICI
	How to Finance a Growing Business	4th	$24.95	GROW
	How to Form a CA Nonprofit Corp.—w/Corp. Records Binder & PC Disk	1st	$49.95	CNP
	How to Form a Nonprofit Corp., Book w/Disk (PC)—National Edition	3rd	$39.95	NNP
	How to Form Your Own Calif. Corp.—w/Corp. Records Binder & PC Disk	1st	$39.95	CACI
	How to Form Your Own California Corporation	8th	$29.95	CCOR
	How to Form Your Own Florida Corporation, (Book w/Disk—PC)	3rd	$39.95	FLCO
	How to Form Your Own New York Corporation, (Book w/Disk—PC)	3rd	$39.95	NYCO
	How to Form Your Own Texas Corporation, (Book w/Disk—PC)	4th	$39.95	TCI
	How to Handle Your Workers' Compensation Claim (California Edition)	1st	$29.95	WORK
	How to Market a Product for Under $500	1st	$29.95	UN500
	How to Write a Business Plan	4th	$21.95	SBS
	Make Up Your Mind: Entrepreneurs Talk About Decision Making	1st	$19.95	MIND
	Managing Generation X: How to Bring Out the Best in Young Talent	1st	$19.95	MANX
	Marketing Without Advertising	1st	$14.00	MWAD
	Mastering Diversity: Managing for Success Under ADA and Other Anti-Discrimination Laws	1st	$29.95	MAST
	OSHA in the Real World: (Book w/Disk—PC)	1st	$29.95	OSHA
	Taking Care of Your Corporation, Vol. 1, (Book w/Disk—PC)	1st	$26.95	CORK
	Taking Care of Your Corporation, Vol. 2, (Book w/Disk—PC)	1st	$39.95	CORK2
	Tax Savvy for Small Business	1st	$26.95	SAVVY
	The California Nonprofit Corporation Handbook	7th	$29.95	NON
	The California Professional Corporation Handbook	5th	$34.95	PROF
	The Employer's Legal Handbook	1st	$29.95	EMPL
	The Independent Paralegal's Handbook	3rd	$29.95	PARA
	The Legal Guide for Starting & Running a Small Business	2nd	$24.95	RUNS
	The Partnership Book: How to Write a Partnership Agreement	4th	$24.95	PART
	Rightful Termination	1st	$29.95	RITE
	Sexual Harassment on the Job	2nd	$18.95	HARS
	Trademark: How to Name Your Business & Product	2nd	$29.95	TRD
	Workers' Comp for Employers	2nd	$29.95	CNTRL
	Your Rights in the Workplace	2nd	$15.95	YRW

 Book on disk

CONSUMER

Fed Up With the Legal System: What's Wrong & How to Fix It	2nd	$9.95	LEG
Glossary of Insurance Terms	5th	$14.95	GLINT
How to Insure Your Car	1st	$12.95	INCAR
How to Win Your Personal Injury Claim	1st	$24.95	PICL
Nolo's Pocket Guide to California Law	4th	$10.95	CLAW
Nolo's Pocket Guide to Consumer Rights	2nd	$12.95	CAG
The Over 50 Insurance Survival Guide	1st	$16.95	OVER50
True Odds: How Risk Affects Your Everyday Life	1st	$19.95	TROD
What Do You Mean It's Not Covered?	1st	$19.95	COVER

ESTATE PLANNING & PROBATE

How to Probate an Estate (California Edition)	8th	$34.95	PAE
Make Your Own Living Trust	2nd	$19.95	LITR
Nolo's Simple Will Book	2nd	$17.95	SWIL
Plan Your Estate	3rd	$24.95	NEST
The Quick and Legal Will Book	1st	$15.95	QUIC
Nolo's Law Form Kit: Wills	1st	$14.95	KWL

FAMILY MATTERS

A Legal Guide for Lesbian and Gay Couples	8th	$24.95	LG
Child Custody: Building Agreements That Work	1st	$24.95	CUST
Divorce & Money: How to Make the Best Financial Decisions During Divorce	2nd	$21.95	DIMO
How to Adopt Your Stepchild in California	4th	$22.95	ADOP
How to Do Your Own Divorce in California	21st	$24.95	CDIV
How to Do Your Own Divorce in Texas	6th	$19.95	TDIV
How to Raise or Lower Child Support in California	3rd	$18.95	CHLD
Nolo's Pocket Guide to Family Law	4th	$14.95	FLD
Practical Divorce Solutions	1st	$14.95	PDS
The Guardianship Book (California Edition)	2nd	$24.95	GB
The Living Together Kit	7th	$24.95	LTK

GOING TO COURT

Collect Your Court Judgment (California Edition)	2nd	$19.95	JUDG
Everybody's Guide to Municipal Court (California Edition)	1st	$29.95	MUNI
Everybody's Guide to Small Claims Court (California Edition)	12th	$18.95	CSCC
Everybody's Guide to Small Claims Court (National Edition)	6th	$18.95	NSCC
Fight Your Ticket ... and Win! (California Edition)	6th	$19.95	FYT
How to Change Your Name (California Edition)	6th	$24.95	NAME
Represent Yourself in Court: How to Prepare & Try a Winning Case	1st	$29.95	RYC
The Criminal Records Book (California Edition)	5th	$21.95	CRIM

⌨ Book on disk

HOMEOWNERS, LANDLORDS & TENANTS

Dog Law	2nd	$12.95	DOG
⬚ Every Landlord's Legal Guide (National Edition)	1st	$29.95	ELLI
For Sale by Owner (California Edition)	2nd	$24.95	FSBO
Homestead Your House (California Edition)	8th	$9.95	HOME
How to Buy a House in California	3rd	$24.95	BHCA
Neighbor Law: Fences, Trees, Boundaries & Noise	2nd	$16.95	NEI
Safe Homes, Safe Neighborhoods: Stopping Crime Where You Live	1st	$14.95	SAFE
Tenants' Rights (California Edition)	12th	$18.95	CTEN
The Deeds Book (California Edition)	3rd	$16.95	DEED
The Landlord's Law Book, Vol. 1: Rights & Responsibilities (Calif. Ed.)	5th	$34.95	LBRT
The Landlord's Law Book, Vol. 2: Evictions (California Edition)	5th	$34.95	LBEV

HUMOR

29 Reasons Not to Go to Law School	1st	$9.95	29R
Poetic Justice	1st	$9.95	PJ

IMMIGRATION

How to Become a United States Citizen	5th	$14.95	CIT
How to Get a Green Card: Legal Ways to Stay in the U.S.A.	2nd	$24.95	GRN
U.S. Immigration Made Easy	5th	$39.95	IMEZ

MONEY MATTERS

Building Your Nest Egg With Your 401(k)	1st	$16.95	EGG
Chapter 13 Bankruptcy: Repay Your Debts	1st	$29.95	CH13
How to File for Bankruptcy	5th	$25.95	HFB
Money Troubles: Legal Strategies to Cope With Your Debts	3rd	$18.95	MT
Nolo's Law Form Kit: Personal Bankruptcy	1st	$14.95	KBNK
Nolo's Law Form Kit: Rebuild Your Credit	1st	$14.95	KCRD
Simple Contracts for Personal Use	2nd	$16.95	CONT
Smart Ways to Save Money During and After Divorce	1st	$14.95	SAVMO
Stand Up to the IRS	2nd	$21.95	SIRS

PATENTS AND COPYRIGHTS

Copyright Your Software	1st	$39.95	CYS
Patent, Copyright & Trademark: A Desk Reference to Intellectual Property Law	1st	$24.95	PCTM
Patent It Yourself	4th	$39.95	PAT
⬚ Software Development: A Legal Guide (Book with disk—PC)	1st	$44.95	SFT
The Copyright Handbook: How to Protect and Use Written Works	2nd	$24.95	COHA
The Inventor's Notebook	1st	$19.95	INOT

⬚ Book on disk

RESEARCH & REFERENCE

Law on the Net	1st	$39.95	LAWN
Legal Research: How to Find & Understand the Law	4th	$19.95	LRES
Legal Research Made Easy (Video)	1st	$89.95	LRME

SENIORS

Beat the Nursing Home Trap: A Consumer's Guide	2nd	$18.95	ELD
Social Security, Medicare & Pensions	6th	$19.95	SOA
The Conservatorship Book (California Edition)	2nd	$29.95	CNSV

SOFTWARE

California Incorporator 2.0—DOS	2.0	$47.97	INCI2
Living Trust Maker 2.0—Macintosh	2.0	$47.97	LTM2
Living Trust Maker 2.0—Windows	2.0	$47.97	LTWI2
Small Business Legal Pro—Macintosh	2.0	$39.95	SBM2
Small Business Legal Pro—Windows	2.0	$39.95	SBW2
Nolo's Partnership Maker 1.0—DOS	1.0	$47.97	PAGI1
Nolo's Personal RecordKeeper 3.0—Macintosh	3.0	$29.97	FRM3
Patent It Yourself 1.0—Windows	1.0	$149.97	PYWI
WillMaker 6.0—Macintosh	6.0	$41.97	WM6
WillMaker 6.0—Windows	6.0	$41.97	WIW6

SPECIAL UPGRADE OFFER

Get 25% off the latest edition of your Nolo book

It's important to have the most current legal information. Because laws and legal procedures change often, we update our books regularly. To help keep you up-to-date we are extending this special upgrade offer. Cut out and mail the title portion of the cover of your old Nolo book and we'll give you 25% off the retail price of the NEW EDITION when you purchase directly from us. For more information call us at 1-800-992-6656. This offer is to individuals only.

VISIT OUR STORE

If you live in the Bay Area, be sure to visit the Nolo Press Bookstore on the corner of 9th and Parker Streets in West Berkeley. You'll find our complete line of books and software, all at a discount. We also have t-shirts, posters and a selection of business and legal self-help books from other publishers. Open every day.

ORDER FORM

Code	Quantity	Title		Unit price	Total
				Subtotal	
		In California add appropriate Sales Tax			
		Shipping & Handling ($5 for 1st item; $6 for 2-3 items, 7$ for 4 or more)			
		UPS RUSH delivery $7-any size order*			
				TOTAL	

Name

Address

UPS to street address, Priority Mail to P.O. boxes

* Delivered in 3 business days from receipt of order. S.F. Bay area use regular shipping.

FOR FASTER SERVICE, USE YOUR CREDIT CARD & OUR TOLL-FREE NUMBERS

ORDER 24 HOURS A DAY   1-800-992-6656

FAX US YOUR ORDER   1-800-645-0895

e-MAIL   cs@nolo.com

GENERAL INFORMATION   1-800-549-1976

CUSTOMER SERVICE   1-800-728-3555, Mon.-Sat. 9am-5pm, PST

METHOD OF PAYMENT

☐ Check enclosed

☐ VISA   ☐ MasterCard   ☐ Discover Card   ☐ American Express

Account #   Expiration Date

Authorizing Signature

Daytime Phone

Send to: Nolo Press, 950 Parker Street, Berkeley, CA 94710

PRICES SUBJECT TO CHANGE

Take 2 minutes & get a 2-year
NOLO NEWS subscription free*

With our quarterly magazine, the NOLO NEWS, you'll
- Learn about important legal changes that affect you
- Find out first about new Nolo products
- Keep current with practical articles on everyday law
- Get answers to your legal questions in
  Ask Auntie Nolo's advice column
- Save money with special *Subscriber Only* discounts
- Tickle your funny bone with our famous
  Lawyer Joke column.

It only takes 2 minutes to reserve your free 2-year subscription or to extend your NOLO News subscription.

*U.S. ADDRESSES ONLY.
TWO YEAR INTERNATIONAL SUBSCRIPTIONS: CANADA & MEXICO $10.00;
ALL OTHER FOREIGN ADDRESSES $20.00.

REGISTRATION CARD

NAME

DATE

ADDRESS

PHONE NUMBER

CITY   STATE   ZIP

WHERE DID YOU HEAR ABOUT THIS BOOK?

WHERE DID YOU PURCHASE THIS PRODUCT?

DID YOU CONSULT A LAWYER? (PLEASE CIRCLE ONE)   YES   NO   NOT APPLICABLE

DID YOU FIND THIS BOOK HELPFUL?   (VERY)   5   4   3   2   1   (NOT AT ALL)

SUGGESTIONS FOR IMPROVING THIS PRODUCT

WAS IT EASY TO USE?   (VERY EASY)   5   4   3   2   1   (VERY DIFFICULT)

DO YOU OWN A COMPUTER? IF SO, WHICH FORMAT? (PLEASE CIRCLE ONE)   WINDOWS   DOS   MAC

We occasionally make our mailing list available to carefully selected companies whose products may be of interest to you. If you do not wish to receive mailings from these companies, please check this box ☐

FLD 4.0